A THIRST FOR WINE AND WAR

Intoxicating Histories

Series Editors: Virginia Berridge and Erika Dyck

Whether on the street, off the shelf, or over the pharmacy counter, interactions with drugs and alcohol are shaped by contested ideas about addiction, healing, pleasure, and vice and their social dimensions. Books in this series explore how people around the world have consumed, created, traded, and regulated psychoactive substances throughout history. The series connects research on legal and illegal drugs and alcohol with diverse areas of historical inquiry, including the histories of medicine, pharmacy, consumption, trade, law, social policy, and popular culture. Its reach is global and includes scholarship on all periods. Intoxicating Histories aims to link these different pasts as well as to inform the present by providing a firmer grasp on contemporary debates and policy issues. We welcome books, whether scholarly monographs or shorter texts for a broad audience focusing on a particular phenomenon or substance, that alter the state of knowledge.

A THIRST FOR WINE AND WAR

THE INTOXICATION OF FRENCH SOLDIERS ON THE WESTERN FRONT

ADAM D. ZIENTEK

McGill-Queen's University Press

Montreal & Kingston • London • Chicago

ISBN 978-0-2280-1992-3 (cloth)
ISBN 978-0-2280-1993-0 (paper)
ISBN 978-0-2280-1994-7 (ePDF)
ISBN 978-0-2280-1995-4 (ePUB)

Legal deposit first quarter 2024
Bibliothèque nationale du Québec

Printed in Canada on acid-free paper that is 100% ancient forest free
(100% post-consumer recycled), processed chlorine free

We acknowledge the support of the Canada Council for the Arts.
Nous remercions le Conseil des arts du Canada de son soutien.

McGill-Queen's University Press in Montreal is on land which long served
as a site of meeting and exchange amongst Indigenous Peoples, including
the Haudenosaunee and Anishinabeg nations. In Kingston it is situated on
the territory of the Haudenosaunee and Anishinaabek. We acknowledge
and thank the diverse Indigenous Peoples whose footsteps have marked
these territories on which peoples of the world now gather.

Library and Archives Canada Cataloguing in Publication

Title: A thirst for wine and war : the intoxication of French soldiers
    on the Western Front / Adam D. Zientek.
Names: Zientek, Adam D., author.
Series: Intoxicating histories ; 9.
Description: Series statement: Intoxicating histories ; 9
    Includes bibliographical references and index.
Identifiers: Canadiana (print) 20230487246 | Canadiana (ebook) 20230487416
    ISBN 9780228019930 (paper) | ISBN 9780228019923 (cloth)
    ISBN 9780228019954 (ePUB) | ISBN 9780228019947 (ePDF)
Subjects: LCSH: Soldiers—Alcohol use—France—History—20th century.
    LCSH: Wine and wine making—France—History—20th century.
    LCSH: Operational rations (Military supplies)—France—History—
    20th century. | LCSH: World War, 1914–1918—Social aspects—France.
Classification: LCC D639.D74 Z54 2024 | DDC 362.292094409/041—dc23

CONTENTS

Table and Figures

Acknowledgments

This book would not have been possible to write without the financial and moral support of many institutions and people. As for institutions: my research in France was supported by the Georges Lurcy Charitable and Educational Trust, the Josephine de Kárman Fellowship Trust, Stanford University, and the University of California Davis. I owe a debt of gratitude to my mentors at Stanford: Paul Robinson, James Sheehan, Amir Weiner, and most of all JP Daughton, all of whom encouraged and advised me in graduate school while giving me a large degree of freedom. I owe a similar debt to my colleagues at Davis: Ian Campbell, Gregory Downs, Stacy Fahrenthold, Sally McKee, Daniel Stolzenberg, and Ted Margadant, all for reading and providing comments upon drafts of my material. The feedback of my students – in particular those whose honours theses I have advised, who have taught me much – has been invaluable. Outside of Davis, I would like to thank Deborah Bauer, Randall Collins, Martha Hanna, Robert Merges, and Srijita Pal, again for providing detailed comments on drafts of chapters. Thanks are also due to the anonymous evaluators who read this book's manuscript for McGill-Queen's University Press, whose comments greatly improved the book. Similar thanks are due to my editor Kyla Madden and her team at MQUP for guiding me through the process of publication.

Finally, I would also like to thank my family: Geri Zientek, Neil Zientek, Amanda Kamali, and my son Alexander Zientek, for invaluable support and encouragement. And, above all, my late father, Brian Zientek, for sparking my interest in history.

Some of the material in chapters 1–5 appeared, albeit in mostly different form, in my "Energizing Munitions for the Body: French Alcohol Policy on the Western Front," in *Journal of Modern History* 95, no. 1 (March 2023), as did some material from chapter 6 in my "Affective Neuroscience and the Causes of the Mutiny of the French 82nd Infantry Brigade," in *Contemporary European History* 23, no. 4 (2014).

A THIRST FOR WINE AND WAR

INTRODUCTION

The First World War's Western Front presented a grim picture to the men it held captive in its trenches. The fertile fields of France had become a wasteland of sand, refuse, and mud. Forests of mutilated trees stood amid lakes of putrefaction. Once-living towns were reduced to pitiable rubble and ash. Soldiers passed most of their waking hours repairing and maintaining the trenches, endless work that left them fatigued and filthy. Long weeks and months of drudgery were punctuated with bursts of terror, helplessness, and madness. At any moment, the enemy could launch bombardments of shells that might explode at soldiers' feet, maiming or killing men in scenes of indescribable horror. Many were blown to pieces – in the words of French infantryman Louis Barthas, they were "pounded into marmalade."[1]

The situation in which men like Barthas found themselves was often unbearable to contemplate. As Étienne Tanty, a French infantryman whose letters home to his family are some of the war's most poignant, explained in June 1915, when the war was still young but felt ancient:

> The duration of this catastrophe chips away at hope bit by bit. The sun, the dust, the thirst, the filth, the lack of rest and sleep, all of it, all of it coalesces together; the perpetual shelling, the misery of the spectacle – the frightful things we must see – all of this puts one's nerves in an unbearable state of tension. It is a war of exhaustion, in effect, that will last until nothing but human tatters remain. It is no longer war, it is carnage and torture, scientifically and mathematically organized.[2]

Those who dwelled within these kinds of "black thoughts," as Tanty described them, could find themselves falling prey to *le cafard* [the cockroach], which was French soldiers' slang term for the state of profound physical lassitude and emotional depression that accompanied life in the trenches. The *cafard* left trench-fighters in paralyzed despair. "I have times of black, black *cafard*," Tanty wrote of the affliction in late 1915, "[and] I do not know how I will resist this torment. There is nothing left that gives reason to live."[3]

Yet according to Barthas, Tanty, and France's other *poilus* (the "hairy ones," as the French affectionately called their unshaven soldiers), their condition had an antidote: *pinard*, which is the name that French soldiers gave to wine. The word itself was a vulgarization of *pinot*, a type of grape; the trench etymologist Albert Dauzat traced its first use to 1886 in the 13è *Régiment d'Artillerie*.[4] But it was not a popular word in France until the war, after which *pinard* conquered the army and French popular culture more generally.[5]

Of course, many of France's civilian-soldiers drank wine in their daily lives before the war, and wine was recognized as a national drink. But in the context of the fighting, it took on even more patriotic connotations – in the trenches, it came to represent the moral community of French soldiers, their blood and France's in common. The trench poet Jules Pech explained:

Le pinard du poilu n'est autre que le vin	[The *poilu's pinard* is nothing but wine]
Or le vin, c'est le sang, le sang pur de la terre	[But wine is blood, the pure blood of the earth]
Où la flame du ciel répand dans notre artère	[Where the flame of the sky beats through our arteries]
Le soleil de la France et son charme divin[6]	[The sun of France and its divine charm]

Indeed, *poilus* imbued the word *pinard* with deep meaning. It was wine, but it was also more. Soldiers idolized it as a source of inspiration and comradery, and as a symbol that bound their bodies to the land they defended.

As of late November 1914, each soldier in the French army received a daily ration of *pinard* from the army. The amount started out modest, a quarter-litre per man, but grew larger as the war dragged on: it was raised to a half-litre in 1915, and to three-quarters of a litre in 1917 – a full bottle's worth for each of the 2.75 million Frenchmen in the army. This required an immense apparatus that, over the course of four and a half years, sucked up billions of litres of wine not only from France's traditional wine-producing areas, but also from Algeria, Spain, and Portugal. There were efforts to procure wine from as far afield as Argentina, Brazil, and even California, for the army's thirst was unquenchable. *Pinard* was one of the few joys permitted to men in the trenches and its daily distribution was central to the maintenance of morale. "We can hold on [*tenir*], if we can drink," recounted one *poilu*.[7]

The daily *pinard* ration, the rituals that accompanied its distribution, and the army's strategic intentions behind it underwrote what I will call the "daily system." The daily system sought to use wine to raise and sustain morale, to make bodies robust and vital, to make minds energized and alert – all in the interest of preparing men to fight and endure suffering in the trenches. It took the physiological and sociocultural effects of wine consumption and harnessed them to the war effort, working through a biocultural mechanism to elicit certain emotions and encourage certain behaviours. The army's wine distribution can be likened to an experiment in emotional and behavioural manipulation and control via the mass distribution of a psychotropic drug – and alcohol is a psychotropic drug, even if its use was normalized in France. The experiment was a success. As one *poilu* concluded, when *pinard* arrived in the trenches, "morale leaps in a single moment to 100 degrees."[8]

The daily system was key to the maintenance of morale in the French trenches, but it was just one part of French alcohol policy on the Western Front. It was accompanied and reinforced by another system – the "battle system" – in which soldiers were given distilled alcohol right before attacks. Consider the scene soldier André Tanquerel recalled of a battlefield from 1915. As he awaited the order to attack, the exploding French shells made terrible flowers of heat and fire bloom over the German positions. This was a moment of acute fear and tension, and he was not eager to go over the top. As Tanquerel and his comrades counted down, the army distributed the requisite *eau-de-vie*, or *gnôle*, as French soldiers called the rough overproof alcohol they received before attacks.[9] According to Dauzat, the trench etymologist, the word *gnôle* was a slang corruption of the Franco-Provençal word for fog [*niola*], although, like *pinard*, it was not especially popular before the war.[10] The *gnôle* was "taken down all at once," Tanquerel explained, and soon began to do its work. The drink turned in the men's bellies and their "overheated brains lost all notion of what was happening." Fired up by adrenaline and alcohol, they attacked in a swarm, led by an officer who had been transformed into a "brute, the biggest brute of them all; a maniacal murderer [who] kills anything without pity."[11]

Here the French army was supplying its citizen-soldiers with a dose of a psychotropic drug to condition their responses to violence: to prepare them to kill and to be ready for the prospect of being killed. Such distributions of *gnôle* before battle were frequent: similar scenes – some highly dramatized like Tanquerel's, others more laconic – are common enough in personal narratives of the war.[12]

Yet alcohol's transformative power had to be carefully controlled, confined to the trenches, and unleashed only when necessary and beneficial to the war effort. Distilled alcohol in particular was a tool that *poilus* could not be permitted to use whenever they felt like it, for, the army believed, they could then become a danger to themselves and their fellow soldiers. Hence the third element of the French army's alcohol policy: the "prohibition system," which sought to regulate *poilus'* consumption of alcohol in the awkwardly named "rear-front" [*arrière-front*], the relatively shallow strip of land behind the front lines where soldiers went into rest [*en repos*] between their tours. The prohibition system was a set of regulations and surveillance networks that controlled what and where men drank when in the rear. It aimed to ensure that the power of alcohol to modulate experience and behaviour did not escape the control of the army, resulting in drunkenness and indiscipline.

The army began issuing prohibitions on alcohol consumption in March 1915, when Commander-in-Chief Joseph Joffre banned the importation of distilled alcohol to the rear-front, as well as its sale to soldiers.[13] Soon after, the army banned sales of distilled alcohol in the army zones in their entirety.[14] More robust prohibitions followed: in December 1915, the army forbade the opening of new alcohol shops in the rear-front; in April 1916, it gave officers the power to close existing alcohol shops there; in September, it began to expel alcohol-sellers from the army zones for the duration of the war.[15] To enforce the prohibitions, the army developed a surveillance network that employed customs agents, plain-clothed army officers, gendarmes, and cavalry detachments.[16] To limit supply, the army kept detailed records of civilians' distilled alcohol stocks and regularly requisitioned whatever they believed might end up in the hands of *poilus*.[17] By the end of 1916, it was difficult for soldiers to find distilled alcohol on the Western Front outside of officially sanctioned distributions thereof. The army's position, as one *poilu* recounted with irony, was that while in the rear areas *eau-de-vie* was considered a "poison for civilians," at the front *gnôle* was a "military beverage and weapon of war."[18]

This is not to say that France used alcohol to turn its citizen-soldiers into doped-up automatons, nor that French army policy was secretive or coercive, or even explicitly intended from the war's outset. Indeed, as we will see, the army did not enter the war with a plan to distribute alcohol strategically to soldiers. Rather, the daily, battle, and prohibition systems were improvised solutions to the problems of morale that came with trench fighting. They emerged as a response to the war and maintained a dialectical relationship. Notwithstanding this absence of explicit intention, the result of interactions among the daily, battle, and prohibition systems was to enmesh *poilus* in a framework of emotional and behavioural conditioning and surveillance that shaped their experience of the war in profound ways.

DRUGS AND WAR

Combat effectiveness depends upon physical resilience and emotional control. Hence the value of training and drill, whose purpose is not only to condition soldiers' bodies and teach them how their weapons ought to be used, but also to teach them how to regulate themselves emotionally. Hence also soldiers' frequent use of psychotropic drugs immediately before and in combat, a subject occluded by myths about battle that historians have only recently begun to investigate.[19] The recent work of Lukasz Kamienski in *Shooting Up* (2016) and Peter Andreas in *Killer High* (2019) has shown that psychotropic drug use among soldiers before, during, and after battle has been frequent, if not universal, throughout history and across cultures.

The types of psychotropic drugs soldiers have employed come in a bewildering variety. Some have used stimulants, such as Túpac Amaru II's coca-chewing Incan warriors and Hitler's methamphetamine-chomping Wehrmacht.[20] Others have used hallucinogens, such as the Siberians who consumed muscimol-containing mushrooms to make themselves berserk and Napoleon's hashish-smoking infantrymen in Egypt.[21] Yet others have used opiates, such as Greek nepenthe-drinkers and American opium-eaters during the Civil War.[22] Reviewing evidence across different historical periods and cultures, Kamienski concludes that soldiers have frequently used drugs "as a means of fighting the most dangerous enemy of combatants, which is to say their shattered nerves." In this sense, he insists that soldiers are "pharmacologically constructed."[23]

The psychotropic drug most frequently used by soldiers is alcohol, which has long been associated with soldiering and warfare. Kamienski notes how alcohol was prevalent on battlefields in the ancient, medieval, and modern periods: Greek hoplites and Roman legionnaires frequently went into battle drunk; French knights "drank themselves into a stupor" before the Battle of Agincourt; and Napoleon's lucky men received triple rations of brandy at Austerlitz, as did Wellington's at Waterloo.[24] According to Kamienski, alcohol has played four distinct roles in war. First, its use has been medical, both because it acts as an anesthetic and because alcohol itself was often held to have medicinal properties. Second, it has been used as a stimulant that "alleviate[s] the stress of battle, raise[s] courage, and bring[s] self-confidence in combat." Third, it has been used as a therapeutic to "relax, induce sleep, numb emotions, and offer reward for the hardships of battle." And finally, it has been used to provide caloric energy.[25]

Peter Andreas has surveyed the role of alcohol consumption among soldiers from antiquity to the present, focusing especially on how prevalent drinking was in the British, German, and Soviet armies during the Second World War, and how frequent alcohol abuse was among Americans in Vietnam.[26] For Andreas, like for Kamienski, alcohol has served as a "lubricant" in war that has "helped soldiers prepare for combat, boost their confidence and willingness to take risks, anesthetize the injured, celebrate wins, and cope with losses."[27]

In his *Drunk on Genocide* (2021), Edward B. Westermann has shown that alcohol consumption among Nazi soldiers and ss men was inseparable from the violence of the Eastern Front and that of the concentration and extermination camps, where the physical state of alcohol intoxication was, among the killers, linked psychologically to brutal acts of human destruction. Nazis, he argues, drank copiously and so drunkenness became "a routine part of the rituals of humiliation in the camps, ghettos, and killing fields of Eastern Europe."[28] Not only did drinking dull men's physical and moral senses and thus provide them with a mechanism that distanced them from their crimes, but it also fuelled celebrations of masculine camaraderie and shared violence. Alcoholic intoxication,

Westermann concludes, not only made mass violence possible, but could make it feel like a party.

Thus it is not surprising that all the belligerents on the Western Front of the First World War drank. Indeed, many men drank whatever they could whenever they could.[29] Once the trenches were dug and the front was established, drinking became part of the German army's culture, most particularly behind the lines, where soldiers frequented alcohol shops run by French civilians in the occupied territories as well as canteens run by the German army. For instance, in his classic autobiographical account of the war, Storm of Steel (1924), Ernst Junger describes parties behind the lines in which "beer and grog flowed," as well as taking and sharing the occasional gulp of cherry brandy he carried with him into battle, which was useful in recovering nerves after an encounter with the enemy.[30]

Yet while German soldiers were known to drink, there is reason to conclude that alcohol distribution in the German army was unsystematic and generally limited to what men could find and purchase themselves. Some German army units started the war with beer or schnapps rations on their books, but this was not the case army-wide.[31] Moreover, Germany faced significant difficulties in supply. Its national drink was beer, which was carbonated and had a low alcohol content. It spoiled easily in transit and could freeze in the winter, making its transport difficult. When Germans drank beer in the trenches, it was in bottles they (laboriously) brought up on their own. Also, distilled alcohol is a key solvent in the manufacture of armaments. This meant that industrial alcohol production that might have been diverted into the manufacture of alcohol for soldiers at the front was instead directed to munitions factories, a pressure that only became greater with Britain's blockade in 1916. Despite its reputation for drunkenness in French war culture, Germany was likely the most sober of the three main belligerents.

British and Commonwealth soldiers also drank behind the front lines. Their drink of choice broke along class divisions. British officers frequently brought whisky with them when they rotated in and, like rankers, they could also drink to excess. The memoirist Robert Graves wrote of several officers who became "dipsomaniacs" because of the stresses of trench life, with one man consuming two bottles a day and becoming incapable of making decisions as a result. Graves admitted that he became a bottle-a-day man himself for a short while during the Somme. "It certainly helped me then," he admitted.[32] But the whisky was neither provided by the army nor officially sanctioned, even if it was tolerated.

On the other hand, enlisted men in the British army received rum rations. The rum British soldiers received on the Western Front was Royal Navy stuff, thick and over-proof.[33] It was carried to the front in earthenware jugs labelled "SRD" for "Supply Reserve Depot," but which wags at the front said stood for "Service Rum, Diluted."[34] In theory, each enlisted man in the British army was entitled to an eighth gill (about two ounces) of rum per day, although in reality the ration was distributed infrequently.[35] Officers and rankers unsurprisingly agreed that rum's effects were mostly beneficial. The War Office's 1922 Shell Shock Commission ranked the rum ration ("especially in the morning") as one of the approved treatments for nervous exhaustion, although it ranked last for effectiveness in a list of fourteen treatments.[36] One medical officer from the Black Watch, JSY Rogers, testified to the commission that rum soothed damaged nerves. Without it, he declared, "I do not think we should have won the war."[37] A soldier's song made the same point in lovely doggerel:

But the RUM—
But the RUM—
Yes, there's naught to be said;
If it weren't for the Rum,
All the troops would be dead.[38]

So did another, which also lamented how infrequently the rum came up:

Now mark my word, it fills us with delight,
To drink our tot of rum.
Hurrah! Hurrah! Hurrah! We'll all get tight
The day that the Rum does come![39]

Yet British soldiers did not often receive enough rum from the army to get truly drunk. As historian John Ellis highlights, the amount of rum distributed was not excessive, with each BEF division receiving around 300 gallons a week. This came to about a third of a pint per man, which was, Ellis notes, "hardly enough to create an army of drunkards."[40] Unhappily, rum could be withheld by officers, either as punishment for misbehaviour or per commanders' teetotalling sensibilities. The latter was the case in the much-lamented Canadian 11th Brigade, who were called the "Pea-Soupers" because they received soup rather than rum.[41] As historian Tim Cook has argued, in the British and Commonwealth armies rum was considered not so much a beverage as a medicine – an antiseptic and tonic – with incidental happy morale effects.[42] Throughout the First World War, rum distributions were not quite regular or systematic.

While some British soldiers described taking a "tot" of rum before an attack, it was most often just that: not much more than a mouthful, perhaps two or so ounces. Ellis quotes one soldier who admitted that men drank but denied that they received enough to get drunk when they went over the top: "Well we got a stiff tot after struggling to reach the firing step of the take-off trench … and it has [sic] very little effect on any man after the night march."[43] Indeed, Britons could be jealous of how much alcohol the French army supplied its soldiers. As Bourne, the protagonist of Frederic Manning's *Her Privates We* (1930), demanded: "Why don't we get a rum issue every night, or a bottle of beer with dinner? The French get their wine … And we have to be content with that filthy stuff they sell us in the estaminets [as places that sold alcohol were called in Belgium and the north of France]."[44]

Indeed, the French case was different – *poilus* were regularly supplied with substantial amounts of alcohol in a systematic fashion. While French historians have long recognized that French soldiers drank considerably, it is only recently that the subject has received detailed attention. In *Le Pinard des poilus* (2015), Christophe Lucand provides an overview of the origins of the wine ration, the means of its distribution, and its central importance in maintaining morale in the French trenches.[45] Lucand also contends that the wine ration served as a tool of social control that kept up soldiers' aggression and consent for the war, though he does not develop the argument in depth.[46]

In his *L'Ivresse du soldat* (2016), Charles Ridel seeks to provide a "total history" of alcohol consumption during the war, one that encompasses its "economic, political, social, cultural, and anthropological" aspects.[47] Unlike Lucand, Ridel takes into consideration soldiers' consumption of distilled alcohol, as well as the army's anti-alcohol policies in the rear areas and their relationship with the French temperance movement.[48] Ridel notes that men who drank together not only recharged and readied themselves, but also formed a connection between "present and past," "front and rear."[49] For Ridel, the army's alcohol distributions were less a means of behavioural control and more a complex expression of France's national culture of drinking confronting the horrors of the war.

While both these works are empirically rich and inform the present study, they overlook what is arguably most important about French alcohol policy on the Western Front: that it was an experimental program of emotional and behavioural conditioning that constituted a unique and particular kind of biopower deployed on a massive scale. This was not because soldiers had never drunk to cope with the hardship of war, nor because armies had never before supplied soldiers with alcohol, but because of the unprecedented scale, regularity, and centrality of alcohol distributions to the experience of soldiering in France's conscript army. Even if the implementation of the daily, battle, and prohibition systems had not been the army's intention before the war, and had emerged only haltingly and reflexively to deal with the contingencies of trench life and prolonged fighting, these measures together produced a psychotropic regime on the Western Front in the service of France's war effort.

French soldiers recognized that alcohol consumption influenced their mindset and behaviours and understood that the army was giving it to them with this intention, but they accepted the rations because they believed these helped them to endure and do their duty: *pinard* and the rituals of its consumption gave men succour and fostered trench comradery while *gnôle* gave men courage (or stupefied them) in preparation for attacks. The question of *why* this was the case – why the consumption of alcohol affected the men in these supposedly predictable ways, and why various kinds of alcohol were thought to condition different responses – was less well understood.

ALCOHOL, PSYCHOTROPY, AND BEHAVIOUR

There is an abundance of scientific literature regarding the effects of alcohol consumption.[50] Ethyl alcohol (ethanol), the type that people consume, is very similar in molecular structure to water, which allows it to go where water does in the body, which is to say, everywhere. Yet alcohol's electrical properties are different enough from water's to cause it to interfere with cell-signalling in the nervous system, especially in the brain, where it serves as an agonist in some neurological pathways and an antagonist in others.

Indeed, there is hardly a neurological system whose properties are not modulated in some way by alcohol consumption. It is a very powerful drug.

Alcohol has physiological, psychotropic, and behavioural effects. As far as its purely physiological effects are concerned, a half-litre of wine contains about 400 calories, while an eighth to a quarter of a litre of distilled alcohol contains about 300 to 600 calories, so alcohol rations gave soldiers energy in this most basic sense.[51] Moreover, alcohol is a dose-dependent analgesic whose robustness is approximately equivalent to that of intravenous morphine, so drinking it eased the physical discomfort of sore muscles and bruises.[52] Finally, in the doses at which *poilus* consumed it, alcohol acts as a vasodilator, increasing blood flow, which gives a subjective sense of warmth.

Alcohol's psychotropic effects in mild to moderate doses are biphasic. While blood alcohol concentration is rising, which it does for approximately twenty minutes to half an hour after ingestion, alcohol acts as a stimulant, giving the drinker a feeling of increased energy and vigilance. But once the drinker's blood alcohol concentration has begun to drop as the alcohol is metabolized, its effects become relaxing and sedative for several hours.[53] Importantly, this subjective sense of stimulation *and then* relaxation is accompanied by a decrease in overall fear, tension, and anxiety because alcohol is a potent anxiolytic. This is the one of the most important direct consequences of alcohol consumption for our purposes: in a literal sense, alcohol makes danger look and feel less dangerous by prohibiting the electrochemical processes in our brains that cause anxiety.[54]

These physiological and psychotropic sensations within the body and mind then interact with "alcohol expectancies" to shape behaviour. Alcohol expectancies are, in brief, socially learned and culturally shaped responses to the interoceptive and affective sensations that come with alcohol consumption: they tell drinkers what these sensations mean in a given context and what ought to be done with them.[55] Put another way, expectancy theory holds that just as important as the pharmacological properties of a psychotropic drug – alcohol included – in the experience of intoxication are our expectations of its effects. This is what psychiatrist Norman Zinberg referred to as the "set" (meaning the drug-taker's personality and assumptions about how the drug will affect them) and the "setting" (meaning the drug-taker's social and physical environment).[56] All three variables – drug, set, and setting – work together to define the types of emotional and behavioural changes that come with intoxication.

Thus, what must be considered when investigating intoxicated behaviour is not only the pharmacology of the "head-change" (psychoactive effects) a given drug produces, but what the head-change signals in this or that specific context. This helps to explain how such a wide variety of drugs can play a role in readying soldiers for combat. The head-change signals to the mind and prepares the body for the experience to come; the emotional changes it produces are read through set and setting and then felt as readiness, power, and permission to use violence.

The effects of psychotropic consumption on experience and behaviour intersect with recent research into the history and neurobiology of emotions. Until quite recently, the scientific study of emotions was dominated by the "basic emotions" model, which holds that all human beings share a set of core emotions, usually including anger, fear, joy, sadness, surprise, and disgust. These emotions were thought to be produced by specific and dedicated "circuits" in the brain that produced similar facial expressions and subjective emotional experiences in people across time and cultures.

Historians of emotions have vigorously challenged this model and argue that emotions and historical emotion concepts – which is to say, emotion words and taxonomies, as well as the ways people "perform" emotions to make them personally and socially legible in a given historical context – vary greatly over time and culture.[57] Consequently, historians of emotions have concluded that there are no truly basic emotions. One of the leading emotions researchers, Barbara H. Rosenwein, has stated plainly: "Although many scientists today think of emotions as universal, biological, and invariable, this is not true at all."[58]

Recent research into the neurobiology of emotions aligns with what historians of emotions have been arguing. Indeed, an increasing number of neuroscientists have argued for a new paradigm: the "theory of constructed emotion." The most prominent advocate of this paradigm has been neuroscientist Lisa Feldman Barrett.[59] In Feldman Barrett's model of emotional experiences, there is first a physiological, bodily response in reaction to an internal or external stimulus: the heart races, pupils dilate, blood pressure rises, etc. These bodily changes are experienced interoceptively (within the body) as changes in affect, meaning they have valence (they feel pleasurable or uncomfortable) and scalability (they vary in strength).[60] Feldman Barrett insists that such interoceptive and affective sensations have *no meaning in and of themselves*. In her words, the "purely physical" sensations

14

felt in the body "have no objective psychological meaning" until what she calls "emotion concepts" – mental categories that are learned socially and expressed in language – provide "an explanation of where [the sensations] come from, what they refer to in the world, and how to act on them."[61] Thus, people must learn to interpret interoceptive and affective sensations with mental concepts *before* these sensations are experienced as emotions; the emotion concept is the key that unlocks the meaning of the bodily experience. The pith of Feldman Barrett's argument is that while emotions *feel* automatic and natural, they are in fact constructed and cultural. "Emotions," she concludes, "*are* meaning."[62]

The interoceptive and affective effects of the consumption of psychotropic drugs – including alcohol – can be interpreted according to what I will call "intoxication concepts," which are analogous to Feldman Barrett's "emotion concepts" and which help in shaping drug-related expectancies. Intoxication concepts are cultural and historical: they explain what a given feeling of intoxication means in context and what ought to be done with it.[63] Because, as we will see, wine and *eau-de-vie* came with vastly different intoxication concepts in French culture and were consumed in different contexts, drinking them produced different emotional experiences and behaviours despite their shared neurobiological mechanism of action. Such, at least, is the model I propose to elaborate below: the alcohol supplied by the French army generated shared interoceptive and affective sensations that were then interpreted through culturally learned and contextually bound intoxication concepts, making for distinct and entraining emotional experiences and group behaviours that tended to bolster the war effort.

The main argument of this book is that French soldiers were instrumentalized by the army through the distribution of alcohol, which was intended to exert (and did exert) emotional and behavioural control over them, bringing them into alignment with the needs of the war; this was the exercise of what we might call "psychotropic power," a distinct form of biopower.[64] Yet it is also true that the men were not simply passive subjects. Soldiers requested, and often demanded, alcohol. They had the freedom to decide whether or not to drink (though most men did), and their consumption was within their individual control. Ultimately, the power relations were bidirectional, if mainly top-down. The army created the system, established the rules, provided the alcohol, regulated men's drinking, and countered internal resistance (if imperfectly and not without some severe challenges). Yet the system also required soldiers' consent to participate. This consent was manufactured collaboratively and shaped the system over the course of the war.

CHAPTER OVERVIEW AND INTERVENTIONS

This book consists of seven chapters. The first five chapters argue that French alcohol policy on the Western Front can be thought of as creating and enforcing a psychotropic regime of emotional and behavioural control over soldiers. The final two chapters argue that the French army mutinies of 1917 can be thought of as the result of a breakdown in this psychotropic regime, as the great majority of the mutinies involved intoxicated men. It thus provides a new interpretation of those events.

Chapter 1 investigates the origins of the intoxication concepts for wine and *eau-de-vie* through a consideration of French drinking patterns before the war. It argues that while wine was associated with health, vitality, and power, *eau-de-vie* was associated with criminality, violence, and murder. These intoxication concepts were the ones that the daily and battle systems, respectively, would activate and use at the front.

Chapter 2 traces the genesis of the wine ration in the French army, which was the result of several factors: the wine industry's pressure on the army to adopt a ration, the army's construction of an apparatus that could supply one, and French medical elites' justification thereof. It argues that the ration emerged from an unexpected combination of circumstances, such as the wine industry's fear that its biggest consumers were locked away at the front, the nature of trench fighting and need for high morale in 1915 (which was characterized by large French offensives), and the medical consensus about the bodily and moral benefits of wine drinking.

Chapter 3 considers how French soldiers in the trenches experienced their quotidian wine ration. It argues that wine played a central (indeed, perhaps *the* central) role in maintaining morale in the trenches, just as it was intended to do. In their personal narratives and trench journals, soldiers wrote of how wine helped them conquer fear and suffering, and how it brought them together in fellowship. Soldiers understood that wine distribution was a tool of emotional and behavioural manipulation and control, but they also saw drinking as a means by which they might exert agency over their own feelings, experiences, and behaviours.

Chapter 4 considers the French army's practice of distributing *eau-de-vie* to soldiers immediately before attacks, holding that this played a central role in the experience of battle and men's behaviour. Through analysis of personal narratives, trench journals, and interviews with veterans, the chapter shows that such distributions were frequent and substantial. But, again, the effects of distilled alcohol were not only pharmacological. The sensation of intoxication interacted with the intoxication concept for *eau-de-vie*, which held that the drink made men brutal, and so they not only felt their fear and anxiety dampened, but also felt themselves transformed into killers.

Chapter 5 describes the French army's attempts to prohibit men from drinking *eau-de-vie*, as well as to regulate their wine-drinking behind the lines. It argues that in the winter of 1914–15, soldiers consumed large amounts of *eau-de-vie* that they purchased themselves, outside of any army ration. The army responded with a ban on distilled alcohol that made it difficult for soldiers to procure it outside of their official rations. Yet wine circulated freely behind the lines, at least until the spring of 1917, when the army began to crack down on what it considered to be excessive consumption.

Chapter 6 considers the breakdown in French military discipline and subsequent mutinies after the failure of the Nivelle Offensive in 1917. Historians have long recognized that the mutineers, who called for better food and living conditions, and an end to wasteful offensives and the war more generally, often appeared to be intoxicated. But they have tended to regard alcohol consumption as playing a minor role in the mutinies, positing that alcohol disinhibited soldiers and allowed them to burn off negative energy. Through an analysis of several case studies, the chapter demonstrates that men did not mutiny because they were drunk, but rather got drunk because they wanted to mutiny – they harnessed the power of alcohol to motivate and unify and then turned this power against their commanding officers.

Chapter 7 considers the unintended consequences of General Henri-Philippe Pétain's expansion of leave policy in the summer of 1917, which was done to appease the mutineers. In early June, when indiscipline at the front improved, indiscipline in the rear – particularly in the train stations that connected men returning from leave to the Aisne front – spiked, with tens of thousands of men demonstrating and calling for an end to the war. This surge of indiscipline was also fuelled by alcohol, which was available for purchase in the vicinity of the train stations. The chapter shows that discipline was only restored after a more severe prohibitionary regime was put in place.

Finally, the epilogue considers French drinking practices after the war. It argues that *pinard*'s fame helped to establish wine as France's national, patriotic drink. It concludes with some observations about the role of psychotropic power in the later twentieth and twenty-first centuries.

1

PROLOGUE TO THE WAR

QUALITY AND QUANTITY

According to Jacques Bertillon, one of France's most eminent demographers at the *fin-de-siècle*, if his nation were to continue to exist as a major world power into the twentieth century, it had to solve two problems: depopulation and degeneration [*dégénérescence*].[1] The problems were different but interrelated.

On the one hand, depopulation had to do with the quantity of French citizens. Bertillon was one among many observers who noted that, over the nineteenth century, France's birthrate had declined while those of its neighbours had increased. In the Napoleonic era, France was the most populous state in Europe; by the *fin-de-siècle*, it was the least populous of the Great Powers.[2] Of France's rivals, Bertillon fretted: "they are all growing, all becoming more populous, and as a consequence, richer, stronger, more vital."[3] On the other hand, degeneration had to do with the quality of the French population, which was ostensibly declining. Degeneration theory, which was widely accepted in Europe at the time, held that the social and environmental conditions of modernity made at least some of its constitutive human elements evolve in reverse, becoming vicious and criminal, deformed and degraded. Such was supposedly happening throughout France.[4]

Together, depopulation and degeneration formed an existential problem, as for Bertillon and those like him, France's political stability, social harmony, and national power – economic, military, and cultural – were all a function of population size and fitness. Fewer people meant less economic activity and fewer soldiers for France's conscript army; more degeneration meant more crime, feebleness, and social unrest. Sooner rather than later, Bertillon predicted, if left unchecked, depopulation and degeneration would destroy France from within or leave it vulnerable enough to be destroyed from without.

Bertillon's view of French power was thus primarily biological – it was a function of the French population's quantity and quality. The problem was that rather than thriving under the conditions of the *fin-de-siècle*, French bodies were becoming fewer, weaker, and less vital. Moreover, Bertillon's view was racial in a basic sense, although by "race" he meant something like the total human biological content of the French nation rather than some specific racial group. Because history was the story of the pitiless struggle of races and the nations who were these races' avatars, he saw biological knowledge – the knowledge of how to improve the quantity and quality of individuals and populations – as the key to maintaining the French race on the earth.[5] Racial vitality – measured by both the fertility and the biological quality of the population – was national vitality. Racial degeneration – measured by crime, prostitution, alcoholism, and physical deformities – was an existential threat to the nation's continued existence.[6] The competition among nations, in Europe and in their empires overseas, was in this way a competition for racial supremacy. Thus the question of how to ameliorate or prevent the negative consequences of depopulation and degeneration was paramount.

In France, the alcoholic was considered the most perfect and threatening type of racial degenerate.[7] The father of degeneration theory, Bénédict Augustin Morel, defined degeneration as a "moral insanity" resulting from a "deep and all-encompassing biological process" of the corruption of the human body: the environmental and social conditions of modernity warped the body and so turned the personality wicked.[8] Alcohol, he argued, was a primary driver of this process, as it acted directly to pervert the form and workings of the individual's body and consequently pervert his behaviour and nature. Morel held that the "physical decline, the complete perversion of morality and sentiments" that defined the alcoholic were bad enough – such was the problem of quality. But, he insisted, the alcoholic also transmitted his degeneration to his offspring, spreading "idiocy" and "imbecility" through the generations, thus ruining quantities.[9]

In the first decades of the Third Republic, Valentin Magnan, Morel's star student, was chief psychiatrist at the Saint Anne asylum, through which thousands of Paris's ill and suffering alcoholics passed. For Magnan, arguably France's leading expert on degeneration theory at the *fin-de-siècle*, alcoholism was the primary source of France's biological, racial weakness.[10] Bertillon agreed. His research found that alcohol consumption did not decrease fertility as was commonly supposed. This worried him, as it implied that overly fecund alcoholics passed on their degeneracy through their children. Indeed, those concerned with the power of the French nation were remarkably unified in horror: alcoholism was the "most manifest cause of [France's] physical and moral decadence"[11]; "the enemy of the provident institutions that are the strength of our country and the honour of our age"[12]; "a poison destructive of human energy, and through that, all of society"[13]; and had "disastrous economic, political, social, moral, and *ethnic* consequences."[14]

Yet *fin-de-siècle* reformers insisted that alcoholism was quite new to France. "Alcoholism! Who had heard of this illness fifty years ago?" asked one in 1900. "Nobody," came his inevitable answer.[15] "Alcoholism properly defined," claimed another improbably, "was not known to our ancestors."[16] The syndrome, as frightening as it was, was not thought relevant to France, at least not until the *fin-de-siècle*. This was, of course, clearly wrong. But the question is: why did the French – who drank substantially more than any other people in the world – think that their country was untouched by alcoholism until the late nineteenth century?

The Swedish physician Magnus Huss, who studied systematically the physical effects of excessive alcohol consumption from a medical viewpoint, first coined the term "alcoholic" as a substantive noun in 1847. Yet the Swedes who drank excessively and whom Huss studied drank *aquavit*, the local distilled spirit. Thus Huss's data were restricted to men who drank what the French called *alcool* [distilled alcohol], rather than wine. The French conclusion was that the syndrome of alcoholism [*alcoolisme*] was caused by the consumption of distilled alcohol. And because so few Frenchmen in the mid-nineteenth century drank the distilled alcohol known as *eau-de-vie* (the French equivalent of *aquavit*) or wine-derived liquors such as cognac, alcoholism as defined by Huss did not really exist in the Hexagon. At least, so the argument went.

In 1852 Huss received for his studies on alcoholism France's highest award for academic achievement, the Montyon Prize.[17] The presenter praised Huss's research, but noted with pleasure that "chronic alcoholism" was a "condition rarely seen in France" precisely because the French drank wine rather than distilled alcohol.[18] Indeed, as we will see, wine-drinking, according to French folk and medico-scientific thinking, did not – and could not – lead to the syndrome of alcoholism, which was uniquely and perniciously the product of the distilled stuff. Wine might get one drunk, but it could not permanently warp and pervert the body and mind in the same way as distilled alcohol. Moreover, the drunkenness caused by wine and that caused by distilled alcohol were not the same, with the former being benign or even salubrious and the latter deadly and deforming.

CONSUMPTION PATTERNS

Consumption of distilled alcohol was relatively rare in France until the mid-nineteenth century, when innovations in the agricultural and chemical sciences allowed France's beet and potato farmers to use their crops in the industrial-scale distillation of alcohol.[19] Industrial distillation produced clean and pure ethyl alcohol, which was useful not only in industry, where it was used as a solvent; it was also consumed in France's *débits de boissons*, as the cafés, cabarets, bars, and other places licensed to sell alcohol were called. Average per capita consumption of distilled alcohol roughly doubled in France between 1830 and 1879, with nearly all the increase coming in industrializing urban regions, particularly in the northern *départements*.[20] Distilled alcohol increasingly became the drug of choice among the growing urban working classes, for it was cheap and powerful.[21]

Wine consumption in France followed a similar upward trajectory over the same period. Wine was neither a daily nor an affordable drink for most French citizens until the middle of the nineteenth century, when improvements in the science of wine-making and the development of national transportation infrastructure allowed certain regions in the country to specialize in wine production and distribute their products cheaply. This is not to say that every French family had a bottle of wine on their table every night, and the increase in consumption had geographical differences: people in the south and east drank more wine than those in the west and north, whose traditional drinks were beer and cider. Rather, it is to say that by the

Franco-Prussian War, wine was more widely available than ever before and a source of national identity for millions.[22]

Thus, over the third quarter of the nineteenth century, there was a double increase in French drinking patterns: distilled alcohol was introduced and consumed (at first in modest but ever larger amounts) while wine consumption jumped. The French drank more and more – more, indeed, than any other people in Europe, if not the world.

Then, during the last quarter of the nineteenth century, the French wine industry suffered the catastrophic *phylloxera* aphid infection.[23] The blight, brought over on American plants during a mid-century viticultural exchange, infected vines throughout the country and destroyed millions of hectares of vines – around a third of all under cultivation. Wine production plummeted. French drinkers, with wine now dear, turned to industrially distilled alcohol as a substitute. Consumption of distilled alcohol spiked, again especially in urban centres in the north and around Paris. It doubled between 1875 and 1890, a period when wine consumption fell by about a third.[24] There was thus a convergence: distilled alcohol became a substitute for wine at precisely the time that fear of alcoholism began to spread among French social reformers, who were increasingly obsessed with the idea of degeneration.

The wine industry recovered after grafting French vines onto American rootstock, which had resistance to the blight. While purists considered this the equivalent of poisoning France's patrimony and fought the process bitterly, resistance collapsed in the face of necessity. By 1900, two-thirds of the vines in France had American roots.[25] At this time, France had about a third less land under vine cultivation than it had had a quarter-century prior, but the new hybrid vines produced bigger grapes with more sugar. This meant more wine by volume overall, and wine with higher alcohol content. Prices collapsed beginning around 1890, when a flood of cheap wine washed over France. The French soon proved that they did not lose their taste for the national drink during the blight's dry years.[26] Consumption spiked with supply, and by 1914, they were drinking wine at pre-blight levels. Yet as they began to drink wine again, the French did not lose their taste for distilled alcohol, the consumption of which continued to increase apace with that of wine.

The result was a clear quantitative jump in the amount of alcohol French people consumed over the nineteenth century, with a peak in the first decade of the twentieth. Between 1830–39, per capita yearly consumption of pure alcohol was 9.74 litres (1.14 litres from distilled alcohol and 8.6 litres from wine). By 1900–13, per capita consumption had almost doubled, coming to 17.35 litres (3.65 litres from distilled alcohol, an increase of 220 per cent, and 13.7 litres from wine, an increase of 60 per cent). A 1914 article in *Le Matin* stated shortly before the war that a French citizen was (on average) consuming 18.8 litres of pure alcohol yearly when official figures for distilled alcohol and wine were accounted for.[27] This is equivalent to about 200 bottles of wine – no small amount. French figures are double those provided for Germany (9.4 litres), more than twice those for Britain (7.7 litres), and more than thrice those for Russia (5.5 litres). *Le Matin* did not supply its source, so its statistics must be taken with a grain. But recent historical research has suggested that *Le Matin* may have been underestimating: in one estimation, the French number came in at 21.6 litres in the early 1900s (as compared to 15.5 for second-place Italy, and 11.0 for the bronze-winning UK).[28] And these figures do not include the contributions of the *bouilleurs de cru*, France's prolific and productive home distillers, and so are an underestimate, perhaps by as much as half.

Of course, per capita statistics can be misleading, as they obscure differences in individual and regional consumption – women and children surely consumed less and men more, and some men much more than others. But the statistics unambiguously reflect an increased availability in France of both forms of alcohol for those who wanted them, and strongly suggest that more people wanted and drank more. In short, the problem of excessive alcohol consumption was not only a moral panic resulting from the fears and dislocation that came with industrialization and the ostensible arrival of the drunken, degenerate proletariat mob, but also a social and medical issue with some basis in reality.

To review, French social thinking was not able to properly "see" the alcoholic as a site for intervention until the category was invented in the mid-nineteenth century. It only seemed relevant to French reformers afterwards, when the French took up drinking distilled alcohol in quantity in the latter quarter of the century. These new drinking habits took root primarily among the working classes in urban centres, where the patterns of social life that revolved around the *débit* were highly visible. This led reformers and theorists of degeneration to see a link between their fears of national and racial decline and the increased consumption of distilled alcohol.[29]

Put another way, French reformers made sense of the social tumult, deracination, and political unrest that came with industrialization and urbanization by associating them with concept of alcoholic racial degeneration among the labouring classes. They saw reflected in the new urban populations the sinister fears invoked by Le Bon's mob, shadows of the drunken Commune and its *pétroleuses*. Just as this happened, French thinking about alcoholism developed a highly idiosyncratic character. On the one hand, it identified distilled alcohol, new to the scene, as uniquely dangerous and threatening to national well-being; it was the real problem. On the other hand, the same thinking identified wine, which had ostensibly been around forever and never caused any problems, as healthful and beneficial to national well-being; it was the *solution* to degeneration, alcoholism, and national decline.

TWO KINDS OF DRINKS

In *fin-de-siècle* France, the recent changes in drinking patterns and the country's mythological self-understanding as an eternally wine-drinking country led the French to develop peculiar medical and folk-psychological notions about alcoholism that posited the syndrome could only be caused by distilled alcohol, which was uniquely dangerous.[30] This split was of consequence, and not only because it produced different – even opposed – intoxication concepts for wine and *eau-de-vie*.

On the one hand were the so-called *boissons hygièniques* [hygienic drinks], which included naturally fermented alcoholic drinks such as wine, cider, and beer. They were lightly taxed, represented by powerful lobbies, and their consumption was viewed as benign or, more frequently, beneficial. *Boissons hygièniques* were, as their name suggests, healthy and invigorating, with wine being the *boisson hygiènique* par excellence, an "indispensable food" without which France's labourers would be incapable of their work. So long as men drank it in moderation – which one reformer suggested was no more than four (hopefully watered-down) litres a day(!) – wine was no more harmful, and markedly more beneficial, than bread.[31] And too much of this good thing was not always bad. In French popular culture, a man drunk on wine was witty and friendly, a figure to be, at his best, lauded for the conviviality he carried with him, and at his worst, tolerated despite his personal weaknesses. Wine produced a distinct kind of intoxication –

"happy and friendly, the Gallic drunkenness," as historian Michael Marrus has described it – that was to be celebrated rather than reviled.[32] As A. Lafont, an anti–distilled alcohol advocate, argued: "we attribute to [the drunkenness of wine] several benefits, particularly that it engenders good humour, that Gallic spirit which makes our people so proud."[33] Just as crucially, the drunkenness wine produced was thought to be temporary, a transient state of being rather than a fixed condition. It caused no permanent damage to the human organism and thus did not threaten the French race with degeneration.[34]

Indeed, in French discourse about wine, the drink was a powerful tonic and its consumption the *solution* to racial degeneration – wine could prevent, even reverse, this biological process.[35] Its proponents explained, for instance, that wine provided energy while "developing the individual and the race"[36]; that wine, the product of "the ancient soil of our birth," was a germ of coevolution with the French race itself (and its "fiery virtues") that made the French race "joyous and strong"[37]; that wine "gave force to [the French] race" and "pushed men to sacrifice" for their nation[38]; that wine made the French race "gay during peace and brave during war"[39]; and, as the "inestimable product of the Gallic soil," that wine was the foundation of the French race, just as roast beef was for the English.[40] One doctor even proposed that "the Republic ought to assure that to the menu of every Frenchman is added a bottle of good wine" in order to prevent racial degeneration, suggesting a pleasurable national vaccination scheme against the problem.[41] Such citations could be reproduced *ad infinitum*, as the medical and folk-psychological understanding of wine as regenerative and protective, inspiring and unifying – a notion generously underwritten by propaganda from the powerful wine industry – was widely accepted.[42] Wine, Frenchmen were told, was not only beneficial for the French race, but was its necessary, coevolutionary nourishment.

On the other hand were the *boissons alcoolisées* or *alcooliques* [alcoholic drinks], which took as their base industrially produced distilled alcohol [*alcool*] and included absinthe and the flavoured *eaux-de-vie de fantasie*. They were rather heavily taxed, at least as compared to the *boissons hygièniques*, and were also represented by powerful lobbies. *Boissons alcoolisées* were not considered healthy. Indeed, reformers considered distilled alcohol to be a poison at any dose and the alcoholism it caused a debilitating racial disease. It did not just inebriate the drinker but also changed his body in a fundamental and indelible way, rotting him from the inside out on a microscopic scale before leading him to, as one reformer maintained, "mental insanity and death."[43]

The difference in the language the French used to describe what the two drinks did inside the body was stark. According to one reformer, whereas wine comforts and repairs, distilled alcohol "attacks" the stomach, inflaming and ulcerating it. It strikes the liver "rapidly and murderously," turning the organ into a "fatty mass."[44] As a result of his drug of choice's poisonous effects, the alcoholic loses his musculature and posture and becomes frail and stooped. His brain – soaked and bathed in what another reformer called a vile *"poison psychique par excellence"*[45] – is warped in such a way as to turn him against society. And so distilled alcohol's putrefying effects inside the individual's body manifested themselves as harm to the social body: the alcoholic's memory becomes "vague and incoherent," making him useless in commerce or as a labourer[46]; he knows "neither pity nor charity for others" and is willing to sacrifice relationships and people in order to satisfy his "unbridled and savage appetites," making him like "some sort of animal ... with no soul and no heart"[47]; he not only "destroy[s] himself," but is also ineluctably drawn to "commit[ting] crimes of ferocious violence," making him murderous.[48] "The alcoholic," declared yet another reformer, "is brutal, a brute."[49] He was the archetype of villainy, the perfect opposite of the healthy, vital wine-drinker.

Dr Galtier-Boissière's widely distributed temperance poster from 1900 made the point visually and is as economical and eloquent a statement of French thinking about alcoholism on the eve of the First World War as one is likely to find.[50] It compares on the left side wine, cider, and beer, the *boissons hygièniques*, which are natural and good when not taken in excess, with, on the right side, "industrial alcohols" made from beets and potatoes, which are "bad, even when taken in small quantities." The "natural drinks" produce the confident and smooth man with the impeccably bourgeois mustache on the left. The drinks containing distilled alcohol produce the sallow, nearly transparent wraith on the right, whose unkempt beard and red undershirt hint at anarchism. This ghoul is racked with troubles physical (trembling, general decline, paralysis, dementia) and moral (professional incapacity, degradation, violence). His internal organs are pictured as virtually falling apart, the stomach with ulcers, the liver with cirrhosis, and the brain with swelling and rotting – this in contrast to the shiny, healthy organs of the man who drank wine. The consequences of the consumption

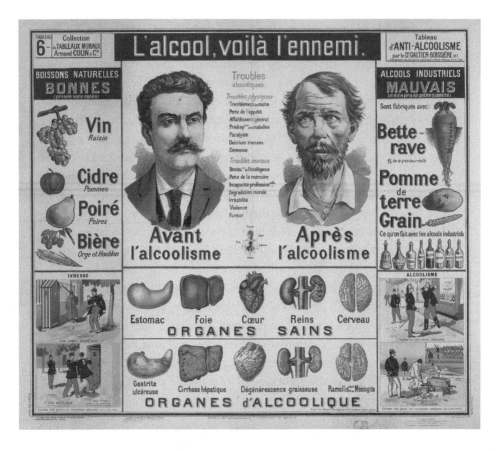

1.1 Dr Galtier-Boissière, "L'alcool, voilà l'ennemi" (1902).

of distilled alcohol are also drawn out. While over-indulging in wine produces, in the very worst case, "bad soldiers" and nights in the clink, drinking distilled alcohol has consequences of a different, more severe order. In small doses, it leads to indiscipline, but in large doses, it leads to penal servitude in the Algerian Sahara or even execution by firing squad, which are depicted for the benefit of visual learners.

Thus the French temperance movement took on a nationally idiosyncratic character.[51] Everybody involved agreed that alcoholism would inevitably cause the hollowing out of the French nation and extirpation of the French race within a few generations if left unchecked. Most agreed that wine-drinking was the *solution* to the crisis of alcoholism in France: not only did wine not cause alcoholism, but wine was the *cure* for alcoholism. Such was the position of the *Société française de tempérance* (SFT), France's largest private temperance organization, which was aligned with the wine lobby. Its line repeated the division: wine was healthy, invigorating, and lively, while distilled alcohol was sickening, debilitating, and deadening. Again, the two were opposites, and the benefits of the first were a natural prophylactic, even a cure, for the diseases produced by the second.

The SFT's mission was shaped by these conclusions. Dr Lunier, one of the group's founders, declared that the SFT's efforts ought to be directed in their entirety to making sure every alcoholic in France had enough of the wine he needed to recover from his malady. Part of Lunier's reasoning was practical. He noted that France thought of itself as a country of wine drinkers, and wine was deeply integrated into the day-to-day lives of millions of French people. It was "scarcely practical," argued Lunier, to propose complete abstinence in France.[52] Part of his reasoning was economic: the more wine the population drank, the better for the SFT's benefactors. And part of his reasoning was medico-cultural: wine really was a biological marvel that improved the quality of the French population. With Lunier, the majority of French temperance reformers generally thought those who preached complete abstinence (i.e., from distilled alcohol *and* wine) to be deluded zealots who, in their priggish and quixotic quest, were doing positive harm to the French nation and race.

Even still, their indulgence of wine notwithstanding, temperance activists were profoundly unpopular, viewed as killjoys, spoilsports, and wet blankets, which, of course, they really were. Private temperance organizations struggled. Their offices were routinely vandalized and their lectures heckled. Their posters did not last long once posted in public places and were torn down from all walls that did not hold up government buildings. More importantly, the powerful alcohol industry lobby, the relatively low capacity of the Third Republic before the First World War, and the strong preferences of the French population made passing anti-alcohol legislation all but impossible, despite the desires of reformers. Reformers ran up against the fact that forms of French sociability translated into a broadly shared assumption that French people had, as free citizens in a free country, a right to drink what they wanted to drink. The interventions that the Third Republic could pursue were limited by the norms of democratic governance, the power of the alcohol lobbies, and popular culture.[53]

But if the private temperance movement in France was piteously weak, there were nonetheless two *state* institutions that provided France's temperance reformers with captive audiences: its secular government-run schools, which most French children attended at least until they were thirteen, and the army, in which all young men were required to serve for two (and after 1913, three) years as conscripts, beginning in their twentieth year. The Third Republic sought to make its mark in these two institutions, turning them into schools of anti-alcoholic racial hygiene.

ANTI-ALCOHOLISM IN THE SCHOOLS

The Third Republic's government-run educational system provided temperance reformers with a captive and credulous audience, and its reformist educators availed themselves of the opportunity to barrage France's schoolchildren with visions of France and its people made toothless and wretched by distilled alcohol. In March 1897, a national educational reform mandated a nationwide program of temperance pedagogy in primary schools. The reasoning behind the program was explicitly racial. The damage alcoholics did was not just limited to their own bodies, but also

> transmits itself amplified and grown larger to their offspring and to theirs, and so on through the generations. Idiots, imbeciles, the feeble, hysterics, epileptics, degenerates of all types are found among the descendants of alcoholics.[54]

The state was obligated to do something to protect France against such transmissions. As one anti-alcohol advocate argued, quoting from a government report: "almost everyone today admits that the state has a right, or even a duty, to intervene in order to protect human life and the future of the race" against the poison of alcohol.[55] The job of protecting French citizens from distilled alcohol and the consequences of its consumption was thus a natural task for the Third Republic and its physician reformers and legislators.

Pedagogical material was designed to shock young charges into hatred of distilled alcohol and fear of the alcoholics it produced. For example, the first lesson in L. Angot's textbook, which was designed for use in primary schools, was titled "The Dangers of Drunkenness." It began with the teacher painting a verbal "portrait of the drunkard," a man wasted inside and out, slovenly dressed and evacuated of human intelligence. Teachers were encouraged to be as vivid as possible to "inspire horror and disgust" among the children. There were dictations, with lower students learning useful phrases like "The drunkard, what a physical degenerate!" Next came math problems that required students to show how much workers wasted on drink, teaching them at the same time how to do sums and that alcohol was a source of familial and racial degeneration. The title of the second lesson – "Alcoholism Will Lead You to Betray All Your Duties Bit by Bit" – aptly summarized its content, the gist being that "alcoholics are naturally indolent, and through their idleness most often become criminals."[56]

The thinking throughout the Third Republic's anti-alcohol textbooks is often racial. Alcoholism, instructed one of them, "left men unable to defend their fatherland, and menaces the French race's very existence"[57]; according to another, it threatened not only the individual, but "the family, the race, and society"[58]; a third noted it "attacks the race" and threatened it with degeneration[59]; a fourth that, through alcoholism, the French race would "extinguish itself."[60] Students were taught not only that they should avoid the bottle, but that alcoholics were socially deviant precisely because their drinking was not a question of individual vice, but of the enervation of France's collective biological power through the corruption of the bodies of its citizens. For good measure, Galtier-Boissière's textbook included an image of a "degenerate child" suffering from fetal alcohol syndrome, holding up a distorted mirror to his child readers as a warning.

Moreover, the Third Republic's young charges learned that alcoholism posed a dire threat to national defense. Textbook exercises taught that "there are no good soldiers without discipline, and the soldier who goes to the cabaret runs the risk of the firing squad," and told stories like that of a conscript who, in a state of alcoholic intoxication, struck an officer and was executed.[61] Galtier-Boissière's textbook, which was the standard, contained an entire chapter titled "A Soldier: Alcoholism in the Army," which described a volunteer soldier of slight physique but great spirit who, tragically, began to drink distilled alcohol once he joined up. Within a year he was in prison, awaiting a court martial for striking an officer while drunk. He faced execution. "Alas," the narrator, his former officer, proclaims upon visiting him in prison, "what a decline!" The narrator is doleful but firm. The French *Code de Justice Militaire* does not consider intoxication to be a mitigating factor: the volunteer "was responsible" and the code was correct

31

in holding him to account. This story, though, ends happily, as the volunteer receives six months in prison, where he dries out and reforms his ways.

The true and good French soldier was not, Galtier-Boissière maintained, fuelled by alcohol, whose consumption caused men to lose their élan and love of country. Rather, it was a sober and earnest love of "honour and *patrie*" that drove the French trooper forward. "It is among sober soldiers," he advised, "that we find the old brave ones." He concluded that to defend the fatherland [*patrie*] "we must be brave men, and the brave are temperate."[62]

ANTI-ALCOHOLISM IN THE ARMY

Fittingly, the Frenchman's education in the evils of distilled alcohol continued when he graduated from school and went into the army. Following France's inglorious defeat in 1870–71, the French army came to see itself as a vehicle for the material and moral regeneration of the country. According to historian Douglas Porch, the politicians of the Third Republic saw in a reformed army an opportunity to rehabilitate the army's reputation and at the same time win its allegiance to republicanism by associating it vigorously with "the patriotic aspirations of the new [Third] [R]epublic." It was to become be a school of republican patriotism and values, where the men of France would learn to become Frenchmen.[63] The republicanizing of the army reached its height in the years after the Dreyfus Affair, when, under a series of aggressively republican Ministers of War, the army sought to purge itself of reactionary Catholics and replace the residue of the professional army of the Second Empire with one composed of self-consciously republican citizen-soldiers. As Porch argues, France's barracks were to become "seminaries of French patriotism and its officers, missionaries of national unity."[64]

Part of this ministry was to spread the gospel of temperance. Conscripts were of course punished for drunkenness, either with jail or by having their leave taken away, but according to officers, this power to repress did little to address conscripts' pitiful moral state or check the spread of alcoholic racial degeneration among them. Moreover, officers feared that putting presumed alcoholics in prison risked "contaminating" other soldiers in some unspecifiable but surely neo-Lamarckian way.[65] A positive program was needed – one that did not merely repress undesirable behaviours with fear of punishment, but rather allowed young soldiers to develop the techniques of the self that were necessary to *become* valuable citizens and soldiers. One such program was put into place in the years before the outbreak of the war.

In 1898, *Médecin principal 1è class* Viry was tasked with producing a study concerning prophylaxis against alcoholism in the army. In his report, Viry argued that the biggest danger was the army's canteens, which sold food, wine, and distilled alcohol to soldiers. The "logical conclusion," he argued, was to ban the sale of distilled alcohol in army camps entirely. This solution, he continued, "would be perfect" if not for the numerous *débits de boissons* that surrounded every camp and escaped army regulation. A ban might drive men into these insalubrious places, where they would fall prey to prostitution and the *péril venerienne*, itself a source of racial degeneration. Viry believed it was impossible to render men completely abstinent but held that the army could teach them the practices of temperance, which they would then internalize. He concluded that the army should launch its war on alcoholism on two fronts: "the moral education of soldiers and the surveillance of the sale of [distilled] alcohol in army camps."[66]

The following year, the French army sent a representative, *Médecin inspecteur* Dieu, to the Seventh International Congress against the Abuse of Alcoholic Beverages in Antwerp with the task of learning as much as he could about what other nations were doing to fight alcoholism in the ranks of their armies and make suggestions as to what the French might do in theirs – the French were not alone, of course, in their fear of racial degeneration among their conscripts. Dieu left Antwerp convinced that France's army had to ingrain the "the habits of sobriety" in its soldiers if the French race were to remain capable of defending itself into the twentieth century. He agreed with Viry that the army ought to launch a pedagogical program but argued that this had to be accompanied by sober activities and distractions. Dieu disagreed with Viry insofar as banning the sale of distilled alcohol was concerned. He recommended immediately banning the sale and consumption of it entirely in army camps.[67]

From these two reports the army drew up a two-pronged strategy to turn itself into a weapon of temperance. It would seek to restrict men's access to distilled alcohol to the greatest extent possible *and* it would deploy a pedagogical program that would teach them why the survival of the race depended on their not seeking it out. Moderate wine consumption would be permitted, but under supervision.

On 3 May 1900, the Minister of War (and the butcher of the Commune) Gaston Alexandre Auguste, the Marquis de Gallifet, banned all sales of distilled alcohol in all army canteens, barracks, camps, and parade grounds.[68] Nationally significant temperance reformers wrote to Gallifet and hailed him as the saviour of the race.[69] Newspapers too reacted favorably, with *La France militaire* holding that Gallifet's action was the "first step" in France's biological regeneration.[70] *Le Temps* assured readers that "all of France applauds" Gallifet's ban, which would help fight against distilled alcohol, "the principle cause of racial degeneration" with its "neurological troubles" and "blind violence." "Let us hope," the journal continued, that the army's anti-alcohol policy becomes "irresistible."[71] Under Gallifet's successor at the Ministry of War, Louis André, the policy was extended to include all soldiers in the empire, both European and colonial, on 21 March 1901.[72]

This was an unpopular move among the troops, and one that came with the very side effect that Viry foresaw, which was that soldiers became more loyal patrons of the *débits* that sprang up around army camps. The army responded by forming consumption cooperatives [*coopératives de consommation*] on the company level. These cooperatives served limited amounts of wine to soldiers during set hours and so provided them with an alternative to drinking at the local *débit*. Rather than go to a bar, where he would learn immoderate habits, a soldier would be drawn to these cooperatives, where he would learn self-restraint and be limited to only the most healthful of libations. The consumption cooperatives' purpose was thus not to initiate a regime of complete prohibition but rather to manage and regulate soldiers' drinking, to keep tabs on and control it by providing soldiers with an alternative – army-supplied wine – to the unregulated and shady *débit* with its distilled alcohol and syphilis. Moderate doses of wine consumed under supervision, besides, would protect soldiers *against* alcoholism. As of 30 May 1907, every army camp was supposed to have had such a cooperative, and the army began closing privately run canteens in June of that year. This had the added benefit of purging army camps of the female *cantinières*, thereby further "virializing" and masculinizing the army.[73]

The army also sought to provide distractions for soldiers to keep them dry. In March 1904, it established funds for units to purchase games – card, board, and ball – to provide soldiers with healthy alternative forms of amusement; this matched well with a more general French medical belief that physical exercise could prevent or even reverse degeneration.[74]

In September 1905, it organized anti-alcoholic libraries with tempting titles such as "The Manual of Anti-Alcoholism" and "Social Hygiene." On 15 April 1909, it began organizing field trips to the countryside on Sundays. On these assuredly profitable excursions, soldiers were escorted to regional sites of note and ordered to interest themselves in the economics, geography, and military history of France, as this would help them understand their own role in history as defenders of the Republic. It also kept them out of the bars.[75]

But moral education was the heart of the army's temperance campaign. The idea was to train men to take care of their bodies to help the race evolve and the nation's power grow. Conscript soldiers would learn to contribute consciously to both processes. Education would not only keep men sober while they were under the colours, but would have, reformers hoped, a life-long influence; it would prepare soldiers not only to fight, but to be productive and reproductive after they finished their time as conscripts.

The educational campaign was formally launched when Minister of War André issued a circular on 15 January 1901 mandating a program of anti-alcohol lectures and conferences. It stated that while the effects of Gallifet's prohibition were helpful, "the abuse of alcohol was always possible outside of army camps." What was necessary was "moral action" among officers and anti-alcohol pedagogy that would help "the soldier acquire the certainty that the use of alcohol diminishes resistance to illness and fatigue." Having gained the habits of sobriety, the soldier would thus assure his and his nation's "physical and moral" development. Among the subjects that would be discussed: the "the diminution of organic strength" distilled alcohol caused, its "devastating hereditary effects," and its negative influence on discipline.[76] One reformer called this the institutionalization of a "veritable anti-alcoholic education[al]" system in the army.[77]

The content of these presentations was unexceptional and hammered home a familiar point: distilled alcohol was a racial poison. One zealous officer recounted proudly the long schedule for a Sunday of temperance pedagogy. First came a "monologue by Soldier N." on the subject of "The Children of Drunkenness." This was followed by "Drinking Too Much at Night," an "amusing" talk illustrated with slides. The next presentation, "The Types of Alcoholic Degeneration," also came with visual aids, these ones depicting human beings in increasing states of penury, filth, and degradation. Fourth was "How We Lose Our Health," and last a surely edifying lecture on "The Contemporary History of Anti-Alcoholism." This, that officer wrote, "was how we passed the sad and often rainy days of winter."[78] Indeed.

Lectures were accompanied by propaganda. Posters decorated with grisly images of alcoholically diseased organs proudly displayed themselves in mess halls and dormitories, where they accompanied conscripts as they ate and watched over them as they slept. A conscript, ideally, ought not to be able to step into a single room without being assaulted with slogans printed on banners: "A good soldier is a sober soldier"; "The majority of insane people and criminals are alcoholics"; "War on alcoholism"; "If France continues to drink so much, in ten years there will be two German conscripts for every French one."[79] One reformer suggested rather ghoulishly that it would be useful to obtain the diseased internal organs of alcoholics (preserved in vats) in order to display them to conscripts.[80] Officers were to set the example by demonstrating sobriety "entirely and continuously." Anything less would be to abandon the conscript to himself, which spelled certain disaster.[81]

But enforcement of the rules regarding sales of distilled alcohol and the closure of canteens, to say nothing of conscripts' interest in the pedagogy or even attendance at its outings, was far from uniform. Some commanders were too lax and failed in their continuous labour of moral rectitude, while others were too strict and fanatical in their war on alcohol. Soldiers, save the keenest for the race, reacted to the temperance campaign the way all young men react to temperance campaigns: with incomprehension and horror. Nevertheless, reformers were pleased with themselves, citing a marked decline in arrests for drunkenness in units with vigorous temperance activity.[82] But in an army camp, drunkenness was the easiest kind of thing to police. The question was whether the temperance message stayed with men after they moved into the reserves and on to civilian life, where distilled alcohol was cheap and plentiful and there was no surveillance. Would they police themselves? They do not seem to have done so, as the per capita consumption statistics tracked upwards from 1901 to 1914, the period that temperance colonized the army's pedagogy.

But the efficacy of the program is not really the point; what matters is its existence and nature. It sought to mold a certain kind of citizen through controlling his environment – forcing him to be mostly dry, if you will – in hopes that this, along with a pedagogical program, would adapt his body and protect it against alcoholism. He would be armoured against his environment once released back into the democratic wilds and strong and sober under fire, which would allow his natural martial characteristics as a Frenchman to lead him to victory. The specifically French nature of the program manifested itself in the focus on distilled alcohol along with a limited promotion of wine. Wine-drinking was tolerated as a hedge against the wild, murderous, undisciplined intoxication distilled alcohol ostensibly produced.

In the Third Republic's first decades, soldiers' rations generally did not include distilled alcohol or wine. On 19 May 1890, a redesigned army ration schedule informed by scientific research into bodily requirements was introduced. It supposedly assured that soldiers would obtain the right number of calories and nutrients.[83] What was most noteworthy about the new ration schedule was that it did not include wine or distilled alcohol, at least not daily and not in peacetime.[84] Only when bivouacking – whether on campaign in the colonies or during manoeuvres – were soldiers to be allotted a quarter-litre of wine *or* two ounces of 47-proof *eau-de-vie*. In these times of exceptional danger and stress, alcoholic drinks might serve as a "spur" to help men in their exertions and could be distributed at the request of a commander. But in ordinary circumstances, alcohol's effects were "noxious."[85] In practice, distilled alcohol was not distributed even when permissible. The army viewed it as a tool, but a dangerous one. And befitting its position as an instrument of temperance, the army made no plans to centrally provision wine or *eau-de-vie* and distribute them to soldiers in the field in the event of a general European war. When just such a war broke out, the army lacked the capacity to store or deliver alcohol of either type in any significant quantity, having no special train-cars, barrels, or cleaning equipment, nor specially trained personnel. Thus – and by design – the French army that went to war in 1914 marched on water.

This set the stage for a great reversal in the French army's alcohol policy when the war began and men interred themselves in the trenches, where the miserable and terrifying conditions made sobriety a liability rather than an asset. As of mid-1915, the army was actively supplying men with both wine and distilled alcohol, the former drink daily and the latter in the exceptional circumstance of battle, to help in keeping up their morale and fighting spirit. Wine was praised to the heavens in the army and French popular culture; distilled alcohol was distributed in silence, a dirty but open secret. In both cases, intoxication was instrumentalized as a biocultural tool of emotional, and thus behavioural, control.

2

THE ORIGINS AND NATURE OF THE PSYCHOTROPIC REGIME

THE EARLY WAR

On 4 August 1914, the right wing of the German army scythed through Belgium, wheeling through the country and into France in a great sweeping motion with Metz as its fulcrum. German heavy mortars threw shells of awesomely large calibres – 380 and 420 mm – that thundered down upon the sophisticated Belgian fort system around Liège, driving the men inside the forts mad with fear. Liège fell on 16 August, opening the door to Flanders and France. In late August, the bulk of the German and French forces met in a series of confused encounters on the border of Belgium and France known as the Battle of the Frontiers. These were the bloodiest weeks of the entire war, costing the French some 330,000 casualties and the Germans a comparable number.

Meanwhile, terrified French civilians abandoned their homes and livelihoods by the tens of thousands and fled along with their retreating army, carrying what they could. This "Great Retreat" not only undermined the morale of soldiers, who felt helpless and impotent rage as they watched their country being overrun, but also destroyed the lives of countless noncombatants. As the war consumed the soldiers of France and Germany, it razed the towns and villages it moved over, leaving them burned-out husks. Such is what happened to Pillon, which Charles Delvert described: "The Germans have literally ransacked the place ... They raped the women, burned down the houses ... Poor folk reduced to the clothes on their backs wander distraught through the wreckage. It looks as if a horde of savages has passed this way."[1] From the rail station at Rambervillers, Henri Désagneaux watched the refugees pour backwards. "These poor people," he lamented, "distressed, leaving their homes and their possessions … It brings tears to your eyes … It's an indescribable mess."[2]

As Germany's army pressed south, it further extended its lines of resupply and strained its logistics. The advance became harder and harder for the increasingly exhausted Germans. Between 7 and 8 September the French and German armies met in a battle that spanned eastern France along the Marne River. The Battle of the Marne was enormous, involving nearly two million French and German soldiers in total; it ended in a decisive French victory. On 9 September, the Germans pulled back to re-establish their line, and their advance was halted. This was followed by a more general German retreat to the Aisne River on 12 September.[3] The "miracle" at the Marne was a great French victory, perhaps the greatest in the nation's long history.[4] That France's soldiers, weary and demoralized beyond comprehension by weeks of defeat and horrific fighting, and at the price of a quarter-million casualties, could and would rally was an event unforeseen by the German General Staff.

What followed was the so-called "Race to the Sea," a series of battles that were less of a race and more of a series of clumsy alternating French and German attempts to outflank one another to the north.[5] In this way, the Western Front – anchored in the east by French forts along the German border and running due west from Verdun to Noyon – slowly grew northward and reached toward the Channel. By mid-October, the war was once again in Belgium. At the First Battle of Ypres in the late fall, the German army, fresh with reinforcements eager to prove their bravery, made one last attempt to break through and turn a flank. The result was the *Kindermord*, the "slaughter of the innocents," when German volunteers fresh from their patriotic training in school were massacred while attacking. By mid-November, the German push had stalled. German commanders recognized that an immediate victory on the Western Front was impossible. They shifted to a strategy of keeping the territory in France they had already taken and letting the French break themselves with attacks.[6]

Three relatively new weapons – the repeating infantry rifle, the machine gun, and quick-firing, breech-loading artillery – fundamentally reshaped the First World War battlefield in ways that commanders did not foresee or immediately appreciate.[7] The rapidity and accuracy of their fire from kilometres away made it hazardous for infantrymen to cross open ground. Their range elongated the battlefield, extending greatly the time infantrymen needed to close with their enemy. And they allowed even small numbers of men to lay down dense fields of fire – a single well-placed machine-gun could cut down hundreds, which is why bayonet fighting was virtually unheard-of during the First World War.[8] Yet the rifle, the machine-gun, and the smaller-calibre artillery pieces (e.g. field guns) all fired their projectiles along a relatively flat trajectory, which meant that jumping in a shell hole, or better yet digging a trench, provided an infantryman with a lot of protection. In seeking to escape the effects of modern firepower, soldiers thus added another dimension to the battlefield: depth.

The experience of the first battles was traumatic in nearly every sense. They were confusing. Soldiers seldom knew where fire was coming from, or where the enemy was, or what was happening at all. Firepower overwhelmed the human sensorium, and battle brought with it, according to the veteran Paul Lintier, a disorienting, "awe-inspiring roar … similar to that of an ocean storm" that drowned out all other sound.[9] The fighting consisted of a series of bewildering, blind movements, of being ordered here and there without knowing why, of being shot at without being able to shoot back because the battlefield was empty of visible enemies. Battle, in short, had neither narrative nor structure and thus denied men meaning; it was like some terrible initiation ritual with no resolution. Courage traditionally construed had little place there, where firepower ruled as a tyrant. It forced immobility upon combatants, who sought shelter in trenches to protect themselves.[10]

The trenches were at first hastily made and provisionary, but as the Race to the Sea wound down, they became deeper and more permanent. By late November 1914, the British and French on the one side and Germans on the other were effectively besieging one another along a front that ran from the Channel to Switzerland. Soldiers were thus interred in a labyrinth of defensive trenches, bound and fixed unto the earth.[11]

Soldiers were uniformly horrified and aghast at the grotesque effects of modern firepower upon the human body, which it mocked and defiled in ways that beggared imaginations. Rifles did not punch clean, neat holes in infantrymen, but rather tore into them, leaving deep channels and gaping exit wounds the size of fists.[12] Machine-guns fired larger bullets with higher velocities than rifles, to say nothing of their rate of fire. A series of hits could tear off arms and legs or rip bodies in two. But neither rifle nor machine gun abused the French infantryman's body or haunted his fears like artillery. Particularly terrifying were Germany's large-calibre howitzers and mortars, which threw bigger shells farther than their fewer-in-number French equivalents. The shells these guns fired, according to Delvert, "hit the ground like meteors, long trails of black smoke mounting to the heavens, echoing with a fearsome clap like thunder."[13] They did vile and unimaginable things to whatever living creatures they landed near. They blew some men into the sky and turned other men inside out, crushing and pulverizing them until nothing human remained.

The fear and anxiety shellfire produced was debilitating precisely because what it did to the body was so obscene. Battle, of course, had always maimed and broken the human body, but those bodies most often remained recognizably human even in death. Modern firepower offered no such reassurance, and its effects shocked men deeply, inspiring a mixture of sorrow, revulsion, and hatred.[14] Indeed, modern firepower provided men with a new and awesome terror, that of disappearing completely, of being cut to ribbons by shrapnel or vaporized by a shell fired from kilometres away. Paul Cazin recalled:

> If a shell falls next to you, at just the right moment, nothing will be left. This is not just a saying; there is literally nothing left. Death makes you disappear. Blood and lymph evaporated. Skin, bone, hair, shoes, belts, every solid part of the individual, reduced to ashes and pulverized.[15]

The soldier's radical powerlessness matched the radical violence imposed upon him, and this sense of powerlessness was coupled with ever-present anxiety and fear that sapped morale and fighting spirit. Thus, in the context of trench warfare, the very meaning of military morale changed: the question was no longer only, nor even primarily, how to attain it in an attack. Rather, the question was how to maintain it in enduring conditions fatal to dignity and hope. Morale needed to last – it needed duration as well as valence. And so, all armies on the Western Front faced a puzzle: how to maintain it?[16] For the French army, the stalemate itself made possible a partial solution to the problem of morale. The war had fixed the belligerent armies in place, and this allowed for regular deliveries of supplies – including, soon enough, wine and distilled alcohol.

As planned, French soldiers were largely sober during the first months of the war of movement, which didn't seem to help them. Granted, there was some extracurricular drinking among *poilus* early on. In early August, after newly mobilized conscripts had debarked their trains, found their units, and begun to march, they were feted and celebrated in the streets, greeted by the cheering and wine-bearing women and children of France and Belgium.[17] Some brought flasks or bottles of wine or distilled alcohol with them to the front, outside of regulations, and passed them around to drink for courage or to fight fatigue, right before or even during battle.[18] Others "requisitioned" alcohol from half-destroyed and abandoned homes, or sought out oblivion during the shame of the Great Retreat. For instance, Maurice Genevoix described his men finding a cache of wine in a ruined village on 5 September. "It had been a long time since they had wine," he recalled, "so they took it and abused it."[19] But, overall, there was – as planned – remarkably little drinking in the French army during the first weeks and months, and what drinking did take place was opportunistic, mercenary, and contingent. This did not last long, for the same unhappy tactical reality that assured the Western Front would remain static also allowed for regular and, soon enough, generous alcohol rations for French soldiers.

THE *VIN AUX SOLDATS* CAMPAIGN AND
THE ORIGINS OF THE WINE RATION

Shortly after the trenches were dug, some of France's wine-makers provided donations of wine for soldiers, although the amount was modest given the size of the army.[20] The wine was very well received, which provided these same wine-makers with a brilliant idea, one that would simultaneously show their patriotism, help win the war, and line their pockets: the *vin aux soldats* [wine for soldiers] public relations campaign, which sought to use donations of wine to show the drink's military usefulness and thus convince the army to adopt a regular ration. The spearhead of the *vin aux soldats* campaign was Pierre Charles Causel, a prefect from the Hérault who called for every wine-grower in his *département* to donate one per cent of his harvest to the army, a request of 140,000 hectolitres in total.[21] Through October and November, the campaign brought to the army about 200,000 hL of wine, 100,000 from the Hérault alone.[22] This provided around 80,000,000 rations of a quarter-litre, enough to supply the army for a month. The gift from France's wine-makers to its soldiers was a public relations boon. The army would receive the first taste for free, and once it saw the value of the ration and could not go without, the wine-makers would start charging.

The language of the campaign was patriotic. If a daily wine ration could be delivered to soldiers, the wine-makers proclaimed, it would protect and revive them, helping them in enduring the war's physical and psychological stresses. Plus, the wine harvest of 1914 was a bumper, and France's wine-makers fretted that their biggest customers were locked away at the front. Finally, what could be a more powerful symbol of the land France's soldiers were defending than wine, the very blood of the soil? It was a persuasive argument. Wine – the national drink – would give men the power to drive Germany from France. Thus, were the army to adopt a daily ration of wine, their argument went, two problems would be solved: morale in the trenches and the wine market's slack in demand.[23]

On 19 October 1914, just as the trench system was coalescing, the wine-maker Louis Martin wrote a short article in the French centre-left's organ, *Le Radical*. The wine harvest was in, and it was big enough – 66 million hectolitres, a near record – and prices low enough to permit "the addition of a bit of wine to the daily fare of our brave soldiers." Those soldiers, whom Martin affectionately called the "valiant little *pioupious*," fought with "ardor, endurance, and heroic gaiety [and] had a *right* to the solicitude of the state" in the form of wine. Martin asked that the Minister of War, Alexandre Millerand, investigate whether soldiers might receive a daily ration, which, Martin held, "would be an excellent thing."[24]

"Our soldiers will get wine!" shouted the former Minister of Agriculture Hippolyte Gomot confidently from the front page of *Le Petit Journal* about a month later, on 13 November 1914. The French nation, he maintained, owed a debt to the citizen-soldiers who defended it and was obligated to "engineer a means to relieve their suffering." But wine did more than just relieve – it had positive, activating emotional and behavioural effects, inspiring men and setting them in motion by "remind[ing] them of their country." Wine was potable patriotism, and its consumption would produce, Gomot predicted, the kinds of behaviours that would fuel the army's victory. "Wine for our soldiers! Who would not agree with this idea?" he asked, either blissfully or intentionally unaware of the army's recent history of promoting sobriety.[25]

And Joseph Garat, a deputy from Bayonne, sent a letter to the Prime Minister that was published in *La Gazette de Biarritz* at November's conclusion. He quoted a soldier from who had ostensibly written to him earlier in the month: "Say it from on high, cry it out loudly, that they [must] distribute to us a bit of wine! [W]hat we lack above all at this time is a soothing drink." Men were asking for it and the Republic owed it to them, for the months to come would assuredly be difficult. "Is not the moment near when we will demand from [our soldiers] that they, with a decisive attack, drive out the invaders?" Garat demanded. France's soldiers, in short, needed a fuel to push them to victory over both the winter conditions in 1914–15 and their German enemies. Wine, that biological marvel, was perfectly suited for the task.[26]

Throughout November, French newspapers throughout the country dedicated column inches to the *vin aux soldats* campaign. *La Petite Gironde* lauded the effort and hoped the Gironde would do its part to assure men in the trenches received what they needed.[27] *L'Écho d'Alger* regularly and joyously reported when Algerian wine was donated to the army: M Despaux gave 500 hL of wine in order to "benefit the soldiers who defend us against invaders of the French fatherland and Algeria"[28]; the Chenu brothers, all three mobilized and at the front, agreed to donate 100 hL from their vineyard[29]; the widow Mme Bernoin donated only six hL, but no gift was too small.[30] The pressure on the army to reverse its stance and adopt a wine ration built.

As happy news of the donated wine's beneficial effects on morale and behaviour came in, a certain "F.V." concluded with authority in the *Revue de viticulture* that the army's policy of temperance had been revealed as a failure. The doctors and commanders who promoted it, he insisted, were misguided fools who, through their "snobbism," divorced Frenchmen from what should have been their natural nourishment and source of power. "In this war of the trenches," he maintained, "where the soldier was submitted to the rain, to the cold, his feet in the water, his spirit constantly stretched," an "abundant ration of wine" would comfort him, energize him, and, through its "antimicrobial" properties, protect him from illness. The war wore men down, but wine recharged them; war filled them with sorrow and fear, but wine gave them joy and courage; and war forced them from their families and loves, but wine provided them with a link to the land they defended, a way to *feel* patriotism. Plus, providing wine for soldiers had the substantial benefit of protecting men against alcoholism.[31] Such was the compelling yet inchoate logic behind the wine ration: it would alter men and so adapt them to the war's unnatural environment; but in doing so it would also bring them together, powering their bodies and energizing their minds collectively.

Yet by mid-fall 1914, French soldiers had, on their own, already discovered that alcohol was an antidote to the miseries of the war and a way to power their labours; they did not need the *vin aux soldats* campaign to sing for them the virtues of drink, which, once the trenches were dug, they began to consume with enthusiasm whenever possible. By the time the army began its regular distributions, it was most likely playing catch-up with realities on the ground.

Recall that the rations schedule from 1914 permitted the distribution of a quarter-litre of wine or .0625 litres of *eau-de-vie* to soldiers at the discretion of commanders in wartime. Some commanders began such distributions once the trench system emerged, probably even before the donations from the *vin aux soldats* campaign arrived. They must have purchased local wine and/or *eau-de-vie* themselves, taking the opportunity to live off the land while they could. For instance, the infantryman Joseph de Fontenioux received an alcohol ration somewhere between 2 and 8 October, which included not only a quarter-litre of wine, but also "some mouthfuls" of *eau-de-vie*. This was well before the army's centralized distribution network was in place. The effect on morale was instant. "Now we are happy as kings," he declared in his journal. "It is impossible to describe the avidity with which those two things were drunk."[32]

Information on these early army distributions is scant in the French military archives, but in one short and telling exchange from 30 October 1914, Ferdinand de Langle de Cary, the commander of Fourth Army, wrote to General Headquarters (GQG) requesting permission to expand the wine ration for his soldiers, who were fighting off German counter-attacks in the Argonne. Maurice Pellé, commander-in-chief General Joseph Joffre's deputy, forwarded the request on to the army's logistical wing and requested a ration of .375 litres be distributed to the men.[33] Unfortunately, the army was incapable of providing the wine, as it lacked the logistical capacity.[34] The brief exchange suggests two things. First, by late October 1914, at least some commanders were distributing wine rations to their soldiers. But they were not getting much if any wine from the army's central stocks, which were virtually non-existent. Commanders must have purchased alcohol locally and distributed it to their men at the front. Second, what deliveries the army managed to send out were irregular and their amount modest because the army lacked the logistical capabilities to store and distribute wine in bulk – indeed, what wine was brought up from the rear was transported by the wine-sellers themselves. These very first wine distributions were, in other words, not systematic in their application; they were neither diligently supervised nor planned, but were rather a spontaneous reaction to the war. Third, and most importantly, the distributions worked: they raised morale.

In November 1914, Minister of War Alexandre Millerand made the fateful decision to supply every soldier in the French army with a daily ration of a quarter-litre of wine, centrally procured and distributed.[35] No longer would the ration depend on donations or local supplies but would rather flow incessantly from the wine-growing regions in the rear to the front. Millerand's decision was a recognition of the success of the *vin aux soldats* campaign, of the reality that men were already drinking, and, perhaps most importantly, of a sense of obligation the Third Republic felt towards its citizen-soldiers, whose bodies it wanted to protect from the war and whose morale it wanted to keep high for the offensives to come in 1915. When word of Millerand's decision to provision and distribute wine centrally spread through the army, the response among soldiers was predictably positive. Zacharie Baqué was jubilant. "Perhaps, in this way, the sun of the *midi* will shine on us," he wrote in his journal. "We have need of it."[36]

The adoption of a regular ration represented a sea-change in the French army's relationship with alcohol. As we have seen, before the war, the army had, at its very wettest, permitted limited wine consumption among conscripts and did not regularly distribute distilled alcohol rations. It was arguably France's largest and most effective temperance organization. But during the war, it would come to act as France's greatest *promoter* of alcohol consumption – of both wine and *eau-de-vie*. The exigencies of maintaining morale in the trenches were paramount, with necessity birthing this hypocritical, improvised reversal.

But the army was not immediately ready for the logistical task of distributing an alcohol ration, as it lacked the necessary infrastructure and planning. Thus, two structures had to be built: the first material and logistical (which would allow for the distribution of alcohol to men in the trenches), and the second discursive and medico-cultural (which would explain how much alcohol was needed and why). In the event, the French army erected the largest wine-purchasing and distribution network in history up to that point, while French doctors, politicians, and wine-makers erected a similarly elaborate physiological-cum-racial justification for the ration. Both were complete by mid-1915, by which time the psychotropic program of emotional and behavioural conditioning was largely in place.

THE LOGISTICS OF A GREAT BIG STRAW

Feeding, clothing, and sheltering millions of French soldiers in wartime was the job of the army's supply wing, the *Intendance Militaire*. Its motto was *vivre sur le pays, vivre sur l'arrière* [live off the land, live off the rear], which aptly describes the *Intendance*'s philosophy when it came to resupply in wartime.[37] On the one hand, once mobilized, the army planned to supply itself partially off the land it advanced over, purchasing or requisitioning supplies as it moved. This was useful for supplies that did not travel well, either because they spoiled (such as fresh vegetables) or because they were very heavy but easy to find (such as hay). The rub was that the army had to advance to keep itself fed, but because the French naturally assumed that they would be advancing into Germany, this was not expected to be a significant problem. On the other hand, the army also planned to supply itself partially from supplies prepared in the rear and brought up to the front by rail. Supplies that kept well and could be manufactured in great quantities – bread, tinned beef, coffee, and sugar – would be delivered in this way. The *Intendance* thus provided an umbilical cord tying the army to the rear.[38]

The backbone of this procurement network was the *stations-magasins* (sms), huge logistical depots and assembly centres in France's interior. There were around twenty of them, placed in cities a comfortable distance from the German border to assure that they were not overrun in an invasion.[39] sms contained rail stations and loading facilities, enormous warehouses, giant ovens, huge roasters for green coffee, and butcher's stations capable of processing hundreds of animals a day. During peacetime, they were quiet, but on the first day of mobilization, they activated and became staffed by thousands of men.

Materials collected from the rear were sent to the sms, where they were processed and packed into special resupply trains. These were directed downstream to the *gares régulatrices* [control stations] located about 100 kilometres from the front, where the supplies were sorted and organized before being sent further downstream to the *gares de ravitaillement* [resupply stations], located about twenty kilometres from the front. There, the

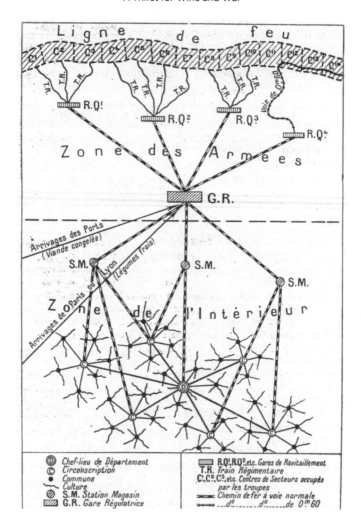

2.1 "How France Subsists Her Armies at the Front" (1917).

Intendance handed the supplies off to regiments at the rear of the trench system. Every day each sm prepared and shipped supplies for more than a hundred thousand men.[40]

In short, the French army's logistical system was designed for a sharp, offensive war of movement in a hostile country, which is to say inside of Germany. In the event, it was tasked with supplying soldiers in a long, static war inside of France. Consequently, French troops were stationed around the same villages for weeks and months. They ate and drank through their local supplies quickly. The French army found itself forced to live off supplies sent from the rear, from provisions collected and readied in SMS and sent to the front. The SMS consequently evolved in function and shifted into a higher gear, soon receiving, processing, and transporting all sorts of supplies.

When the war broke out, SMS were stocked with only basics such as flour, sugar, green coffee, lard, and the canned preserved meat that *poilus* came to call *singe*, or "monkey."[41] They focused on making enough bread, butchering enough animals, and transporting enough food to keep the millions of men in the French army fed.[42] By October, SMS had taken on much more responsibility and greatly expanded what they stocked and delivered, which now included cooking oil, potatoes, cheese, sausage, sardines, chocolate, candles, matches, petrol for lamps, pipes, cigarette paper and tobacco, and soap – a necessary "ingredient for cleanliness," but one that was seldom practical to use in the trenches.[43] In addition, the army's medical wing, the *service de santé*, had logistical troubles in the war's first weeks. Thereafter the SMS were charged with maintaining and delivering medical supplies.[44] By mid-December, the SMS were doing the same for the *service vétérinaire*.[45] This expansion of the SMS' capacities allowed the French rail system to become, one commentator noted, "an organ of resupply" that assured the *poilu* in his trench got what he needed with regularity.[46] The army relied upon them for nearly everything but munitions.

In effect, the Western Front – static, entrenched, fire-swept – created a revolutionary new circumstance in military logistics: it fixed men in place and buried them in its defensive networks, which made it possible to deliver provisions with an unprecedented regularity and capacity. Material could be drawn out of the interior and then pushed into the front as though on a conveyor belt, with the static nature of the fighting making a highly centralized, just-in-time logistical system possible. This set the conditions for the possibility of the systematic delivery of wine and *eau-de-vie* to millions of soldiers all at once, even to men who were in battle fighting, and all from centrally provisioned stocks. Nothing like this had ever before been possible, at least not on this scale.

But, recall, the army was unequipped to provide its soldiers with wine when Millerand made his aspirational pledge in November. SMS had no stocks of wine. Nor did they have any way to process, store, or transport

2.2 Barrels of wine at Dunkerque's *station-magasin* (1916).

stocks, as the army – having never planned to distribute a regular wine ration – lacked barrels, *wagons-foudres* (the special rail stock used to transport wine), barrel-making and cleaning equipment, and trained personnel.[47] The army called up reserves from old classes and gave leave to men at the front with specialized building skills, putting them to work. There were "great difficulties" at first, mostly because the army had only half as many barrels as it needed. Logistical records show that sms were understocked through November, although they had started taking deliveries of wine when the gifts from the *vin aux soldats* campaign began to arrive at the end of October.[48] By December, most sms had been outfitted with the equipment needed to transfer and store great quantities of wine and *eau-de-vie*, including industrial-scale machines for washing barrels and *wagons-foudres*, with the army requisitioning tens of thousands of barrels and thousands of cars for its own use for the duration. Additionally, the army requisitioned a majority of France's *wagons-foudres*.[49]

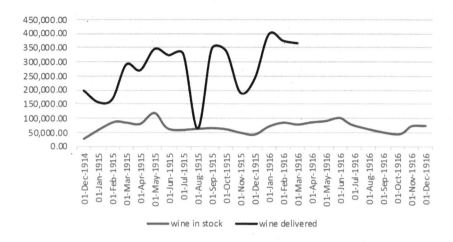

2.3 Wine in stock and delivered to *stations-magasins* (hL), 1914–16.

By winter, centralized distributions of wine began. At the end of December 1914, after the army began to receive government-purchased wine in bulk, SMS held but 27,920 hectolitres of wine in stock.[50] The army required about 6,750 hL per day to provide each man in the army with a quarter-litre of wine, so at the winter's outset the SMS had enough to provide the army with wine for about four days. Stocks quickly rose through the first half of 1915, as SMS grew in their capacity. Between December 1914 and May 1917, SMS kept an average of 72,770 hL in stock, with a peak in May 1915 at 118,500 hL. There could be substantial variation because of the season and delivery schedules, and at no time did the of amount of wine stocked exceed three weeks' worth. The system had a buffer but was built for constant turnover – the wine was sent out shortly after it was received.

The amount of wine delivered to SMS tells a similar story. In December 1914, they took in 198,416 hL, enough to supply the army for a month. Between that month and March 1916, SMS received an average of 255,169 hL, and in every month save August 1915, when there was a precipitous drop-off in purchasing for reasons explored below, SMS received enough to meet about three-quarters of the army's requirements. To make up the remainder, when possible, wine was purchased or requisitioned in the army zones from bulk wine dealers.

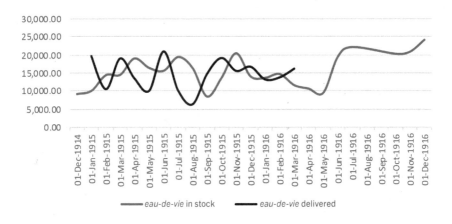

2.4 *Eau-de-vie* in stock and delivered to *stations-magasins* (hL), 1914–16.

The procurement and distribution of *eau-de-vie* followed the same general trend of just-in-time provisioning in which there was monthly variation but a near-constant stream of alcohol flowing into the trenches. *Eau-de-vie* was much easier to move and store than wine, as it was purchased at 95 per cent alcohol by volume and then watered down. It was transported to the front in the same way as wine – through the SMS. However, the distribution of *eau-de-vie* marked a much greater change in the French army's policy than the distribution of wine. The drink, after all, was considered a racial poison before the war. But now, its supposedly antiseptic and antimicrobial properties made it an important prophylactic medicine for trench fighters if it was used responsibly and in the smallest efficacious dose. The adoption of an *eau-de-vie* ration was not trumpeted in the popular press – indeed, it was adopted furtively, without fanfare or publicity. In December 1914, the army held 9,203 hL of *eau-de-vie* in stock, and between that month and December 1916 kept an average of 15,610 hL, with a maximum of 24,154 hL. On average, the army kept about nineteen days' worth of *eau-de-vie* in stock. The deliveries taken by SMS came to an average of 14,655.2 hL, enough to supply the army for seventeen days. A little over half of the army's *eau-de-vie* requirements, then, were met by the SMS. Moreover, unlike wine, *eau-de-vie* could not be purchased in bulk at the front. Soldiers were thus unable to supplement this ration in the field and so must have gone without frequently, around half the time.

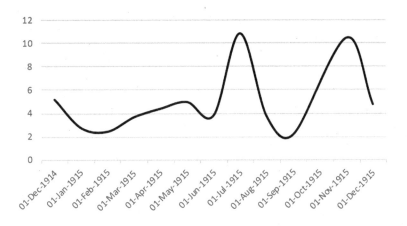

2.5 Average drinks per day supplied by the *stations-magasins*, 1915.

The available data allow for a rough model of how much alcohol from both sources – wine and *eau-de-vie* – French soldiers in the trenches could expect to receive over the course of 1915 from the SMS. Assuming that all the alcohol purchased by the *service de ravitaillement* made its way to the trenches every month, the SMS supplied the average French soldier with 5.1 standard drinks per day, a substantial but not overwhelming amount and just under what the *Intendance* aimed at.[51] Tellingly, there were two months in which the French soldier in the trench received an unusually large amount of alcohol, in July 1915 (during the Second Battle of Artois), when he received an average of 11.2 standard drinks a day, and in November 1915 (during the Second Battle of Champagne), when he received an average of 10.8 drinks a day. While the statistics are necessarily overestimates, as some alcohol was assuredly pilfered, lost, or spoiled, they nevertheless strongly suggest that men received significant amounts that would have powerfully influenced the experiences they had of the war.

THE BIOMEDICAL LOGIC OF PSYCHOTROPIC POWER

While no public rationale was ever given for the *eau-de-vie* ration, which was nearly kept a secret from the public (see chapter 4), there was an elaborate public one provided for the wine ration. To justify the existence of the huge logistical system necessary to procure wine and the similarly huge costs related to it, France's doctors provided a theory of the ration that was anchored in neo-Lamarckian racial science: the ration would not only protect men in the trenches, but also help regenerate the biological quality of the French race by transforming the bodies and drinking practices of soldiers.

Scientific discussions of the ration began in winter 1915. On 1 February that year, Dr Armand Gautier presented a paper to the *Académie des sciences* titled "On the Soldier's Ration in the Time of War" that generated some debate in the French medical community.[52] Gautier, a well-respected biochemist and former president of the *Académie*, spoke in the technical language of nutrition. He analyzed the French rural labourer's diet, which, on average, he claimed (with doubtful exactness), contained 144.3 grams of protein, 77.7 grams of fat, and 753.7 grams of carbohydrates. This came to a total of 4,133.7 calories. He repeated the same process for the diet of industrial workers, finding that they consumed, on average, 4,349 calories. Finally, he dissected the soldier's daily ration, which provided a measly 3,189.7 calories. At least 800 or 1,000 more calories were needed if men were to labour and fight. Gautier argued that if soldiers got more wine, the caloric deficit would be made up.[53] His main point was that the wine ration ought to be raised to three-quarters of a litre, which he considered "indispensable, especially during the cold and the winter."[54]

But it wasn't just about calories. There was also something biologically special about wine that would make its consumption additionally beneficial. Gautier noted that unlike fat and meat, which release energy slowly and make men sluggish, wine explodes with immediacy, being "burned off" right away and providing "momentary ardour [that] facilitates and brings forth effort [*amène l'effort*]." There was also wine's energizing "nervine" effect. It worked directly upon the body's nervous system, somehow simultaneously calming nerves *and* charging them up so as to maintain the "nervous excitement necessary" for fighting. Finally, wine had important hygienic properties that protected men from illnesses such as bronchitis, pneumonia, diarrhea, rheumatism, frostbite, and, of course, alcoholism. Wine, Gautier concluded, "was cheaper than the hospital; it protects soldiers; it maintains their strength and their good spirits; [and] it turns them away from the *cabaret* and [distilled] alcohol."[55]

Gautier's article was well received. Shortly after he presented it, the *Journal officiel* declared that Gautier was right: wine was a "powerful tonic and is recommended" for soldiers.[56] In March 1915, the *Revue de viticulture* reminded readers that the "technicians of nutrition" agreed that wine would preserve soldiers' "physical energy and health"; this was a simple scientific fact. "It is necessary that wine reaches our soldiers," the *Revue* maintained (with a telling choice of words), "[because wine] is an *energizing munition for the body.*"[57] That same month, Dr Émile-Léon Vidal, a member of the *Conseil supérieur de l'agriculture* from Hyères, lamented in *Le Progrès agricole et viticole* that the Ministry of War was not paying enough for the wine it was purchasing for soldiers. He emphasized with Gautier that soldiers needed wine as their nutritive and nervine agent but complained that the army's tight-fistedness was leading to "great discouragement" among wine-makers. Vidal cautioned that the army needed to not abuse its buying power if the wine-makers were to stay in business, and wine-makers needed to stay in business because the health of soldiers and the outcome of the war depended upon it.[58] The *poilu* and his *pinard* were symbiotic; the former would need the latter to triumph.

In the early summer of 1915, the Chamber of Deputies asked France's *Académie de médecine* to discuss the ration and make recommendations as to whether to keep it and if so at what amount. At the 29 June meeting of the *Académie*, Vidal began the proceedings with a new paper titled "The French Soldier's Wine Ration and Its Relationship with Alcoholism" in which he declared his agreement with Gautier's argument that the ration was too little. But Vidal thought Gautier was thinking small regarding what the wine ration could accomplish. The phylloxera blight was, Vidal held, a racial catastrophe for the French because it replaced wine, the "reparative drink of our ancestors," with distilled alcohol, the source of degeneration and its "furious homicides." This process threatened to be replicated in miniature in the trenches, where men were tempted to turn to distilled alcohol for energy or oblivion, as the situation required. Thus, unexpectedly, the spectre of degeneration haunted even the front.

But at the same time, the war – by trapping France's men in the trenches – created the unique opportunity for racial regeneration through the army-wide use of a regular wine ration. "We have been more and more invaded by alcoholism," Vidal reminded his audience, "and the future of the race depends, let us not forget, on what we have at hand to combat it."[59] He thus brought the racial, neo-Lamarckian logic implicit in Gautier's physiological reductionism into the open: the wine ration was, at least in part, conceived of as a wartime program of emergency racial hygiene. It thus had two purposes: to help the individual fight and endure, and to preserve and improve the biological quality of the army, and after the war, the nation. Vidal proposed that the *Académie* adopt a motion in support of the wine ration, now conceived of as a vast exercise in psychotropic power and biological engineering.

Vidal's paper inspired a cascade of follow-ups in the *Académie de médecine*. On 6 July, Gautier himself gave another presentation about soldiers' caloric requirements that was essentially a summary of his earlier paper, but now scented with degeneration theory.[60] On 13 July, after the miraculously named Dr Adolphe Pinard (of the famous Pinard horn) interrupted the meeting with an outburst of outrage at the thought that wine was not getting to soldiers with regularity, Dr Louis Landouzy, a towering figure in French medicine, read a paper titled "Wine, in the Soldier's Ration: A Means of Fighting Alcoholism." Landouzy agreed with all who came before that wine was an inexpensive and "agreeable stimulant" that "gives heat to the chest, joy to the heart, and gaiety and humour." "As a physiologist, a physician, a nutritionist," he continued, he had no hesitation prescribing wine for France's soldiers to protect them against the trenches and alcoholic racial degeneration. "They all are wise who, in taking care of the richness of the soil, in taking care of public health and the vigour of the race, in the interests of national defense," Landouzy advised, "think like with our colleagues E. Vidal and Armand Gautier that wine is one of the best weapons against alcoholism."[61] And so, as these papers built off one another, they built a cohesive theory of the ration, one that framed the health of the individual, the wine industry, and the French race together into a single problem whose elegant and eminently French solution was simple: *vin aux soldats!*

On 24 August, Gautier put forward for discussion the proposition that "the minimum required for a soldier in combat is fifty centilitres of wine [per day]." Dr Anatole Chauffard – whose concern for the health of the French race knew no bounds[62] – objected and took the unpopular position that wine was "a condiment, agreeable and euphoric," but not a true source of energy. He suggested that a wine ration might serve as a free supplement to other "voluntary libations less wisely limited" and so contribute to the problem of alcoholism rather than combatting it. Landouzy found this outrageous, retorting that *even psychologists* knew that wine was both a source of nutrients *and* a stimulant that cured alcoholism. Dr Barrier, a veterinarian, asked why, if wine was so energizing, nobody ever gave it to draught animals. A real spoilsport, he called the idea that "wine and alcohol give strength, vigour, and health" an "enormous error, a profound illusion," and regretted that no institution could disabuse the French of it.

Thus, France's doctors were not of the same mind insofar as how they thought about the ration – they were not universally or uncritically enthusiastic. And even though the good doctors Chauffard and Barrier were in the minority, they made their influence felt. To propitiate them, Dr Ballet offered some compromise language. The science was clear, Ballet maintained: "all the evidence shows that wine, taken with food and in moderate doses, is good for soldiers." But the key was moderation. Soldiers should always get and drink their ration of wine, but not get or drink more. The point was to find a physiological and psychotropic sweet spot, enough to keep soldiers happy, active, and protected, but not enough to undermine discipline or reduce combat effectiveness.

The final version of a motion in favour of the wine ration stated that "the *Académie* is of the view that natural wine should be introduced, in moderate quantities [of at least half a litre] … into the soldier's daily ration, and that precautions be taken to prevent soldiers from consuming more." It was adopted unanimously, with Dr Valentin Magnan, France's most eminent neo-Lamarckian theorist of alcoholism and racial degeneration, presiding. In this way, the minimum therapeutic dose of *pinard*, the patriotic drug *par excellence*, was established.[63]

Dr Pierre Viala, Professor of Viticulture and Viticulture Inspector General, followed the discussion in the *Académie de médecine* with delight. The wine ration had no greater friend than Viala, who, from his position as founder and editor of the *Revue de viticulture*, approvingly reprinted Gautier and Landouzy at length.[64] Then, on 26 March 1916, he presented a paper to the *Association française pour l'avancement des sciences* titled "The Vinicultural Future of France," a remarkable defense of the wine ration later republished as a stand-alone volume that contains a distillation of the psychotropic and racial logic behind it.[65] Viala conceived of nations as essentially biological entities that transform and are transformed by their natural environments. They were meta-organisms, manifestations of the complex relationships among body, race, and *milieu*. "The characteristic genius of a race," he argued, "is the physical and psychological result of an ensemble of factors, traditions, and habits."[66] Because the French race co-evolved with the vine in a symbiotic relationship, its vitality was a function of how much pure, natural wine it consumed. Viala had but scorn and venom for those like Chauffard and Barrier, who, he claimed, imported dangerous "anti-French" understandings of wine.[67]

In Viala's thinking, French wine's value came from its near-miraculous properties in the body. It was, he held, a "complex colouring material in which organic substances bind to phosphoric bodies and amino acids to make a nutrient of the highest order." And this is "to speak only of its general nutritive character and [say] nothing about its direct effects on the nervous system," which wine of course "excites" with its "nervine properties."[68] In fact, wine had a beneficial and "direct effect on *all the functions of the body*"; it made the entire human organism stronger and more energetic.[69] Viala argued that the wine ration not only protected soldiers in the present, filling them with "courage and patriotic faith," but also trained them to become wine-drinkers for life, and so would protect the French race against degeneration in the future.[70] This was a distillation of the biomedical logic behind the wine ration: it would defeat Germany *and* degeneration at the same time.

PROBLEMS OF QUALITY AND QUANTITY

Yet over 1915, there were pressing problems of quantity and quality that threatened to defeat the purpose of the system. For example, early in that year, the Director of the *Intendance* for the 21è Army Corps wrote several times to his superiors – once each in February, March, and April 1915 – alerting them to the low quality of the wine that was reaching his soldiers. He submitted a sample of the wine to an army lab for analysis and appended the report. The wine in question was reddish, slightly cloudy, and tasted lightly astringent and bitter. It was low in alcohol content at just over eight per cent and had been adulterated with both distilled alcohol and water [*vinage* and *mouillage*]. The lab concluded with all the majestic authority of science that it "tasted bad."[71] An internal review revealed that the poor-quality wine was coming from the SMS, meaning the problem was with the centrally provisioned stocks. The wine sold at the front on the open market that soldiers used to supplement what they received from the rear tended to be expensive but of reliable quality.[72]

The problem was that, in early 1915, the army's resupply wing [*service de ravitaillement*] purchased wine in a highly irregular, ad hoc, unprofessional, and undisciplined fashion. It sought and negotiated contracts from individual wine-sellers, primarily in the *midi*, on the open market. Because the wine harvest from 1914 was huge and sellers were eager to find a market for the overproduction, the army was able to purchase moderate-quality wine relatively easily and at a good price, at least at first.[73] The market responded and the price of wine climbed upwards, from 2 fr/hL before the war to 10 fr/hL in November 1914 to 42.50 fr/hL a year later, an increase of some 2,000 per cent.[74] At the same time, unscrupulous wine-sellers routinely committed fraud and took advantage of the army's inexperience in wine-purchasing, leading to wide variations in quality mid-year. In July 1915, the Ministry of War faced disaster as it could no longer find enough quality wine on the open market in the rear to supply soldiers at half a litre, and the amount provisioned by the sms was temporarily reduced to a quarter.[75] Army deliveries of wine to the trenches plunged almost seventy per cent in August 1915, while receipts at sms fell more than eighty per cent.[76] But the following month the army received more wine than it had at any time up to that point in the war.[77] It had found a brute-force solution: requisitions, which allowed it to raise the ration back up to half a litre.[78]

As of September 1915, between one-fifth and one-third of every wine-maker's harvest became the army's. In wine-growing *départements*, commissions appointed by prefects evaluated the stocks available and recommended an amount and price for purchase. This was forwarded on and evaluated in Paris. If a purchasing order was approved, the wine-producer would receive one-tenth of the payment up front and the rest upon delivery. Local mayors were charged with assuring that the wine got delivered.[79] To ensure quality, the *Intendance* sent specialists to inspect and approve each purchase, effectively professionalizing the wine-procurement system. Wine was also sampled for purity and alcohol content. By 1 January 1916, just months after the requisitions began, the army had requisitioned, although not taken possession of, 3,133,575 hL of wine, enough to supply it for about three-fifths of a year at a half-litre per man. This was a startling exercise of state power over – even a partial nationalization of – an industry long considered the Third Republic's protected darling.

Logistics officers worried that, even with requisitions, the army might not be able to supply enough wine to meet army needs in 1916. The harvest of 1915 was small, coming to 23 million hL for both the Hexagon and Algeria. One army report estimated that this, combined with the leftover stocks from the year before, left France with about 30,000,000 hL for the whole country in 1916. The army needed around 5,000,000 hL of wine to supply all its soldiers at half a litre per day. Prudence required that an additional 5,000,000 hL be kept in reserve for the army. This left about 20,000,000 hL for France's 35 million civilians, which came to an average one-sixth of a litre per resident per day; the figure from the year before was half a litre. The language the army used in the report suggested it considered wine a strategically essential commodity, as though it were a munition. The interior *had* to supply it if the army were to fight.[80] Consequently, France's civilians were forced to reduce their wine consumption by two-thirds.

The army briefly entertained an alternative to the wine ration. In December 1915, *Intendant* Général Savoye proposed what he presented as an ingenious alternative solution to the supply problem. In "certain regions" of the north, he explained, it was common for men to drink a mixture of wine and cider, and a recent experiment he performed in mixing the two produced a drink whose taste was "frank and admirable." Savoye suggested the army distribute such a *mélange* to soldiers where it could. He noted that doing so would take no special equipment, just a pump and a few men, and could be done in the *stations-magasins* or downstream at the *gares de ravitaillement*. He proposed to distribute the experimental mixture to the men of Second Army. Savoye was confident that his scheme would save money and reduce the strain on wine markets. Soldiers, he suggested, would not even notice.[81] The Ministry of War approved Savoye's proposal for a trial on a small scale.[82] For eight consecutive days in the early winter of 1916, two divisions from Sixth Army received a mixture of three-quarters wine and one-quarter cider. Unhappily, the men "appreciated the mixture very little," found it "barely drinkable," and preferred to receive their wine and cider unmixed. A report understated the unhappy effects: several who drank the mix experienced "intestinal troubles" that were unfortunate from the "sanitary point of view."[83] There were no further experiments.

Foreign markets were a more useful source of wine, and in early 1916, the army dispatched purchasing agents to Spain, Portugal, Argentina, Chile, and even California.[84] Lieutenant Taupeñas – who assuredly had the best job in the French army – led the four-man expedition to Spain and was charged with procuring 300,000 hL.[85] Spanish merchants were eager for French army contracts, but they demanded a premium to carry wine up to the French border via rail.[86] Taupeñas used the sea, buying from

Barcelona, Tarragone, Valencia, and Alicante, and sending the wine to the nearby French ports of Cette and Cerbère. The wine purchased was tested for quality and alcohol content in a laboratory at Montpelier, and Taupeñas recorded purchasing wine of 10.5 per cent alcohol content or above.[87] He bought a total of 273,700 hL of wine at an average price of 46.56 fr/hL, which was just over what the *Intendance* was paying for French wines of similar quality.[88] The smaller Mission Lalou focused on Portuguese wines. It purchased 177,000 hL at an average cost of 37.54 fr/hL, which were added to 200,000 hL of Portuguese contracts negotiated in October 1915.[89] The total amount obtained by the Iberian missions came to about 650,000 hL. A good portion of the wine that sustained men at Verdun and the Somme was not French at all.

The mission sent to South America encountered more difficulties. In February 1916, a wine-grower from the *midi* named F. Mathieu wrote an unsolicited letter to the Ministry of War. Mathieu was concerned about the effects of requisitions on the French wine industry and proposed that the army purchase wine from Argentina. The idea seemed at first blush to be a stroke of genius: Argentinian wine was of good quality and had high alcohol content, allowing it to travel well; it cost about half of what French wine cost; and it was grown on the other side of the equator, meaning it would be available right when French production was out of season. Mathieu estimated the stocks available for purchase at 11,000,000 hL. A bonus: Mathieu's son owned a winery in Mendoza, Argentina's main wine-growing region.[90]

Mathieu's venality aside, the army decided to try his idea. Its agent Baraton arrived in Argentina in early spring 1916 to find there were only 200,000 hL available at a cost of 40 fr/hL. Baraton could not find ships to transport the wine to France charging less than 30 francs per hectolitre, making Argentinian wine prohibitively expensive.[91] Nevertheless, he purchased 10,000 hL so that he did not return empty-handed. Paris had to dispatch its own vessel, the *Latouche Tréville*, to pick him up. A disappointed Baraton arrived in Bordeaux in August with enough wine to supply the army for about one day. The failure of the Mission Baraton led the army to recall its agents in Chile and California.[92] Even if they failed, these foreign missions show how dedicated the army was to assuring its soldiers got their wine. The logistical tail of the system covered France and Iberia and tried to reach across the Atlantic. Indeed, the army's pretentions and thirst were boundless – it sought to build a global alcohol procurement system.

Table 2.1 Wine requisitioned by the French army (hL)

Département	1914	1915	1916	1917
Hérault	1,032,000	1,188,000	1,346,000	3,014,000
Aude	234,000	632,000	827,000	1,825,000
Pyrénées-Orientales	169,000	244,000	502,000	747,000
Gard	180,000	120,000	220,000	435,000
Gironde	156,000	127,000	316,000	815,000
Others	367,000	631,000	898,000	739,000
Total from France	2,138,000	2,942,000	4,109,000	7,575,000
Algeria	10,500	1,438,000	1,693,000	1,978,000
Total requisitioned	*2,148,500*	*4,380,000*	*5,802,000*	*9,553,000*

Source: Lebert, "Rapport," Sénat no. 413; Charles K. Warner, *Winegrowers of France and the Government since 1875*, 60.

But, in the end, foreign sources were just adjuncts to the great requisitions from the *midi*, and those requisitions proved adequate. Between 1915 and 1916, the amount the army requisitioned increased from at least four and a half million hL (of which three and a half passed directly through the sms) to at least six million, then to nine and a half million in 1917, before falling to four and a half in 1918. These figures do not include purchases made in the field, which likely came to at least a third of the amount requisitioned. Nor does it consider wine that men purchased on their own while in the rear. It thus underestimates total consumption, perhaps by as much as half. In some years, requisitions accounted for up to twenty per cent of France's wine harvest.[93] In 1917, when local purchases are added in, the army likely drank close to a third of all the wine made in France, which itself came to around a sixth of the world's production. The straw the *Intendance* built was big.

Logistical records for First Army over 1916 show that the system worked. Its soldiers were well-supplied with wine and reasonably well-supplied with *eau-de-vie*.[94] Between 10 December 1915 and 30 October 1916, First Army, which had around 200,000 men in it, delivered a total of 78,950,793 wine

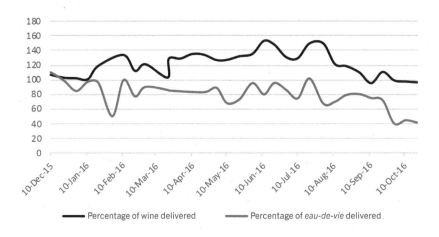

2.6 Percentage of wine and *eau-de-vie* required delivered to First Army, 1915–16.

rations and about 24,110,000 *eau-de-vie* rations. On average, First Army supplied 121.3 per cent of the wine required over any ten-day period in 1916.

Indeed, wine was important enough that First Army only failed to deliver all of what was required in October, when it supplied 97.8 per cent of what was needed. In June 1916, when the battle of Verdun reached its climax and that at the Somme was about to begin, this number reached more than 150 per cent. The figures were somewhat less impressive for *eau-de-vie*, but still adequate. First Army supplied, on average, 79.7 per cent of the *eau-de-vie* required for any ten-day period.

Granted, the averages for both drinks obscure variations in consumption patterns, as some men naturally drank more than others. Moreover, some amount of alcoholic drink was invariably wasted through spoilage, loss, and pilfering, meaning that soldiers received less than the averages imply. The figures in fact reveal less about how much any particular man drank on any given day than they do about the army's commitment to providing soldiers with alcohol. This commitment was consistent, real, and durable: by 1916, the army was supplying its soldiers with half a litre of wine or more every day, and .0625 litres of *eau-de-vie* some of the time.

The theory of the ration justified the use of psychotropic power to solve some of the problems of trench warfare: wine was used both as a tool in a massive program of biocultural engineering and as a public health intervention. French distributions of alcohol were thus conceived of as a biochemical intervention that was also a system of emotional and behavioural conditioning. In the language of the theory of the ration, wine was supposed to fill men with courage and patriotic faith, to help them *tenir* [hold on], to "energize" and "enliven" them, to "ready" and "prepare" them. But for what? Courage: for the attack, for overcoming the fear and tension that come with fighting and having to take lives. Patriotic faith: to endure the proletarianization of the front without complaint, to believe that one's sacrifices and suffering were not in vain. Energy: to power men through the drudgery and pain, and to enliven them. Not only would wine to protect and improve men, but in so doing, it would lead them to *do* certain things and behave in certain ways: be pliant in the face of command, aggressive towards the enemy, silent in their wretchedness.

But that the alcohol ration was a psychotropic tool of emotional and behavioural conditioning does not necessarily make it nefarious. The wine ration in particular was anything but a secret. The whole nation was involved in the project, even schoolchildren such as Suzanne Ferrand, who won a nationwide contest and designed a mass-produced poster urging French citizens in the rear to "save wine for our *poilus*". Moreover, the point of this experiment in psychotropic power was not to turn men into zombies or drunkards, but rather to, by treating their bodies as biological machines needing certain inputs, recharge the very human qualities the trenches degraded. And so, when the army offered alcohol to soldiers, they availed themselves of it both because the war was horrible, and because they wanted to do their duty but needed help to do so. In the French army, alcohol became a partial solution to the emotional trauma and sapping of morale wrought by modern firepower. And by drinking what was provided, these soldiers embedded themselves in a complex set of power relations.

2.7 Suzanne Ferrand, "Reservez le vin pour nos poilus" (1916).

3

THE DAILY SYSTEM AND *PINARD*

LE PÈRE PINARD

"Wine," explains philosopher Roland Barthes, "is felt by the French nation to be a possession which is its very own … It is a totem drink." It is universal in French culture and folklore, and so implies a "kind of conformism: to believe in wine is a collective coercive act." And to believe in wine is to believe it can do anything. It cools in warm weather and warms in cold; it energizes the nervous system while it relaxes it. Wine is "above all," Barthes insists, "a converting substance, capable of reversing situations and states," of "extracting from objects their opposites."[1] Such is why it was so prized on the Western Front. Suffering into succor, stagnation into activity, silence into speech, disorder into meaning: wine transformed men and their experiences. French soldiers took what Barthes called wine's "philosophical power to transmute and create *ex nihilo*" and changed themselves with it.

Indeed, French soldiers welcomed the wine their Republic supplied for them with open mouths and did not worry overmuch about the theory behind it. They experienced drinking the wine they received not as a medico-scientific intervention or even necessarily as an exertion of psychotropic power. Rather, they experienced drinking wine on their own terms, ritualistically, with the sensations the wine produced given emotional and meaning by culture and context, set and setting. These sensations, in turn, gave men a feeling of agency and control over their experiences. For France's *poilus*, *pinard* was a word that was their very own and meant much more than just "wine." As one trench poet asked:

S'il est un nom bien doux fait	[If there is a sweet name fit
pour la poésie,	for poetry,]
Oh! Dites, n'est-ce pas ce beau nom,	[Oh, say, is it not that beautiful
le pinard![2]	name, *pinard?*]

For the *poilu*, *pinard* was what Mary Douglas, taking a cue from Victor Turner, has called a "condensed symbol," one that is "so economical and highly articulated" as to have the power to "recognize orchestration on a cosmic scale" after striking "one single chord."[3] The word served as a single reference that evoked an entire world of hardship and suffering while promising relief, sociability, and victory. *Pinard* represented the experience of the front as well as escape from it. It also represented the moral community of French soldiers – it was their blood and the blood of France at the same time, a patriotic symbol they could feel coursing through their bodies and transforming their emotions. The delivery of the ration became the central ritual in the cult of *pinard*, a great secular republican sacrament of communion in which *poilus* drank the protective and powerful blood of the soil, which is to say, the blood of France.

It is easiest to appreciate the power of this cult and the importance of *pinard* in the daily lives of *poilus* in their personal narratives and trench journals. Personal narratives – which is to say, autobiographies, sets of letters and journals, and semi-fictional novels – overflow with references to *pinard*. Seldom does one fail to have a scene in which the drink is consumed to everyone's great relief and joy. Trench journals were newspapers written and edited by soldiers at the front that contained poems and stories about life in the trenches. They were alternatively humorous and moving and were often accompanied by lovingly made and curated cartoons and pictures. Trench journals were vehicles for the expression of what historian Stéphane Audoin-Rouzeau calls "national sentiment," a set of core ideas about France and its role in the war: the German invasion was a world-historical injustice, France suffering represented civilization itself suffering, and the Republic would invariably if only eventually triumph.[4] Their creators and primary audience were the *poilu* himself, but their circulation level was low, so they did not drive opinion. Rather, they reflected the *poilu*'s self-image.[5] They too are full of references to *pinard* in their poems, songs, and stories. Seldom is there an issue that does not mention the drink. The trench journals provided the cult of *pinard*'s hymnal, and in them the *poilu* proclaimed its mysteries.

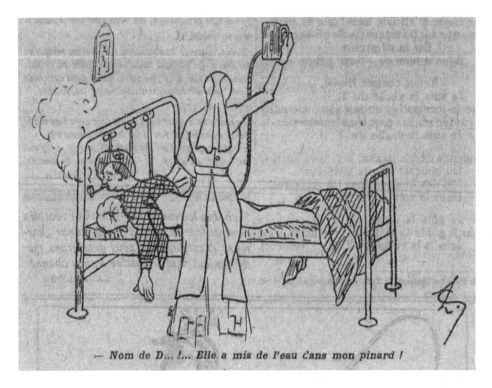

— *Nom de D... !... Elle a mis de l'eau dans mon pinard !*

3.1 "God-damn it! She watered down the pinard!" (1918).

THE MEANS AND RITUALS OF DISTRIBUTION

The roots of the ritual of wine distribution lie with the spatial organization of the trenches, so it will be useful to get an overview of their layout by following wine on its journey from the rear to the *poilu*. Recall that, under the *Intendance*, the wine passed first through the *stations-magasins*, then through the *gares régulatrices*, where it was directed downstream to this or that *gare de ravitallement*, itself around twenty kilometres from the front lines. At the *gares de ravitallement*, the wine was pumped from the *wagons-foudres* into barrels, which were in turn loaded into lorries, horse-carts, or specialized cars on miniature .60 m railways.[6] This marked the end of the wine's civilian career and the beginning of its term of service as *pinard*, as it entered the army zone [*zone d'armée*], where military ordinances and discipline ruled. The army zone itself was divided into three parts.

First and usually farthest west was the rear-front [*arrière-front*], where there were towns, logistical hubs, and hospitals. Then came the staging area [*zone des étapes*], where there were camps, transit centres, and villages, and which was populated by the rear-echelon troops whom the *poilus* called *embusqués* [shirkers]. And finally came the front proper, which began where German shells started to fall.[7]

The front proper was only three or four kilometres thick. On its far reaches, farthest back from the fighting, were divisional headquarters and artillery placements. Another kilometre on came regimental headquarters, and about a kilometre on from there the beginning of the trench system, where the barrels of wine were unloaded. They passed into the possession of the army cook [*cuistot*], who set up his mobile kitchen on the border between the war above ground and that below. The army cook's primary job was to make the meat stew *poilus* relied on for most of their calories. He was invariably filthy, described here as "dingy, dirty, beyond sloppy … covered in grime," and there as "defiled with fat and blood."[8] A talented one was a "king" while a bad one was a "princess."[9] The cook was powerful because he controlled not only who got what kind of meat, but also who got *pinard* and how much.

After doling out the stew to rations parties from the trenches, the cook transferred the *pinard* to either buckets or *bidons*, as soldiers called their gourd-shaped metal canteens.[10] The *bidon* had two holes in its top, one to drink from and the other to aerate. It produced a charming and satisfying "glug-glug" sound when wine poured out from its mouth:

Ô pinard, ô merveille	[Oh *pinard*, oh miracle]
J'aime écouter tes petits glouglous	[I love to hear your little glug-glugs]
Divin jus de la treille	[Divine juice of the vine]
Viens, buvons un coup…[11]	[Come, let's have a drink…]

Indeed, the *bidon* itself, along with the soldier's cup, the *quart* (so named because it held a quarter-litre), were minor deities in the cult of *pinard*. The former, sometimes covered in blue canvas, became:

C'est l'oiseau bleu dont l'âme bien	[The blue bird whose generous soul]
Chauffe le coeur—soutient dans	[Warms the heart – comforts]
l'abandon[12]	without end]

While of the *quart*:

Tu surgis complaisant,	[You arise happily without
sans te faire prier	being asked]
Redonnant à chacun courage et	[Giving to each courage
confiance[13]	and confidence]

Both were stand-alone symbols for the *poilu* in French war culture, with their own miniature mythologies.[14] These most quotidian objects, through their contact with *pinard*, became symbols charged with heroism.

The *bidons* were harnessed to the half-dozen men from a section's rations party [*corvée de soupe*], who emerged from the earth to gather provisions to take back to men in the trenches.[15] The scene at the distribution site was chaotic. Men fought over choice morsels of food and volumes of wine to bring back. One soldier observing a distribution of food and drink wrote that the "bedlam" was "impossible to describe," and resembled nothing as much as a "poultry market."[16] Rations duty – according to one *poilu*, "always painful, often perilous" – could be punishing physically, as the supplies were heavy.[17] Twice a day, each man in the trenches received in his stew between a quarter and half a kilogram of meat with about as much starch and a handful of assorted vegetables, along with about half or three-quarters of a kilogram of bread, all of which had to be carried by hand into the trenches. For drinks, there was of course the precious quarter-litre (or likely more) of *pinard*, and perhaps some *gnôle* or "juice" [*jus*], as *poilus* called their coffee. It was a lot to carry, and it turned the half-dozen or so men who rotated through its duties into, according to one *poilu*, "monstrous hunchbacks" weighted down with enormous loaves of bread and big vessels full of stew, their shoulders cut into by the straps of the *bidons* full of *pinard*.[18]

Rations duty was especially unwelcome at night, when it was easy for men to get lost in the dark while stumbling through gluey mud, under German bullets and shells. Neither was it a short trip – rations parties could leave at midnight and return at seven the next morning and vice versa, taking many hours to cover a few kilometres.[19] "The rations party is something heroic," concluded Eugène Pic, enough to make the "poor devils" who set out on it weep, and as such they deserved a *"pourboire"* [tip] for their labours.[20] Indeed, extra *pinard* was a perk of going on rations duty. As the veteran Sulphart explains to the newcomer Demanchy in Roland Dorgelès's

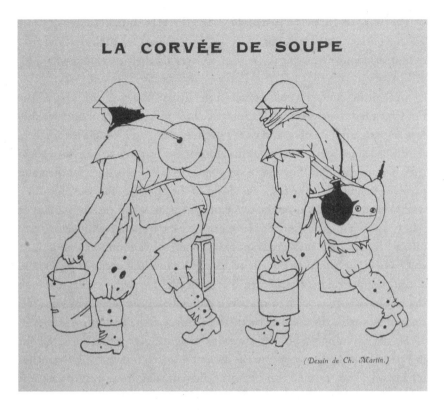

LA CORVÉE DE SOUPE

(Dessin de Ch. Martin.)

3.2 "La corvée de soupe" (1918).

novel *Les Croix de bois* (1919), a man on the *corveé* had a right to a *quart* full of wine for his efforts. Sulphart took his off the top of his section's share, felt no guilt, and encouraged Demanchy to do the same.[21]

Less frequent than the regular rations parties were the informal *pinard* duties [*corvées de pinard*], when men loaded themselves up with their section's *bidons* and went back to the rear – sometimes without permission – to find wine and bring it back to the trenches. Many of the *bidons* they carried were inflated beyond their ordinary capacity by a neat trick: a *poilu* often increased his *bidon's* volume by firing a blank cartridge into it, which blew out the metal some. This allowed him to cheat the *cuistots* and *mercantis*, as men called the wine-sellers in what remained of villages immediately behind the trenches who measured out wine by the *bidon*.[22] The men on the *corvée de pinard* then turned back to the trenches,

Par trois, par quatre, en ribambelle	[By three, by four, in swarms]
Ils repartent vers leur destin	[They depart for their destiny]
Emportant leur tresor de vin.[23]	[Carrying their treasured wine.]

In their descent, the *poilus* entered the first of the *boyaux* [guts], as the French called their communication trenches.[24] These were about two metres across and three deep and were relatively straight, ideally with smooth, reinforced sides and wooden boards along their bottoms to help men avoid sinking into the mud. They were supposed to be like pipelines for men and materiel flowing into the trenches closer to the fighting, but were not often well kept up, and could be the scene of confusion when rations parties or reliefs coming or going into the support or firing trenches collided or came under fire. Spilling was a constant fear. When he went out on *pinard* duty, René Nicolas claimed to put the corks tightly into the necks of his *bidons*, sealing their precious contents in "hermetically" for their journey through the *boyaux*. He thus assured that even if men fell into the mud or were terrorized by shells, the *pinard* would "arrive intact, to [the *poilus'*] great joy."[25]

As the *pinard* moved closer towards the fighting, trenches sprouted out in a perpendicular fashion from the communication trenches, like branches off a trunk. They formed three bands called, moving from west to east, the third line of "reserve" trenches, the second line of "support" trenches, and the first line of "firing" trenches. The bands were spaced several hundred metres apart and connected to one another through numerous communication trenches and tunnels, creating a vast labyrinthine network. The firing trenches abutted No-Man's-Land, the lifeless, empty deadzone that firepower created between the end of the French trench system and the beginning of the German. It was anything from less than hundred metres to a few kilometres in width. The Germans themselves were invisible.

Support and firing trenches were kinked and crooked with traverses, which prevented anyone firing down their length, and were two or three metres deep and two across. They tended to be below the water line, which meant their bottoms were constantly flooded and muddy.[26] It made for slow going for any *corvée de pinard*, which could take hours to wind its way through to its destination in the firing trenches. These, Paul Fussell acidly noted, were, in the French case, "nasty, cynical, efficient, and temporary" so as to discourage men getting too comfortable and

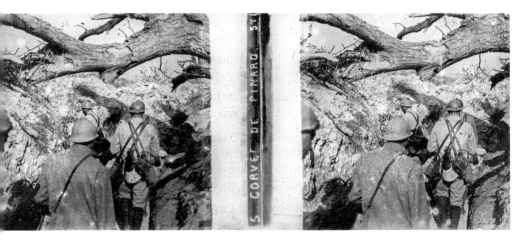

3.3 "Corvée de pinard."

taking up a defensive mindset.[27] In the front-line trench, two rises protected the soldier's head, the parapet on the side that faced No-Man's-Land and the parados on the other. Belts of barbed wire – sometimes a hundred metres thick or more – lay in front of the parapet to discourage or slow down attackers. The *poilu* who wanted to gaze into the lunar desert of No Man's Land stood on a firing-step, which boosted his head over the parapet. The view was uninspired, and it could look as though the land itself were coughing up blood, as one *poilu* noted: "burned earth, devoid of vegetation, indented with old yellow craters and new ones in which the clumped earth remained red."[28]

Pinard, in short, could be a real pain to get. Men struggled and suffered for it. Sometimes they died for it, as did Jean Giono's rationers in his novel *Le Grand troupeau* (1937), whom a shell hit directly whilst they were amid their duties. They became but smears of flesh, a "mortarboard of wine and blood" to be enjoyed only by hungry crows.[29] Yet men went and got *pinard* regularly, whenever they could, despite the danger. When it arrived, they changed; the change was worth the risk and the labour because without *pinard*, the front was unbearable. Indeed, the *poilu* began to feel *pinard*'s effects and emotional energy before it even passed into his mouth. Proximity, sound, and anticipation were enough to elicit a head-change, providing energy and focus:

Quand le bidon, plein de liqueur vermeil	[When the *bidon*, full of vermillion liquor]
Au bord du quart murmure son glouglou	[Whispers its gurgle into the *quart*]
Le poilu dont l'ardeur se réveille	[The *poilu*, his ardor awakened]
Sent au corps un désir fou.[30]	[Feels in his body a crazed desire.]

The main work in the trenches was maintaining the trenches, which consisted of placing and keeping up barbed wire, digging new trenches and repairing dilapidated ones, and constructing shelters. In the wet, the trenches collapsed in on themselves and needed to be constantly excavated, making the labours Sisyphean. There was nothing warlike or glorious about it, and it resembled punitive labour more than anything else.[31] One *poilu* declared the daily labours to be the "tarantula that poisoned our existence." "*Le travail c'est la captivité!*" he lamented.[32]

Building one's own prison was thirsty, dehydrating work. Although the *Intendance* attempted to provide front-line soldiers with trough-like receptacles with bleach-disinfected water, soldiers do not remember them often in their personal narratives. Louis Chirossel, for instance, explained in a letter to his wife that the water in the trenches was "very bad" and gave soldiers typhoid fever if drunk. He absorbed only the coffee and wine that he was served, to be safe.[33] He was not alone, and *pinard* was often the *poilu*'s main source of hydration. He thirsted for it in a literal sense because it met a basic physiological need. He was always tempted to quaff it down all at once, but this was poor planning. As one *poilu* noted of his comrades, "sometimes, one of them accedes to the temptation and drinks down his *pinard* all at once, but then the thirst, the horrible thirst..."[34]

Time in the trenches moved in strange ways, speeding and slowing but always spinning in the same grey loop. The hours circled and eddied into each other with few distinguishing marks. The arrival of *pinard* imposed temporal order. According to the soldier-priest Joseph Raymond, it was an "event" that broke up and punctuated time, giving it direction.[35] It thus broke the draining, endless cycle of sameness with the promise of pleasure. Men had little to look forward to during their days and nights in the trenches other than the distribution of *pinard*, and so they focused on it intently, obsessively. They became impatient, sometimes wild with the expectation of receiving a distribution. Not receiving one could leave them down and listless or frustrated at the unfairness of being denied this one pleasure afforded them. Albert Jamet explained that a lack of *pinard* meant sure discouragement: without it, "the fever increases and the suffering becomes unbearable."[36] Indeed, *pinard* was, another *poilu* maintained, the "sole joy permitted" to men in the trenches.[37] It was *the* common object of attention when it arrived. Everyone took part in the distributions and received his dose, and so all felt the effects of the *pinard* collectively.

One trench poet described the welcome voice of the *pinard* rationer as a clarion call that broke men of their isolation and fitful dreams, waking and bringing them together:

"Debout, là-dedans! Au pinard!"	[Get up everyone, get your pinard!]
Chacun, bénissant l'Intendance	[Each one, blessing the *Intendance*]
Dans le seau, mais avec prudence	[From the bucket, but with care]
Lentement, vient remplir son quart.[38]	[Slowly, comes to fill his *quart*.]

"*Au pinard!*" were words that for René Benjamin – winner of the *Prix Goncourt* in 1915 for his novel *Gaspard*, friend of Maurras, member of the *Action française*, and future supporter of Vichy – announced the arrival of goodness itself. There was, he confirmed, "nothing so affecting as the arrival of *pinard* at the front." Benjamin recalled that when the *pinard* appeared, men woke themselves up and, in a "religious daze," watched the precious nectar being poured out. They did not jostle or bump into one another for fear of spilling, and they were forced to form a rough line. It made for a "solemn" procession.[39] The trench journalist Snop used similar religiously inflected language when he reported that men gathered together with a "certain solemnity" to fill their *quarts* during the distribution. "Everybody advances his container to get what he already considers a healing and re-pairing balm," he assured readers.[40] Francisque Vial noted that when the *pinard* arrived, "nobody was absent, everybody was on their feet." Once men got their *pinard*, even the "most horrible grimaces relaxed and cleared up." The men "savored" it, taking "little nips" to "rewarm their insides."[41]

In effect, the spatial organization of the trenches imposed constraints on how men could arrange themselves during the distribution. They had to line up and wait their turn, and so the mechanics of the distribution provided men with the skeleton of a ritual that was already familiar and waited to be filled with meaning: the Catholic sacrament of communion.

Indeed, the distribution of *pinard* was a ritual in Emile Durkheim's sense. As Durkheim argued in *The Elementary Forms of Religious Life* (1912), rituals are patterned forms of social interaction that give people a sense of common identity and solidarity. The centre of the ritual is the "totem," a sacred object (but not necessarily a divine or religious one) filled with power.[42] During a ritual, people come together and interact with the totem in some stereotyped way. They then emerge emotionally changed and charged. The presence of the totem and the ritualized forms of interaction with it produce what Durkheim termed *effervescence*, a collective, shared feeling of emotional "electricity" that leads to particular forms of group cognition and behaviour.[43] Durkheim's crucial insight was that the totem is a representation of the community of worshippers, and so ritual was the community worshipping itself.[44] Its story was their story, and its energy was the energy the worshippers themselves created.

The influential American sociologist Randall Collins has made use of Durkheimian concepts and applied them on the scale of microsociology to develop what he calls "interaction ritual chain" theory, a model of social interactions that provides a useful way to think through the work that the ritual of *pinard* distribution did in the trenches.[45] Collins argues that when people come together in an "interaction ritual" – a concept he borrows from Irving Goffman and modifies[46] – they undergo bodily and emotional "entrainment," meaning they enter a sense of shared, collective experience through their interactions.[47] The ritual focuses their attention and thoughts on a common object, but it also makes them aware that others are doing and thinking the same. The core function of the ritual is thus to make the group highly conscious of its own intersubjectivity.[48] This raises the group's "emotional energy," which Collins defines as a "feeling of confidence, courage to take action, boldness in taking initiative" that comes from knowing that one is not alone, but rather is part of a moral community.[49] It is not an emotion, but rather a valence that "pumps up" emotions.[50]

In Collins's model, the common object of attention takes on symbolic meaning as a representation of the group through its presence and representation in repeated iterations of the ritual, which "charges" the object and the participants in the ritual. The object becomes a reservoir of emotional energy, and its presence – even if just imagined or remembered – recharges that of the subject.[51] When an interaction ritual is repeated consistently, Collins maintains, it forms an "interaction ritual chain," a constant replenishing of emotional energy and reaffirmation of the unity of a moral community. The daily distributions of *pinard* surely formed an interaction ritual chain in Collins's sense.

If *poilus* were solemn as the *pinard* was poured, they were not solemn for long afterwards, as the increased emotional energy it provided came with increased volubility. *Pinard* encouraged men to talk, to laugh, and get to know one another:

On rit, on chante, on oublie	[We laugh, sing, forget]
Tous les chagrins de la vie	[All the pains of life]
Dans les litres de pinard[52]	[In some litres of *pinard*]

It broke their isolation and gave them an intersubjective boost:

Pour l'homme pauvre et solitaire	[For the poor and lonely man]
Il est la force et la gaîté[53]	[It is strength and happiness]

Pinard, wrote a third *poilu*, turned "the taciturn [into] a babbler."[54] And so the ritual of the *pinard* distribution inspired sociability; it brought men together to talk and bond over the stories they told. Moreover, because letters were distributed and gossip passed along immediately after the *pinard*, *poilus* had things to talk about: their families, farms, and shops; their hopes and shames; the war and its hunger for men. Benjamin, for instance, observed that after the distribution, "stomachs were calmed, thoughts grew less dark, [and] faces lost their cadaverous aspect." "*Pinard*!" he exclaimed, "what an aide in this war, and what a joy! … And to drink is to toast [*trinquer*], to stand together, to love one another, to bring health to one another." When the men get their wine, he enthused, "they roll their eyes, wag their tongue, and say, 'Hey old man, this wine isn't half bad'!"[55] The social interactions during the ritual generated feelings of affection, and so it performed literal face-work, spreading smiles on open mouths, as Jean Galtier-Boissière reported: "the daily *quart* brings to the lips [of the *poilu*] the smile of a gourmet."[56] A trench poet sang of *pinard*'s power to open men to one another affectively:

Par toi, la fatigue s'oublie,	[Through you, we forget our fatigue]
Par toi, la langue se delie[57]	[Through you, our tongues are loosened]

3.4 Detail from Poitevin, "Le Pinard" (1917).

And with the edge taken off, *poilus* came together to talk and celebrate that they were not yet among the dead in No-Man's-Land.[58]

All this is to say that the ritual of the distribution produced mutual bodily and emotional entrainment that was experienced socially. The Durkheimian elements are all there, as if arranged purposefully. *Pinard* was undoubtedly a totem, a sacred substance not of the profane grey world of the trenches. It brought colour and movement, and men reacted to its presence with enthusiasm. During the *pinard* distribution, *poilus* showed "the grasping, thrilled agitation of a supplicant / before whom the tabernacle where a God appears."[59] They called *pinard* a "sacred liquid"; claimed "sacred *pinard*" was the "source of life"; and were confident that "sacred *pinard*" gave strength on the "day of the charge."[60] They drew themselves worshipping the very word.

WINE AND BLOOD

Pinard came in both white and red varieties, but was most often red. When it was white it frequently appeared rose, as the *Intendance* did a poor job of cleaning the residue out of barrels before refilling them.[61] Soldiers showed little practical preference for colour:

Pour nous, qui importe l'origine	[For us, the origin matters not]
Du vin rouge, blanc, ou pisseux	[Of the red, white, or pissy]
Qu'il soit de Bourgogne ou de Chine	[Whether it comes from Burgundy or China]
Touts les Pinards rendent heureux![62]	[All *pinard* makes us happy!]

Pinard's taste varied widely, but usually was that of ordinary table wine that had been roughly handled, which is exactly what it was. As we have seen, its quality was worst at the war's outset, when the *Intendance* struggled with logistics and the wine tended to be of low alcohol content. For example, the wine Jean-Louis Beaufils received in late 1914 was "black coloured, [and] had but a vague taste" of grape, while in mid-1915, Émile Morin reported that the *"gros rouge"* he was receiving was "beaten up, foamy, [and] almost un-drinkable."[63] But the wine improved, getting stronger in alcohol and cleaner in taste as the *Intendance* got better at purchasing and delivery. In any case, most *poilus* were like Jules Mazé's Sergeant Lefèvre, who was not particular-ly discriminating. *Pinard* might have been of "inferior quality" and mishan-dled, but nevertheless it still "conserved all its virtues." "The most savored," Mazé assured, was the "dark red, often loaded with alcohol"; this was the "real *pinard*."[64]

Indeed, *pinard* as a symbol in soldiers' culture was always coloured red, for red was the colour of blood. *Poilus* found the symbolic equivalence be-tween *pinard* and blood an easy one and made it readily. *Pinard* "made blood redder"; it was "the vermillion colour / of blood!"; the "perfumed blood of crushed grapes"; and "the blood of our beloved France."[65] One trench poet waxed eloquent:

Le vin délicieux, à la couleur vermeille	[Delicious wine, the vermillion colour]
Du sang! Que dis-je, vin coule mal à l'oreille	[Of blood! What am I saying, "wine" is hard on the ears]
La bouche de poilu moderne dit: <u>Pinard!</u>[66]	[The mouth of the modern poilu says: <u>Pinard!</u>]

In the event, two distinct discourses about wine and blood proved to be of primary importance to the cult of *pinard*. On the one hand, wine and blood were associated with Christ on the cross and the sacrament of communion. *Poilus* adopted this Catholic discourse in which wine and blood meant suffering, sacrifice, and eventual redemption. Within this discourse *pinard* came to represent the moral community of French soldiers, whose shared, spilled blood linked them together and to the land they defended. It was easily grafted upon the mechanism of the distribution, which already appeared as a secular analogue of the sacrament of communion. On the other hand, wine and blood were associated with energy and strength, vitality and power. This came from blood's ancient Galenic definition as a heat-carrying *spiritus vitalus*, from nineteenth-century physiology's understanding of blood as the carrier of oxygen and glucose, and from French convictions about wine's nervine properties. Blood was the basic currency of biological energy, and wine energized the blood directly. With this discourse, *pinard* came to represent power and resilience.

Men experienced the war as though it were a boundless natural catastrophe. It held them pinned them to the earth and killed them in devastating and shocking ways, forcing vile secrets from their bodies. The endless monotony of the days and the expected but always shocking horrors combined to give men a sense of suffering without progress or reason, and they became estranged from the meaning of their own deaths.[67] Let the words of Étienne Tanty substitute for the experience of millions:

> The marl, the mud, the water, the manure, the lice, the *poilus*, DT ["Dérange-Tout," a despised officer], the trenches, the barbed-wire, the fields of beets covered in cadavers, the woods without trees, trees without branches, branches without leaves, the soiled and torn *kepis* [caps] flung about by the wind that lashes down rain on the poor forgotten graves, the departed; the smell of all forms of rottenness and decay, the spectacle of all manner of misery … physical misery, mental misery, misery of men and things …![68]

The cult of *pinard* provided the *poilu* with a narrative that gave this suffering patriotic meaning. The story it told portrayed the *poilu* as a Christ-like figure who, by sacrificing himself on an upside-down Calvary, ensured the eventual triumph of his *civilisation* over the German's *Kultur*.

There was much levity as regards *pinard* in men's trench journals, but the cult could be somber and serious. *Pinard* meant sacrifice. This is clear in Pierre Causse's long piece "*Le Pinard*" from the trench journal *La Poilusienne* in January 1916. "Civilians," Causse begins, "will never understand the passion that *poilus* have for wine, this exquisite liquor that is known by the name *pinard*." The experience of the front was so fully removed from ordinary life that wine – a quotidian substance for civilians – served a completely different role there, and one of fundamental importance. "*Pinard!*" he continued, "it is the highest of the beatitudes in the *poilu*'s life, [a life that is] ordinarily full of torments, privation, and much suffering." This "sacred blood of the vine" was "essentially French … the national drink *par excellence."* For Causse, *pinard* represented the *poilus'* shared suffering, loss, and, for some, martyrdom. He explained:

> *Pinard* reflects the shared blood spilled by our brothers-in-arms [that] incites us to vengeance; it is a living, tangible, and undeniable symbol *of the sacrifice to which we have nobly consented*, and it is in its blue limpidness that reflects the azure sky, we see the synonym of the Ideal and of Hope.[69]

The blood spilled on the battlefield, another *poilu* went so far to say, nourished the earth and made it more fertile, thereby completing a circle of life and death, generation and regeneration:

Il donne son sang à la terre	[He gives his blood to the earth]
Elle en fait, pour lui, ce nectar:	[She makes of it for him this
le pinard![70]	nectar: *pinard!*]

Thus, in the cult of *pinard*'s mythology, men were not killed at random, annihilated and evaporated by shells, but rather gave themselves in a great act of selflessness to redeem the world by ensuring France's triumph. Neither were those who were killed forgotten, but rather they continued to live on in the pulsing hearts of their countrymen; *pinard* mocked death and promised everlasting life, and so one of its cult's functions was to reconcile men to the possibility of their own end.

Poilus were fond of Noah, the first drunk, and – like them – the helpless victim of a senseless and vast destruction. He was *pinard*'s father, and theirs:

O Noë, notre Père!	[Oh father Noah!]
T'étais plus malin que tous	[You are more cunning than
les médecins!	all the doctors!]
Leurs sal's drouges, pourqoui faire?	[What good are their dirty drugs?]
Si vous tombez pale, un petit	[If you feel faint, drink a shot
coup de vin![71]	of wine!]

Pinard was not, of course, a "dirty drug" but was rather pure blood. And not just any, but the pure blood of France itself – the *poilus'* blood and the land's, shared amongst them now and backwards and forwards in time. When soldiers drank *pinard*, they felt the soil of France itself call out to them, each and all, per Émile Roudié:

"*O vous qui combattez*	["Oh you who fight]
Pour mon honneur, ma gloire	[For my honour, my glory
et pour vos libertés	and for your freedoms]
Buvez mon vin, c'est tout mon sang,	[Drink my wine, it is my blood
je vous le donne;	that I give you]
Buvez-le!—rutilant de vaillance	[Drink it – in will rush bravery
et de gloire	and glory]
Il donne 'le moral' qui force	[It raises the morale that will
la Victoire!"[72]	result in victory!"]

Pinard, *poilus* were happy to repeat, was a blood wholly French:

Pinard, sang de la France aimée	[*Pinard*, blood of our beloved France]
Je devais te chanter ici:	[I must sing your praises]
N'est-tu pas la force principale	[Are you not the principal force
de notre belle armée?[73]	of our beautiful army?]

Indeed, it was France's sun and soil concentrated and made potable:

Mais ce pinard, c'est du soleil	[But *pinard*, it is the sun]
Mis en flacons, mis en futaille[74]	[Put in bottles, put in barrels]

As such, it was a symbolic unifier. *Pinard* dissolved regionalism because everyone loved it entirely. "The *Nord* and the *Midi*," wrote Louis Hourticq, "agree on the question of wine. *Pinard* reconciles the latitudes."[75]

One trench poet went a step further: *pinard*, drawn into the trenches from all over France, represented all of France at the same time. It was the *poilus'* shared blood circulating in common:

C'est un vin de partout	[It's a wine from all over]
De Gironde d'Anjou,	[From the Gironde to Anjou,]
De Bourgogn' du Poitou	[From Burgundy to Poitou,]
C'est un mélange de tout	[It is a mixture of them all]
Comme les poilus[76]	[Like the *poilus*]

The army *was* in fact a great *mélange* of France's men, made of priests, anarchists, university professors, barrel-makers, farmers, and bourgeois dandies. Sections were made of men who would not typically have mixed. The great proletarianizing force of the Western Front victimized them all equally, making peacetime social distinctions less important.[77] All were bent to the war's will. Together they ate the same cold stew and suffered the same bombardments, and together they found refuge and inspiration in *pinard*, which represented and linked all of them together.

The wine ration also served to bind at least some of France's many thousands of colonial soldiers to the army and its mission through the ritual of distribution. As of April 1917, Black colonial soldiers hailing from certain regions, namely the "old colonies" (i.e., Guadeloupe, Martinique, and Réunion) and the four subdivisions of Senegal (i.e., Dakar, Saint-Louis, Gorée, and Rufisque), were given wine rations just as were white soldiers from the metropole, so long as they were integrated into non-colonial military units. Indeed, one 1917 circular specified that these men were to be treated "exactly like other French soldiers" insofar as the army's alcohol policy was concerned, showing how – at least in this case – *pinard* functioned to overcome racial barriers and integrate Black soldiers into the army's culture. However, this treatment applied only to soldiers from the old colonies: those from "Algeria, Tunisia, Morocco, Indochina, or others," as well as colonial labourers brought to the metropole from Asia, were forbidden from receiving wine rations or drinking in *débits*. Such soldiers were to receive coffee, tea, beer, or cider rather than wine. The official explanation was that this prohibition ensured the maintenance of discipline, but it also served to police racial boundaries, particularly in the rear areas.[78]

But not only did the cult of *pinard* give the *poilu*'s suffering meaning and purpose; it also marked him off from the Germans. Indeed, this was central to *pinard*'s intoxication concept – drinking it provided the bodily sensations of Frenchness. The poet Guillaume Apollinaire explained:

J'ai comme toi pour me réconforter	[I would like that you comfort me]
Le quart de pinard	[*Quart* of *pinard*]
Qui ment tant de differences entre	[Which makes all the difference
nous et les boche.[79]	between us and the *boche*.]

The trench poet Stello made explicit the latent implications of *pinard* being the blood of France and equated what men drank, their blood, and the spirit of the French race. "Oh *pinard*! Oh *pinard*!" he cried, "are you not the blood of our blood, the flesh of our flesh? Do you not contain in you, because of your origins, the traditions of our old provinces, [and] all the qualities of our Race?" On a roll, he continued: "Oh! *Pinard*, you whose shared blood has flowed for centuries in the veins of our noble ancestors ... is it not you who will soon bring us victory over the barbarians ...?" The Germans, in contrast, drank beer, that "hideous and heavy drink that weighs down the spirit and closes it to Beauty and Goodness."[80]

Drinking *pinard* made the *poilu* different and feel different from his enemy. Per one trench poet, "insipid and heavy beer" was the "drink of Bavarian slackers," while in contrast:

Le clair rayon d'espérance	[The clear beam of hope]
Le sang généraux de France,	[The shared blood of France,]
C'est le vin, c'est le pinard![81]	[It is wine, it is *pinard*!]

Another *poilu* explained that this distinction between national drinks had consequences biological and martial:

Contre la horde germanique	[Against the Germanic horde]
De son corps faisant un rempart,	[Of his body he makes a rampart,]
France! Ton Poilu héroïque ...	[France! Your heroic *poilu*]
Que tu devras cette merveille? ...	[To what will you owe this wonder?]
C'est ton sang, le jus de la treille[82]	[It is your blood, the juice of the vine!]

Here, the *poilu* who drinks is changed bodily and made hard; he becomes the wall upon which the barbarians break themselves. And so the cult of *pinard* provided French soldiers with a way to narrate the bodily experience of intoxication and direct the emotional energy the ritual produced at the enemy. As such, the *poilu* felt the interoceptive and affective effects of *pinard* in his body both as a tonic preparation for the sacrifices to come and as proof of his membership in the moral community of patriotic French soldiers.

WINE AND ENERGY

Poilus claimed that *pinard* was *the* source of their physical strength and resilience – they believed that it charged up their blood with almost electrical energy. *Pinard* had the ability to power and repair men, and this influenced the experience of intoxication it provided, giving it direction and intentionality. Indeed – and this is crucial – they experienced their intoxication as the feeling of their patriotism and power growing, and, because the distribution was a group ritual, they experienced it together, at the same time. The process was biocultural, with the body forming an experiential substrate upon which culture built and gave meaning through the iteration of an interaction ritual chain. Mazé, for instance, explained that the idea that *pinard* "is the only French drink, an energetic nutrient" was "so forcefully anchored in the spirit of soldiers that to lessen the ration would be to invite a disastrous fate."[83]

Once *pinard* entered the *poilu*, expectation and suggestion built off the effects of both alcohol's pharmacology and the emotional energy generated by the ritual to create a profound, exaggerated sense of bodily relief, one far beyond anything that could plausibly be explained through chemistry alone. *Pinard* was the *poilu*'s omni-medicine, a biological marvel, "the drink without equal" that "made miracles" and a "panacea" whose "endless tenderness cultivates the soldier."[84] Men claimed that it took away all their pains and replaced them with joy. It filled them with power:

Et donne à celui qui le boit	[And it gives to he who drinks it]
Regain de vigueur, de valliance[85]	[Renewed vigour and bravery]

The trenches made them feel weak, distraught, cowardly, and dark, but *pinard* changed this:

Ésprit de Poilus à la guerre	[The spirit of *poilus* at war]
Force, éspoir, valliance, et lumière[86]	[Strength, hope, bravery, and light]

And it modified their bodies, making them stronger and more resilient.

Ça m'met du fer dans les tendons	[It puts iron in my tendons]
Et ça m'enflamm'comm'un brandon[87]	[And enflames me like a firebrand]

85

Indeed, *pinard* was the *poilu*'s solution to all the physical evils of trench life. It protected him from the elements, comforting him as the "fine fuel / who so well warms the human motor," or the drink that "rewarms our carcasses / when we have our feet in the water."[88] The millions of unwashed bodies on the Western Front, along with rivers of trash and waste and the cadavers decaying in No-Man's-Land, smelled extraordinarily bad. Gabriel Chevallier described the odor as having several notes, like an awful perfume, being "at first rather sweet and sickly and then … richer notes of a still-contained putrefaction."[89] But *pinard*, according to one *poilu*, "perfumed the meals in the trenches," giving men appetite and allowing them to eat while the smell of death and decay lay over them like a fog.[90] Even the shoddy shelters the men constructed in the trenches could be transformed into happy spaces when they provided men with places in which to drink *pinard* and the drink was present:

Que la guerre au fond de ce trou	[This war from the bottom of a hole]
Où notre pauvre coeur s'ennuie	[Where lassitude fills our hearts]
Tandis que, du casque, la pluie	[While, upon the helmet, the rain]
Nous dégouline dans le cou …	[Dribbles down our necks]
Mais voici qu'une voix appelle;	[But then a voice calls out;]
"Au pinard" clame le cabot	["Get your *pinard*" shouts the corporal]
Soudain notre sort semble beau	[Suddenly our lot seems good]
Notre caverne semble belle![91]	[Our cave seems beautiful!]

Pinard was not just the solution to the physical discomforts of the war, but also to its emotional evils. Its consumption gave men a feeling of power over their own experiences, awful as those experiences might have been. *Pinard*'s power to give men this sense of agency is best seen in its relationship with the *cafard* [literally "cockroach"]. The *cafard* was the *poilu*'s most persistent and dangerous enemy in the trenches, one as omnipresent as the Germans but more insidious and insistent. It was a sense of emotional emptiness, a hopeless and existential vacancy that could overwhelm men and drown them in black and fog.[92] The *cafard* had a nineteenth-century colonial pedigree: it afflicted French soldiers stationed in North Africa who dreamt of home as well as imperialists in Vietnam who were in constant anxiety about their health. Indeed, historian Michael Vann has translated the word *cafard* as "the colonial blues."[93] The word was then adapted for the experience of the Western Front. In their trench journals, *poilus* sometimes shielded themselves from the *cafard* with humour:

Ça rend taciturne et maussade	[It makes you taciturn and glum]
Étourdi, fainéant, grognon	[Scatter-brained, lazy, grumpy]
Sans énergie, insupportable	[Without energy, unbearable]
Le cerveau deviant marmelade	[The brain becomes marmalade]
Et le sang deviant jus d'oignon[94]	[And blood like the juice of an onion]

But in their personal journals, they spoke of the *cafard* with respect. Marc Boasson wrote hauntingly of the feeling: "The nothingness of [my] existence has taken on a frightful character … I barely think anymore. I feel empty." He confided in his journal that he "could not describe the horrible lassitude that the war has created in me … I feel erased, depressed."[95] Joseph Bousquet described it analogously. When he wrote to his *"Chère Petite Mère"* of the *cafard*, he described it as a "great wave of black crashing into [his] soul." "An infinite sadness gathers within me," he confessed, "and tortures me so strongly that I quiver. I have an immense need for tenderness, to feel myself cradled in the warmth of physical and moral rest."[96]

The *cafard* was a syndrome both bodily and emotional, or more precisely, emotional because it was bodily. The neurologists Huot and Voivenel described it as a real physiological syndrome in their 1917 treatise on the subject. It had two psychological manifestations – a sense of "troubled cenesthesia," meaning a feeling of being detached from one's own body, and an "insidious attack on the nervous system and slow corrosion of the personality."[97] Life in the trenches themselves was to blame as it produced a "series of small emotional shocks repeated over weeks, months, years" that physically depleted the nervous system of its vital energy, effectively emptying out neurons through overuse. "The bullets, the shells, the rockets, the mines, the watches, the patrols, the suddenly unleashed barrage … it is emotional overwork in its purest form," the doctors advised.[98] Charles Delvert arrived at the same conclusion through experience. The constant threat and unrelenting violence "exert such a strain on the soldier that he becomes more, rather than less, apprehensive over time … Future military historians take note," he demanded.[99] *Pinard* supposedly provided the *poilu* with the energy needed to charge his brain into the right electro-molecular state to navigate these feelings. Such is why Huot and Voivenel could claim in a later work that *pinard* was one of the "primordial factors in the resistance of the *poilu*": it worked on a microscopic, chemical scale in the nervous system to refill and energize neurons.[100]

Soldiers, who made happy use of the ready rhyme between *pinard* and *cafard*, were less scientific but more vivid in their descriptions of the emotional and bodily effects of the drink: it was the anti-*cafard*. *Pinard* "puts the *cafard* in the ground"; it "cuts the *cafard*"; it "hunts the *cafard*"; and as the "king of insecticides," it "destroys the *cafard*."[101] Stello wrote:

Verser, versez, jusqu'à l'ivresse	[Drink, drink to the point of drunkenness]
Oncques le Cafard et la Détresse	[Never did the *cafard* and distress]
Au pourpre jus n'ont résisté.[102]	[Resist against the purple juice.]

Another *poilu*, in the same sense:

Pour combattre le cafard,	[To fight against the *cafard*,]
Il n'est tel que le pinard	[There is nothing like *pinard*]
Qui vous chauffe et vous enflame	[That warms you and enflames]
L'coeur et l'âme[103]	[Your heart and soul]

Thus *pinard*'s emotional effects were positive and generative – *pinard*, men wrote, filled them with exactly what the trenches and their *cafard* took from them. They maintained that *pinard* made them brave, "stimulating courage" or "bolstering courage" so that men could "put their heart into the task"; it was courage "most ardent" in liquid form.[104] Drinking it was something the *poilu* could do to make himself feel braver, and so it allowed him a tiny piece of power over the war:

En sortant de la tranchée	[When leaving the trench]
Parfois je tremble, j'ai peur	[Sometimes I tremble with fear]
Mais ma gourde caressé	[But my caressed canteen]
D'un coup me donne du coeur[105]	[Gives me courage in a flash]

3.5 Detail from "Ode au Pinard" (1916).

Poilus drank to firm themselves up, to make themselves hard and confident when they felt soft and weak:

Et pour sortir en patrouille	[And when going out on patrol]
Je ne suis pas fixé, j'ai peur!	[I feel lost and afraid]
Mais je m'dis "Espèc' de nouille	[But I say to myself, "Noodle-legs]
Bois un coup, ça rend du coeur"[106]	[Have a drink, it gives you heart"]

It allowed them to overcome themselves by changing themselves, and so overcome the war's effects on them:

Qui que tu sois, pinard étrange	[Whatever you are, *pinard* so strange]
Lorsqu'on te boit notre humeur change[107]	[When we drink you, our spirits change]

In effect, drinking *pinard* produced the experience of a willed flight to courage. It allowed weakened men to feel themselves made strong ("It makes our blood more vermillion / and our arms stronger for the battle"), just as it gave hope to the distraught ("it is a drink of crazed hope"), joy to the lugubrious (it "drowns" the "dark flowers of black dreams"), and rage to the indifferent (it gives "manly strength and courage / and if not strength, then rage!").[108] It gave men the power *to generate* emotional experiences that were the opposite of those the trenches imposed, just like Roland Barthes suggested: exhaustion into energy, fear into courage, pain into pleasure. And men could not get enough of it.

EMOTIONS, CONSENT, AND COERCION

Through its interaction ritual chain, the cult of *pinard* produced and sustained certain collective emotional experiences among French soldiers that were beneficial to the further prosecution of the war. Indeed, its rituals functioned in such a way as to help in generating what historian Barbara Rosenwein termed an "emotional community" among *poilus*. Rosenwein defines an emotional community as group in which people "adhere to the same norms of emotional expression or value—or devalue" certain ways of feeling and expressing feeling.[109] The ritual of the ration undoubtedly helped in forming *poilus* into an emotional community in Rosenwein's sense, as the forms of sociability and emotional entrainment it produced were crucial in forming interpersonal, affective bonds among French soldiers. These horizontal linkages were themselves necessary to maintain cohesion and military effectiveness under grievously poor conditions – *pinard* was the liquid predicate for the formation of the bonds that created "primary groups," the micro–affective communities of a half-dozen or a dozen men from a section who drank, lived, and suffered together and upon which combat effectiveness depended.

The cult of *pinard* did not just bring men together and help create bonds among them. It also served to generate and enforce what William Reddy has called an "emotional regime." Reddy defines an emotional regime as "the set of normative emotions and the official rituals, practices, and emotives that express and inculcate them," with an "emotive" being Reddy's technical term for an emotional expression.[110] The language of the cult of *pinard* – its songs, poems, and iconography – effectively produced a discursive field that *poilus* used to express and organize their emotional responses to the war. It privileged particular kinds of emotional experiences (i.e., courage, righteous hatred) and discouraged others (i.e., fear and anxiety) and so served to undergird particular clusters of emotions among men.[111]

Here, the history of emotions sheds light on one of the French historiography of the war's central debates, that between the schools of *consentement patriotique* [patriotic consent], which sees French soldiers as willing agents, and *contrainte* [social constraint/coercion], which sees them as socially conditioned and controlled victims.[112] Those of the *consentement* school argue that the French soldier felt a deep and enduring patriotism and duty to defend his fatherland. He was not a victim driven to slaughter, but an agent choosing to fight and perhaps die out of love of country.[113] Those of the *contrainte* school argue that, while the *poilu* was undoubtedly patriotic, patriotism alone was not enough to keep him in the trenches, whose horrors outweighed the tricolour's calls to duty. Rather, men were kept in the trenches by a system of social and cultural pressure that made resisting the war all but impossible in practice. In the *contrainte* school's view, the war's horrible and gargantuan gravity locked men in its orbit: men did not really consent to be there but could find no escape because of a repressive state apparatus and French war culture that did not tolerate dissent.[114]

Historian François Cochet has argued for a middle position – *micro-consentement* – in which men consented not to the idea of the war, but to fighting for their and their comrades' survival. After the horrible experiences of 1914 and 1915, Cochet argues, a sense of lassitude and alienation replaced that of patriotic resolve among French soldiers. What kept men fighting were the affective bonds the war itself created among them. "Soldiers," Cochet holds, "effectively consented. They consented to live the war. Their war, with their officers and their comrades."[115] Cochet's point is that we ought to look not to ideas, but to social realities and horizontal links among *poilus* to determine why men fought. The cult of *pinard*, through its ability to inspire and direct emotional experiences that were felt collectively, helped men endure because it linked them to one another through a ritual of *micro-consentement*.

Military morale – which we might define as a willingness to suffer, endure, and fight – springs from two founts: on the macro-level, from identification with the army, the nation it represents and its political ideology, and the goals of the war; and on the micro-level, from the personal relationships resulting from affective interactions among soldiers in their primary groups, which is to say, with the ten or twelve men from their squad with whom they passed the time in daily life.[116] Put another way, morale and thus fighting power depend on maintaining a sense of corporate identity and moral unity within two overlapping emotional communities, that on the macro-level of the army and that on the micro-level of the squad. This roughly corresponds to the levels of analyses pursued by the patriotic consent school, which focuses on war culture and political ideology, and the constraint school, which focuses on the situational, micro-sociological aspects of daily life.

The ritual of the distribution brought men together and symbolically recognized that, should they want to survive, they would have to stick together, regardless of whether they believed deeply in the war and its justness or saw it as senseless slaughter. All faced the same physical and psychological pressures and saw their personalities degrade in the same ways. Each *poilu* knew he had to be there in the mud because he already *was* there. He was forced to be satisfied with that tautological answer, as the ruthless tyranny of the actual was total.[117] And so he used *pinard* to coerce his body and constrain his emotions to give him the ability to do what he believed necessary to survive.

The *poilu* willingly enmeshed himself in the system of control the wine ration represented because the distribution provided him with fellowship and meaning and allowed him to feel that he had some power over the war – issues of consent and coercion are mixed here in a complex set of power-relations. Drinking *pinard* was experienced as an act of agency; it was an expression of the *poilu*'s desire to control his body and experiences. Nobody was forced to drink, but nearly everybody did. In this sense, the distribution, the central ritual of the cult of *pinard*, was a performance that expressed renewed consent to the prosecution of the war, one that involved millions of men. But it was also coerced, as the daily system emerged from the top down. It thus sits at the bridge between consent and coercion (and between micro- and macro-levels of morale). By coming together and drinking the blood of France, men simultaneously confirmed their willingness to suffer their republican martyrdom *and* generated the emotional energy this required. And this ritualized form of *micro-consentement* radiated out in billions of personal interaction ritual chains, which in turn produced a kind of manufactured or constrained consent for the war.

Pinard, the *poilu* wrote, is what gave life to the wasteland of the front. Without it, his life was reduced to mere mechanism – bare life, absent of vital impulse.[118] Tanty, ever eloquent, made the point:

At present, it is anguish without hope. This will be your existence until you are killed or injured; always marching, tired from a year of campaigning, no hope of peace, when you fall you will be replaced.

We are nothing more than machines for suffering; it is an abomination, it demands more than human forces can give, that which they are imposing upon us.[119]

Pinard was a way to augment that human force, to endure though what was imposed. Few men, if any, wanted to be at the front, but most believed they needed to be. They loved *pinard* because it transformed them and their experience of the war and so allowed them to do their duty. Indeed, the cult of *pinard* provided men with a unified frame that explained why they were where they were and what they had to do, a single definition of their shared situation. And it did this through its ability to change them, together, at the same time, and in the same direction. As one *poilu* maintained, putting words into *pinard*'s mouth and letting it speak:

> *Je te change et tu peux m'accueillir*   [I change you, and you can welcome
> *pour ton prêtre*   me as your priest][120]

4

THE BATTLE SYSTEM AND *GNÔLE*

THE SCANDAL OF DISTILLED ALCOHOL DISTRIBUTIONS

On 2 February 1916, during a debate in the Chamber of Deputies in which legislators discussed the question of soldiers' access to *débits de boissons* while they were on leave in the rear, Bernard Cadenat, a deputy from the Bouches-du-Rhône, made the mistake of asking a good, truthful question.[1] In two parts of France – the Fifteenth and Sixteenth military recruitment districts (Provence and Languedoc-Roussillon, respectively) – civilian administrators had issued circulars prohibiting all soldiers from entering *débits de boissons* between the hours of 9h00 and 17h00, as well as forbidding the sale of distilled alcohol [*alcool*] to them at any time. Cadenat, who believed that soldiers had the right to drink whatever they wanted to drink when on leave, objected to these prohibitions and noted that "in the army zones, we give our soldiers [distilled] alcohol ... so that they have the courage to launch the assault." Why, he asked, would the Republic deny men on leave the very drink it was serving to them at the front?[2]

While his comment went unremarked-upon during the meeting, Cadenat shortly came under fire in the popular press. On 4 February, the weekly magazine *Excelsior* published a piece by the novelist Georges Lecomte that lambasted Cadenat for slandering the honour of the French army. Lecomte glossed Cadenat's argument, and not entirely in good faith, as "when our soldiers attack, it is not the sentiment of duty that animates them, but rather that alcohol pushes them forward." What Cadenat said, Lecomte continued frothily, was the "most impious, most odious, most revolting sentence ever uttered in the French Parliament." It was not true, he insisted, and France and her suffering soldiers "deserve not to hear words that belittle the sacrifice of these fallen heroes and outrage their memory." Lecomte professed his shock and disappointment that not a single deputy in the meeting stood up and challenged Cadenat's "blasphemy" there on the spot.[3]

A small journalistic pile-on followed. The patriotic right, which saw Cadenat's comments as a near-traitorous slander of the French army's honour, was particularly hostile. The Catholic newspaper *La Croix* was incredulous, and under the headline "Deputy Insults Soldiers," it called Cadenat's words an "insult to every parent whose son has been killed on the field of honour."[4] *L'Express du Midi* called Cadenat a "defiler" who "gravely insulted our children, who are killed for a sublime ideal."[5] The nationalist journalist Maurice Barrès weighed in, calling Cadenat's words "horrible" and asserting that the French soldier was driven forward not by alcohol, but by "the spiritual element." Barrès quoted a "young hero" from the trenches: "We will not allow [Cadenat] to disparage the effort we have put forth, [or] the great moral monument of our sacrificing ourselves for honour and for France."[6]

At the end of February 1916, a repenting Cadenat wrote a letter to *Excelsior* which was published in full. He claimed that he meant only to say that "the [distilled] alcohol so decried [in the rear] is nevertheless sometimes judged necessary, by the government itself, to maintain or increase soldiers' physical strength at the moment of attack." But this was not nearly enough: Lecomte penned *Excelsior's* doubtful response, which called upon Cadenat to repent with a formal apology and retraction of his statements from the floor of the Chamber.[7]

It was not that *Excelsior* was afraid of discussing soldiers' drinking. For example, Pierre Mille, one of its columnists, wrote an article in December 1915 (just before the Cadenat kerfuffle) criticizing the army's wine-requisition system that, at the same time, eulogized the *poilu's* "precious *pinard*."[8] On 7 February, soon after it published Lecomte's letter, *Excelsior* published a half-page picture of men drinking together in a devastated village inn at the front, with the caption "they all raise their *quarts* of *pinard* and toast to the victory to come."[9] The very next day, 8 February, it published a humorous short story from the front whose plot involved a wine-seller that charged *poilus* too much for wine.[10]

Thus, just as rage against Cadenat for suggesting that soldiers drank distilled alcohol before attacks was reaching its zenith, the magazine unselfconsciously sang from the cult of *pinard*'s hymnbook. Indeed, as everyone knew, Mille wrote in a June 1916 column, soldiers were enamored "only of wine, the venerated *pinard* [that] reigns in the trenches." *Eau-de-vie*, "better known by the popular name of '*gnôle*,'" he assured readers, was given out only in rare and exceptional circumstances.[11] Drinking distilled alcohol before attacks was something the Germans did, Mille suggested, and this was a mark of their inborn cowardice. Hence the double outrage of Cadenat's comment: it insulted the courage of the French army as it equated the French race with the German.

Indeed, in French war culture, the German soldier had been since the invasion associated with drunkenness, alcoholism, and degeneration. In August and September of 1914, German soldiers frequently "requisitioned" alcohol when they came across it, and the French vilified them as drunken vandals. The propagandist Stephane Lauzanne described the scene in the village of Vincy-Maneouvre in mid-September, after a German withdrawal. "Bottles covered the ground everywhere," he wrote, "in the streets, along the highways, in the fields." They were of all types, "absinthe, brandy, rum, champagne, beer, and wine," as the Germans – "drunken, bloodthirsty brutes, thieving, sickening, nauseous beasts [who] descended upon France"[12] – did not respect the French distinction between good wine and bad distilled alcohol. Purpleness aside, the gist of Lauzanne's argument tracks with those provided in more reliable personal narratives. Joseph de Fontenioux, for instance, reported in his war journal on 11 September that his unit followed a trail of empty bottles to the village of Chéniers, where it found a scene of "indescribable disorder." Things were torn to shreds, graffiti was everywhere, and "the street was covered in bottles." "Evidently," he concluded, "*Messieurs les boches* had been here."[13]

Exaggerated or not, the image of the German formed from the invasion's trauma – of a drunk, pillaging and destroying – crystallized early in French war culture, in which it played a prominent part. Political cartoonists and propagandists made the German's drunkenness a defining feature of his character and evidence of its deficits. *Le Rire rouge*, a "humorous" political magazine, provides an outstanding example with its 20 March 1915 cover illustration, "The Kaiser's Soldier." It features a marauding German soldier dragging a boy in one hand and a naked woman in the other. Sausages

4.1 "Le soldat du Kaiser" (1915).

dangle from his square jaw, which is set in his square head. His skin is greenly sallow and his backpack full of pilfered wealth and wine. France burns in the distance. Very similar is "The Road of Glory," also from *Le Rire rouge*. Here, the boy has been bayoneted and the woman is dying in a field while it is Reims that burns in the distance. But the Kaiser's man is not there. There is just a trail of bottles, which is sure evidence, as we have seen, of the presence of *Messieurs les Boches*.[14] The trope even made its bloody way into mass-produced postcards produced (appropriately) by the *Société des vins de France*.

But it was not only alcohol; the Germans, *poilus* reported repeatedly, were often drunk *and* drugged during attacks.[15] Marcel Marie claimed that the German corpses that littered the ground in October 1914 "had been made drunk with alcohol and drugged with ether."[16] Their bodies, he insisted, gave off a smell of offal and chemicals that "disturbed."[17] Marcel Raymond Recouly declared the Germans he faced in the Argonne in January 1915 not only "reeked of alcohol" but also of ether, which they must have drunk for courage before they attacked. That this was Germany's practice, he claimed, was a well-known fact widely accepted among *poilus*.[18] Maurice Genevoix, one of the Western Front's most reliable narrators, claimed that during the Battle of the Marne, German soldiers had "been made drunk with alcohol and ether." At least such was what German prisoners supposedly explained to their French captors – Genevoix had no first-hand evidence.[19] One trench poet made the point:

Là-bas, au pays de sauvages	[Over there in the land of the savages]
Les soldats s'énivrent d'éther	[Soldiers dope themselves with ether]
C'est ainsi qu'ils prennent courage	[That is how they get their courage]
Et qu'ils insultent notre terre.[20]	[And how they insult our land.]

The problem, of course, was that, by mid-1915, the French army *was* regularly giving its soldiers extraordinary rations of *eau-de-vie* before attacks, a practice that continued to the end of the war. The French thus did precisely what they claimed the Germans were doing. Not only were extraordinary distributions of *eau-de-vie* before attacks frequent in the French army, but their effect was so strong that some soldiers believed what they received was mixed with ether – *poilus* thought that their own army too might dope them up. For instance, in Léon Lebret's war journal we find the following entry from 25 July 1915, when his unit attacked at Moiremont-sur-Marne:

> Day of the offensive, we are in the attacking division's reserve and they gave us a *quart* of *gnôle* that was half ether, and so we were all close to halfway crazy and there were some rolling on the ground and at 9h00 they gave the order to attack with the whole division and the cavalry behind us that will pursue the Germans.

But then, fortunately for Lebret, whose regiment suffered heavily during the assault:

> Our colonel wanted us to go up, us and the [neighbouring section of infantry] but at the moment that he was giving the order, a shell came down and blew him up, him and the captain from the general staff who was with him and their ordnance, which meant that we kept the trench but didn't have to attack and [were] very happy.[21]

Gilbert Belloc was less fortunate. He wrote in his war journal on 12 June 1916 from Verdun, where he confronted "terrible visions of the war in all its horror" and suffered through shortages of all rations. That is, shortages of everything save *gnôle*, which was "distributed in quantity and had a very pronounced taste of ether."[22]

There is little evidence beyond anecdote that the French army was serving its men alcohol mixed with ether, just as there is similarly little evidence that the German did. Nothing in the French military archives, for instance, suggests ether was distributed. The basis of the rumour was more prosaic. As the *poilu* Roger Roche explained, the *eau-de-vie* given out on days of attacks could be very strong, much stronger than what men received in daily rations (when they received daily rations). The most likely explanation is that men, surprised at the harsh taste and the level of intoxication these extraordinary distributions produced, and not entirely trusting the army that distributed them, surmised they must be drugged.[23] Yet it is not the truth of rumour but its very existence, to say nothing of its popularity, that is telling: it suggests that men were aware that the distribution of extraordinary rations of *eau-de-vie* before attacks was intended to stupefy and derange them, and that the distributions did what was intended. Which is to say, *poilus* were aware of how what I call the "battle system" – which used extraordinary rations of *eau-de-vie* to push men through the bottleneck of fear and tension that held them back from attacking – rendered them objects of psychotropic power.[24]

As François Potin recounted in an interview, when asked whether he received such a ration before an attack:

> There was *gnôle*. And there was something in it ... Something to get you excited. That, it didn't bother me. It had a taste that wasn't quite right ... They surely put a drug in it, to get the men to go over. Because when you leave to attack, you leave for death. Because [the Germans], they are waiting twenty metres away![25]

After drinking, he explained, he was transformed:

> Me, I was able to kill a hundred men ... Me, I was a lion! When I attacked, I was a real lion! Ah! I took a *boche*, but wouldn't take him prisoner, no! I would cut him into pieces! Yes! I took out my knife and I would cut him up! I would cut off his ears, his eyes, everything! We were electrified, we were electrified! We were crazy, we weren't normal men any longer ...![26]

And so the second effect of the battle system: it made men feel changed into something other than men, something more animalistic, brutal, and merciless. It thus not only provided *poilus* with a way through the bottleneck of fear and tension that came before going over the top. It also provided them with a moral distancing mechanism that separated them from their actions on the battlefield.

The battle system was the dark reflection of the daily system. It followed a similar psychotropic logic, seeking to use alcohol to transform men bodily and psychologically and thus generate emotional experiences and behaviours that benefited the war effort. But the battle system employed *eau-de-vie* (and good amounts of it) rather than wine, which made all the difference; this is why it was little spoken of during the war. The idea behind the daily system, as we have seen, was not to get men drunk, but rather to use wine to power their labours and give them comfort. The battle system was different. It sought to intoxicate men and help them kill. Indeed, and paradoxically, it was precisely that which made *eau-de-vie* a poison behind the lines that made it such a valuable tool in them – there, its antisocial properties, the very ones that according to its intoxication concept turned men senselessly violent and murderous, could be used for good. As one *poilu* stated simply: "*eau-de-vie* kills; *gnôle* helps us kill."[27]

EVIDENCE OF THE BATTLE SYSTEM'S EXISTENCE

That the French army distributed extraordinary rations of *eau-de-vie* before attacks is no secret: historians have occasionally noted that men received them. In his *La Guerre censurée* (1999), Frédéric Rousseau highlighted as much, as did François Cochet in a 2006 essay. More recently, historians Charles Ridel and Stéphane Le Bras have mentioned the topic.[28] But the descriptions of *eau-de-vie* rations that historians have provided tend to be sketches rather than analyses. As a result, they miss what is most important about these distributions, which is that they were an exercise of psychotropic power.

Soldiers and journalists could be, much like their politicians, rather reticent about extraordinary distributions of *gnôle*, at least compared with the volume of verbiage they produced about *pinard*. Some denied entirely that such distributions took place, suggesting with Lecomte and his supporters that the idea of giving alcohol to men before attacks was an insult to the French army. The journalist René Arcos, for instance, claimed that there was never the "smallest drop of *gnôle*" poured out before attacks. Frenchmen, he declared, echoing Barrès's friend from the trenches, did not need such aid, fired as they were by love of country.[29] Similarly, in his novel *Under Fire*, Henri Barbusse denied that men were drunk before attacks.[30]

Yet there is plentiful if scattered evidence in soldiers' personal narratives that the army distributed *eau-de-vie* to *poilus* before battle. Louis Barthas, for instance, describes one of his officers, a certain Sub-Lieutenant Rodière, as manically drunk before an attack in the winter of 1914–15.[31] It did not help Rodière much. He was shot in the head and killed immediately.[32] Barthas also mentions receiving a ration from the army sometime in May 1915, as does Victor Chantenay.[33] We have already seen how Léon Lebret received a ration in July of that year. So did Antoine Négroni, who, after having his last gulp of *gnôle* before an attack on 20 July 1915, shouted along with the rest of his comrades the "savage cry" of "*à la baïonnette!*"[34] Étienne Tanty reported receiving one before he went into battle in September 1915, just before he was shot in the jaw and invalided out of the war.[35] Extraordinary rations were also reported at the "hyper-battles" of Verdun in 1916 and the Chemin des Dames in 1917.[36] Louis Hobey, for instance, recounted that the night of 15–16 April 1917 – the eve of the Chemin-des-Dames offensive – "passed like a nightmare." The morning featured "the ritual of the distribution of the day of the attack: *gnôle* mixed with ether, distribution of poison."[37]

There is also literary evidence of extraordinary distributions of *eau-de-vie* that matches what is found in soldiers' journals. Two particularly memorable scenes from veterans' novels, the one set at Verdun, the other at the Chemin-des-Dames, feature the distribution of extraordinary rations of *eau-de-vie*. The first is from poet Joseph Delteil's *Les Poilus* (1926):

One day, we went up to attack. It is zero-hour [*heure-H*]. The *gnôle* [spelled *gnolle* in the text] twists in our bellies. The eye of the machine-gun spits. A whistle, and we go. Why? What's the point? Well, whoever falls, falls. The barrage, we know all about it. We jump! We explode! We die! We kill a lot of *boches* in their hole. We take ten metres of trenches. One ten-billionth of France's soil, what! And the next day we do it again.[38]

Here, the distribution is mentioned almost casually, as part of the standard procedure and stock of the dramatic scene – which it was. Its effects are clear: it deadens men to the fear they feel, makes them feel impervious to danger, and fuels interpersonal violence. The second is from Gabriel Chevallier's novel *Fear* (1930):

We drink *eau-de-vie* that has the sickly taste of blood and burns the stomach like an acid. *A foul chloroform* to numb our brains, as we endure the torture of apprehension while waiting for the torture of our bodies, the living autopsy, the jagged scalpels of steel ... We wait for zero-hour, for our crucifixion, abandoned by God, condemned by men.[39]

The tone here is entirely different – the *eau-de-vie* still prepares men for the fighting to come, but here it helps men accept that they might be sacrificed. In a strange, macabre communion, they come together and await their Calvary. For Delteil's *poilus*, the extraordinary distribution helped in preparing men to kill; for Chevallier, it helped in preparing men to die.

Yet the most critical source of evidence about extraordinary distributions of *eau-de-vie* before attacks, and one that has not yet been explored by historians, is Lucien Barou's enormous catalogue of soldiers' experiences, *Les Mémoires de la grande guerre* (2014). Barou began interviewing First World War veterans from his native Forez in the late 1970s for a linguistics thesis. By 2007, he had interviewed 160 veterans about their experiences during the war and collected the written remembrances of about thirty more. In celebration of the war's centennial, Barou edited the interviews thematically and chronologically and published them in five massive volumes, one for each year of the war.[40]

Importantly, Barou asked about half of the men he interviewed (those with experience in battle) whether they received extraordinary rations of distilled alcohol before attacks and what happened to them as a result. Of seventy-five, twelve (16 per cent) reported never receiving rations, four (5.3 per cent) reported receiving them sometimes, and fifty-nine (78.7 per cent) reported receiving them often or always. Barou concludes that while extraordinary distributions might not have been systematic to the point of being universal, they were nevertheless given out most of the time, which fits well with the evidence from personal narratives.[41]

There is, unfortunately, a paucity of material concerning extraordinary distributions of *eau-de-vie* rations in the French military archives, but what evidence there is tracks strongly with the gist of men's personal narratives and Barou's interviews, showing that, although there are but traces of it, the battle system undoubtedly existed. We have already in chapter 1 seen concrete evidence of the logistical system that delivered *eau-de-vie* to men, and that the amount of *eau-de-vie* delivered increased during periods of French offensives in 1915 and 1916. But this is suggestive only, as the records exist only for those two years and they are incomplete. Direct records of requests from field-grade officers for extraordinary distributions are scant, but they exist. A couple in the military archives correspond with the opening of the Battle of the Somme in 1916, when the army established that commanders could distribute extraordinary rations without prior authorization per their judgment – which may help in explaining why there are so few receipts.[42] Others exist for 1917's Chemin-des-Dames offensive. For instance, on 2 May

1917, General Paul Maistre of Sixth Army asked specifically for extraordinary rations of *eau-de-vie* to be given "for the day of the attack."[43]

Because of the lacuna in the archives and the tendency of men to be reticent about this part of their experience in their personal narratives, it is impossible to make any firm conclusions about precisely when such distributions became widespread or why they took place in some contexts and not others. But there is little doubt that they were taking place as of mid-1915 and subsequently defined the experience of attacking for hundreds of thousands, if not millions, of men. Per Barou's interview with Alphonse Solnon, when the former asked the latter whether he received *eau-de-vie* before attacks:

> *Hou!* It was something that was just about general! We often went up to the line with a good *quart* of *gnôle* ... It was to make us crazy! You drink a cup of *gnôle* on an empty stomach: you go crazy! ... We drank the *gnôle*, and then it gave us courage! [stated with emphasis] When we had a glass of *gnôle*, we were crazy, we couldn't even recognize ourselves![44]

This was the power to directly elicit a body-brain state and thus drive experience and behaviour in ways that made men do what they ordinarily would not; this was psychotropic power distilled.

GNÔLE AND THE DAILY SYSTEM

Before examining how the battle system worked in detail, it would be useful to consider the adjunct role of *eau-de-vie* in the daily system, for the drink was, recall, sometimes distributed along with wine as part of the *poilu*'s daily ration. The amount of the *eau-de-vie* ration was set at .0625 litres (about two standard drinks) daily, and only men in the trenches got it (those who were rotated out of the trenches still received their *pinard*). The ration did not require any large logistical apparatus of its own, as it rode *pinard*'s into the trenches: as the *Intendance* built out its capacity to deliver wine, it effectively expanded its capacity to distribute *eau-de-vie*, which travelled over the same rails and through the same logistical stations. The *eau-de-vie* brought up to the lines was ninety-five per cent alcohol and was watered down upon its arrival. It was thus compact and relatively easy to transport. After it was mixed at the mouth of the trench system, *eau-de-vie* was carried into the trenches in *bidons* just as was *pinard*, and usually by the same rations parties.

As the logistical records reviewed in chapter 1 suggest, *eau-de-vie* could not always have been given out daily; the army's commitment to providing it was not as large as that to providing wine. The *eau-de-vie* ration, unsurprisingly, had from the beginning of the war the unwavering support of the powerful distillers' lobby, which swore by its science proving that distilled alcohol was a valuable prophylactic medicine.[45] Yet the army seems to have never debated or discussed what supplying a daily *eau-de-vie* ration would mean, nor addressed its flagrant contradictions with its aggressive prewar anti–distilled alcohol policy – the adoption of the ration marked a fundamental overturning of the prewar system of temperance. Without fanfare, the *eau-de-vie* ration was ushered in along with the wine ration because it was possible and useful, ostensibly for the purpose of maintaining health and hygiene, but also, soldiers claimed, for the purpose of boosting morale. It was, in this sense and much like the wine ration, an improvised adaptation to the war that became a defining feature thereof.

The different prewar conceptions of the two drinks shaped how they were received. Unlike *pinard*, *gnôle* was a spirit with no spirit; while *pinard* had its cult, *gnôle* was more occult. *Pinard* was born of the sun and the soil of France, while *gnôle*'s provenance was less organic. It was an industrial product – a colourless, characterless chemical – pulled from beets and potatoes in the grey north through some unknown and unnatural process. While *pinard* reached back through France's generations to draw its power, *gnôle* lived in an eternal present, without any great tradition of patriotic symbols. It had no rootedness and no history, and there was nothing particularly French about it. Even if its use among *poilus* was not exactly secret, *gnôle* was not trumpeted in the same way as *pinard*, and certainly not in public. Indeed, people behind the lines were largely unaware of *gnôle* and its role in the war. In their letters home, soldiers routinely felt obliged to define the term and explain that they were receiving a ration of *eau-de-vie*.[46] Distributions of *gnôle* had something vaguely illicit and manifestly hypocritical about them.

In some ways, *gnôle* was like *pinard*. When it was distributed daily, it too had the ability to take some of the misery out of the trenches, warming and comforting men:

Avec un'p'tit gnôle   [With a wee bit of *gnôle*]
Un bon jus dégèle un homme blafard[47]   [A good coffee thaws out the pallid]

It consoled them in their losses and loneliness.

Quand je pense à tes caresses   [When I think of your caresses]
Je suis bien triste! Pour oublier,   [I feel such sorrow! To forget,]
Je m'étourdi dans les ivresses   [I drown myself in the drunkenness]
D'un p'tit quart de gnôle bien tassé.[48] [Of a well-poured cup of *gnôle*.]

It too had the power to put down the *cafard*:

Le cafard, insect odieux,   [The *cafard*, that odious insect,]
Prend des ailes d'or et s'envoie   [Takes to its golden wings
                                  and flies away]

Quand paraît le bidon joyeux[49]   [With the appearance of the
                                  joyous *bidon* (of *gnôle*)]

And perhaps most importantly, it gave men courage:

Pour stimuler l'effort en face de péril [To stimulate in the face of danger]
Entre les cordiaux, elle est   [Among the cordials, it is
  le plus viril   the most virile]
Et le dieu Mars, pour nous,   [An ambrosia Mars made for us!]
  en fait un ambrosie![50]

It had its champions. To them, *gnôle* was a "superhuman nectar" and a "divine liquid."[51] The occasional *poilu* even went so far as to claim that he preferred *gnôle* to *pinard*. F.D., for instance, claimed that "in the hierarchy of the *poilu*'s paradises, *gnôle* occupies a level higher even than that of *pinard*," even if over-indulging leads to "prison and the court martial."[52] Similarly, the trench poet Robert Lefort preferred *gnôle* to *pinard* as a morale booster:

Ah! certes, la jus de la treille   [Ah, of course, the juice of the vine]
Le pinard, piquette ou vin vieux   [*Pinard*, *piquette* or old]
En d'autres temps ferait merveille   [At other times works wonders]
Mais ici, la "gnôle" c'est mieux.[53]   [But here, *gnôle* is better.]

Quand je pense à tes caresses,
Je suis bien triste! Pour oublier,
Je m'etourdi dans les ivresses
D'un p'tit quart de gnole bien tassé

4.2 W. Tip, Untitled Postcard.

But these men were in the minority. When it came to daily system, *pinard* was king; *gnôle* was but a minor prince.

Unlike *pinard*, which was given out twice a day, *gnôle* was most often given out only once, in the morning. It was distributed in two different ways, depending on what the rationers carried. On the one hand, *gnôle* could be mixed into the coffee men received, forming a mixture that northerners called *bistouille*. Its taste was remarkable, and its job was to hit men, said one soldier in a letter home, with an "indispensable crack of the whip" and shock them into action.[54] Louis Émile Decamps wrote in his personal journal about *bistouille*: "It sets my stomach on fire, vigorously twisting about the mucous membranes, [but] gives a gentle, prolonged embrace, which jolts the whole being and gives it vigour that endures for a while. The sensation literally wakes you up."[55] Such was the point.

On the other hand, and more commonly, *gnôle* could be given out straight. The stuff distributed had a high alcohol content (around 50 per cent by volume, often more), and *gnôle*'s synonyms – *casse-pattes* [leg-breaker], *tord-boyaux* [gut-twister], *dérive* [adrift], *eau-pour-les-yeux* [eye-waterer], *roule-par-terre* [roll-on-the-ground], and *uppercut* [no translation required][56] – suggest that men respected it for its physicality. When *gnôle* was distributed this way, men got it immediately before they got their *pinard* in the form of a shot. This meant that *gnôle* served as a psychotropic force multiplier during the ritual of the *pinard* distribution – it augmented the sense of intoxication men felt and attributed to their *pinard*, which made them feel more energized and powerful than they did when they received *pinard* alone. The distribution of *gnôle* was thus a miniature ritual-within-a-ritual, a preparation for the distribution of *pinard*, whose powers *gnôle* expanded and helped to exaggerate.

For example, Jean-Louis Beaufils recounted that in the winter of 1914, upon the arrival of the rationers, the first thing distributed was the *gnôle*, which men drank down "right away" for fear of spilling "such a precious thing." The drink, he claimed, "dispelled the hallucinations of the night and rewarmed frozen limbs," and while *gnôle* made Beaufils "grimace" at first – he called it "*macchabée* [corpse] extract" – he grew to "take it with delight, drinking the last drops from the bottom of the *quart*." "It burns like acid in the throat," he admitted, "but it reinvigorates the whole body." Only then, once men were already lubricated and warmed, came the "quasi-sacred" *pinard*, which they sipped while they talked and ate.[57] The feeling that came with drinking *gnôle* thus blended into and became a part of those that came with drinking *pinard*, causing them to surge together. *Gnôle* was, as far as the daily system was concerned, not an independent actor. It was, however, the dread sovereign of the battle system.

PRELIMINAL FEAR AND TENSION: *GNÔLE* AS A PSYCHOTROPIC INTERVENTION

To understand better how extraordinary rations of *eau-de-vie* before attacks served as a psychotropic tool of emotional and behavioural conditioning it is useful to look at the experience of men before and during battle. In his classic study *No Man's Land* (1979), Eric Leed argues that men experienced the war on the Western Front as a rite of passage. Leed adapts anthropologist Arnold Van Gennep's division of the rite of passage into three parts – "preliminal rites," which prepare the subject for the passage; "liminal rites," in which the subject is, as Van Gennep's popularizer Victor Turner writes, "betwixt and between" his old and new social self and thus in a state of flux; and "postliminal rites," which reintegrate the subject into society with a new status – and maps them onto the experience of the Western Front. In Van Gennep and Turner's conception, the liminal phase came with the destabilization or inversion of ordinary social norms and categories – liminality is a state of upside-downness. As Leed notes, if liminality is defined as inversion, then the experience of the trenches – where men lived underground, slept during the day and worked at night, and found their buddies' bodies turned inside out – was undoubtedly on liminality's bleeding edge. Leed posits that because men could never escape the trenches, they remained trapped in a state of anxious liminality that defined the experience of the war and that influenced European culture afterwards.[58]

   While Leed's focus was on the experience of the war as a whole, his thinking can be transferred to the micro-situational level and applied to the experience of battle. In his masterpiece *The Face of Battle* (1976), John Keegan showed how First World War battles divided into three clear phases: the preparatory bombardment, the short flight forward across No-Man's-Land and combat in enemy trenches, and then the consolidation of gains and preparation to renew the attack or fight off a counter-attack.[59] This sequence meant that battle itself resembled a rite of passage, one within the larger rite of passage of the war: the preliminal phase, during which men prepared themselves for the violence to come; the liminal phase, which involved leaving the trenches, crossing No-Man's-Land, and perhaps engaging with the enemy at close range; and the postliminal phase, which, in the case of successful attacks, involved prisoner-taking and abuse and souvenir-hunting.

This meant that the mechanics of battles produced a shared and sequential three-part emotional experience common to the men who fought them. First, during the preliminal phase, came a powerful sense of fear and tension that built to a fever pitch as zero-hour approached; then, during the liminal phase, came a sense of release, when men overcame that fear and tension and attacked; and finally, during the postliminal phase, came euphoria followed by deep exhaustion. Extraordinary distributions were a biocultural intervention that helped in directing and manipulating these emotional experiences, steering them and the behaviours they prompted in certain directions by effecting an emotional and behavioural shift in the men who consumed them. They not only made men unafraid (or at least less afraid), but also helped them do certain things they would not ordinarily do – such as kill.

Large-scale attacks on the Western Front typically took place at daybreak or shortly after – the French launched themselves illuminated by the rising sun – which meant that attackers had to be brought up to the firing or attack trenches and packed into their jumping-off points a night or two before. As they filed awkwardly through the darkness and towards the growing battle, men were assaulted by the sound of the preparatory bombardment, which was intended to pound German trenches and maim or kill as many Germans as possible, and which could last several days. Bombardments lit up German positions with fiery scenes that could make *poilus* feel savage satisfaction, but that also filled them with foreboding, as they knew they would have to travel through the destruction they witnessed. The separate booms blended into each other and created one vast roaring ocean of sound. Henri Barbusse recounted that it "wrapped around" men and seemed to come from all directions at once, while Georges Gaudy compared its omnipresence and deafening power at Verdun to that of absolute silence.[60] In any case, the ordinary aural world was obliterated. The hours and moments before battle produced extraordinary sights and sounds. It was a liminal environment within a liminal environment.

In the high literature of *bourrage-du-crâne* [eyewash], which is what *poilus* called any overly patriotic tripe that glorified the war, men wished desperately for call the call of *"forward with the bayonet!"* so that they might throw themselves at the enemy and prove their manliness. They were portrayed as eager to fight and kill. In a good example of the genre, one soldier-propagandist recounted that before the Second Battle of Champagne, his men's impatient hearts had "swelled with the emotion of victory," and they had to be held back, they were so excited to attack. Driven by a "confidence, an enthusiasm, an incomparable ardor," they crossed the "heroic field" and terrorized the enemy with the bayonet.[61] The popular press behind the lines produced similar claptrap. In a narrative of an attack recounted in *L'Ouest-Éclair*, men took pains to assure that their bayonets were "seriously sharp," the better to run through the *boche*. "The *poilus* wander about like caged bears," the article insisted proudly, "waiting with impatience for the moment when they can get something going [*se dégrouiller un peu*]."[62] This was nonsense.

In his personal narrative, the soldier-priest Paul Tuffrau claimed to have never seen the "impatient joy, [the] mocking lightheartedness, [the] good-humoured energy that the newspapers like to present as the constant attitude of the French soldier." Rather, before an attack, men were subdued and nervous, "silent, thinking of the awful dangers that awaited them."[63] Similarly, another soldier-priest, Joseph Raymond, was emphatic that, in contrast to what one read in newspapers – which would have readers believe that *poilus* treated an attack "like a party," and launched themselves forward in a "torrent of heroism" – the truth was that, when the order came down, some men protested, a few threatened their officers, but most accepted their unknown fate with quiet resignation. Indeed, men before attacks were intensely afraid and the atmosphere was full of tension. While they attempted to remain outwardly stoic, their faces and silent farewells could betray them.

Soldiers' bodies betrayed them too, depriving them of a sense of agency. Historian Joanna Bourke notes the bodily symptoms of fear that military psychologists and physicians during the First World War identified:

muscular tension, freezing, shaking and tremor, excessive perspiration, anorexia, nausea, abdominal distress, diarrhea, urinary frequency, incontinence of urine or feces, abnormal heartbeat, breathlessness, a burning sense of weight oppressing the chest, faintness and giddiness.[64]

This unlovely cluster of experiences was the result of a flood of stress hormones that affected nearly every man at the front before an attack – their fear drove the workings of their bodies in ways entirely outside of their control. In his novel *Fear*, Gabriel Chevallier described these moments, when men spent the final minutes looking one another over, wondering who among them would be ripped apart, their remains made into "objects of horror and indifference." Their flesh betrayed them: "bodies whimper, dribble, soil themselves in shame." For Chevallier, this fear was dehumanizing: "Thought prostrates itself, begs the cruel powers, the demonic forces," he testified. "We are worms wriggling to escape the spade." He concluded that to be a man in the moments before an attack was "the depth of horror," the "consummation of ignominy."[65] This overwhelming feeling of fear and tension defined the preliminary period.

But – and this is crucial – once they left their trenches, men experienced an affective shift; they became detached from the cataclysmic realities around them and were driven forward by the inertia of the attack.[66] Horrible scenes made little impact as their vision grew constricted and tunnelled as they raced across No-Man's-Land. As Chevallier's protagonist Dartemont attacks, he sees around him men "falling, opening up, splitting, shattering." It is incomprehensible, and his mind stops working and shifts into a "kind of unconsciousness."[67] Paul Dubrulle was shocked at the rapidity and completeness of the affective change that came over him and his comrades once they had left the trenches. The fear and tension that had been so crushing just minutes before lifted completely. "I left the sorrowful period of waiting, when one is ground down by fear of the unknown," he recounted, and "thrown into action, I was elevated into the sphere of the Ideal, where I was no longer afraid."[68]

In effect, there was an emotional and behavioural bottleneck at the moment of attack – at the moment of the transition to the liminal state of combat, when men were in the zone of fire, literally betwixt and between two sets of trenches. The trick was to get men out of the trenches and moving forwards, for once an attack started, they plunged forward as though driven over No-Man's-Land by a motive force indigenous to the battle itself. As Barbusse put it, "the blast of death" itself carried men across the fire-swept ground and towards the German trenches.[69]

It was just before men went over the top, around fifteen or twenty minutes before the attack was launched, that the *gnôle* was distributed. Marc Délime described how these distributions worked: "An NCO came around, [and] he poured out about half a *quart*" per man (about four to six standard drinks, depending on the strength of the *gnôle*). Other veterans reported receiving more.[70] Délime recalled that, one by one, the men drank what they received, or at least most of them did. As far as those who did not drink went, Délime was incredulous. "So I asked them," he demanded, "why throw it out? And they told me, you drunk slobs! They want to get you killed!"[71] But, as Marcus Dubuis observed, when you are thrown in the lake you'd better swim, so the men drank what was provided.[72] Roger Roche similarly recalled receiving half a *quart* and noted that he was forced to drink under the supervision of an officer – precisely because men were tossing it away and the army wanted to assure everyone drank what they were given. Roche claimed to have disposed of the first extraordinary distribution of *eau-de-vie* he received, but soon came around to the practice, partially because of the insistence of officers. "It didn't matter what rank you were," he remembered, "all had to drink." He received the dose ten minutes before the attack, and "[i]t took effect right away."[73]

The effects of alcohol consumption immediately before an attack in the doses men reported receiving – on their own, detached (so far as it can be imagined) from the cultural context of the distribution – would have been a quick and powerful relief of physical discomfort, a feeling of increased energy, and a noticeable decrease in the physical and psychological symptoms of anxiety. This head-change – which, Barou's *poilus* emphasized, was felt very strongly because what they received was so strong – was then read through the *poilu*'s intoxication concept for *gnôle*, which gave the sensations meaning and direction. The core of that intoxication concept, as we have seen, was that the drink transformed men into brutes. *Poilus* thus read the interoceptive and affective sensations that the *gnôle* produced as the feeling of becoming brutal, and so prepared for the liminal trial to come. Central to the experience of drinking these extraordinary distributions, *poilus* repeated, was the feeling of becoming "crazy" [*fou*] and losing one's fear of danger and moral sense.

LIMINAL TRANSFORMATION INTO FORWARD PANIC

Fear of killing was perhaps the greatest barrier that men in the attack had to overcome. As sociologist Randall Collins and military psychologist David Grossman have separately argued, interpersonal violence – even the extreme case of battle – is hard to do, and even harder to do competently.[74] Grossman in particular holds that interpersonal violence, especially killing, produces a "universal phobia" in people, who respond physiologically and naturally recoil and run from it.[75] This fear is difficult to overcome, and as S.L.A. Marshall's pioneering if contested work suggested, many men hesitate to use violence on the battlefield, even in self-defense.[76]

Soldiers from all the belligerents on the Western Front reported hesitation towards and regret regarding killing their enemy. Even Ernst Junger – a great fan of the intimate violence of the trench raid – once let a man live who showed him a picture of his family and expressed sorrow at killing a British "boy" in 1918. "The state," he regretted, "which relieves us of our responsibility, cannot take away our remorse."[77] French soldiers too were also often loath to kill. Francisque Ferret, for instance, explained that "whoever is human cannot kill!" and noted that he never did, except perhaps from a distance with a machine-gun, which depersonalized the experience.[78] But trench-fighting during attacks, when it occurred, took place at what Grossman calls the "intimate distance" of killing, when soldiers were physically close to one another; it was highly personalized and thus hard to do. Their enemy, in short, could be close enough to appear human, and this created a high barrier of fear and tension that was difficult to overcome.[79] And when they did kill, men could be wracked with remorse and regret, as was Jean-Marie Quet, who killed a man from close in with a grenade. Only afterwards did he have the thought that the man he killed could have been a father. "I wouldn't have killed him," he wept in an interview with Barou, and "I have regretted it all my life."[80]

Extraordinary distributions of *gnôle* not only worked to get men through the emotional bottleneck of fear and tension, putting them into forward flight, but also helped them overcome their fear of and hesitation towards killing.[81] It did this by making them feel transformed, psychologically and morally, into the very image of the brutal, violent *eau-de-vie* drinker from the army's temperance lectures. François Potin, recall, was insistent, even exultant as to this fact: *gnôle* made men into something other than men, and that could spur them on to kill; it transformed their bodies and minds in such a way as to make them bloodthirsty. He believed that the drink remade him in a fearsome, inhuman image. For Potin, the feeling of intoxication was experienced as the feeling of permission to use violence – it is what transformed him into a pitiless killer. The same feeling provided countless others with a moral distancing mechanism that softened the trauma of killing by making them feel temporarily transformed into killers. The ration simultaneously fuelled and excused their behaviour.

Put another way, the distribution of *gnôle*, by creating a certain psychotropic experience, signalled the moment of transition between the preliminal and liminal phases of the battle just as it prepared men to fight through the latter. The feeling of the head-change was experienced as the feeling of transformation; for at least some men, it physiologically and psychologically marked the moment of a shift between being men and being killers. In this way, the physiological sensations and perceptual changes drinking produced were experienced as a shared change in consciousness that created a powerful sense of entrainment among the attackers, who became prepared, and some even crazed, for the fight to come, together.

Marius Dubuis, for example, knew that the extraordinary distributions of *eau-de-vie* were "to give us strength in order to go over!" He availed himself of them for precisely this reason: they gave him the courage and permission to do what the war required he do.[82] Similarly, Georges Montagne claimed that "[i]t raised morale. We went over like crazies! We were inured to danger! It stimulated us, you see, when it was time to go over."[83] Or Marc Délime: "It made it easy to go over the top, for good reason: we were halfway drunk!"[84] Or Louis Guillaume, who reported receiving a stupendous amount of alcohol: "But if we didn't drink, we couldn't do it! You had to be drunk ... [he begins weeping] to get out of the trench!"[85] And it is no accident that, in all these cases, the *poilus* use the subject pronoun "*on*," a familiar version of the first-person plural, to describe their experiences, as they were shared and emotionally entraining.

Indeed, this group transformation was entirely the point; the bodily sensations and head-change alcohol caused shifted men into a different state of collective moral consciousness, one in which they felt themselves capable of killing. The interoceptive shift provided the physiological and psychological proof that the moral transformation had happened. Caught up in a cascade of emotional and sensory stimulation, pushed forward by the momentum of the battle, and intoxicated with alcohol and destruction, soldiers would arrive in the German trenches to find their enemy, the source of all their suffering, the source of their fear and tension and hatred, in a state of defenselessness and demoralization. In a moment of moral exultation, even euphoria, they could kill, and overkill.

Important here are the tactical realities of a First World War battle. Attacks typically went one of two ways. On the one hand, if the preparatory bombardment failed, the enemy remounted his defenses and tore into the attackers whilst they were still crossing No-Man's-Land. This killed the attackers in such great numbers that it drove them to take cover in shell holes or behind geographical features. Its forward momentum broken, the assault melted away. On the other hand, if the preparatory bombardment did its macabre work well, the enemy on the other side of No-Man's-Land was killed or sufficiently stupefied not to mount much resistance against the assault. In this case, the attackers dropped into the enemy trench relatively unscathed and found the enemy largely demoralized, either still hiding in dugouts or blasted into helplessness by the bombardment.[86] In short, if they managed to arrive in the German trenches, French soldiers usually found their enemy disoriented and dazed and often defenseless.

In the First World War, vanishingly few casualties were the result of the type of close-quarters, hand-to-hand fighting that could take place if the attackers managed to cross No-Man's-Land and drop into the enemy's trenches. Likely some eighty-five per cent of casualties were the result of either artillery or machine gun fire, with most of the rest from desultory rifle fire and small handheld bombs – probably less than one per cent came from hand-to-hand fighting in trenches. As Jean Norton-Cru has noted, soldiers in the attack almost never fought with crossed bayonets – and when they did, they did so after finding their enemy blasted and vulnerable, making it an uneven fight. For these reasons, the degradation of motor skills that came with extraordinary rations of *eau-de-vie*, which undoubtedly reduced the accuracy of the attacking infantry's rifle fire and probably the efficacy of their hand-to-hand fighting, was not of much importance; the success of an attack had less to do with the infantry's fighting power than with artillery preparation and the hardness of German defenses. Indeed, whether men were intoxicated or not probably had little practical effect on their combat effectiveness during battle, as what they were asked to do – occupy space that the artillery had cleared and kill their demoralized enemies – had little dependence on their sober faculties and fine motor skills.

In his *Violence: A Micro-sociological Theory* (2008), Collins, the sociologist, continually hammers one point home: contrary to popular representations thereof, violence is hard to do and even harder to do competently at close range. The fear of injuring or killing others, which for Collins is the product both of "physiological hard-wiring" and the severe disruption of "ordinary processes of [emotional] entrainment and mutual attention," creates a high barrier of fear and tension. Those who want to do violence must overcome "the own bodies, emotions, and nervous systems" to become agents, and this is particularly true when there is little physical distance between combatants.[87] But this resistance can be overcome by, he insists, "transforming the collective tension of combat into moments of entrainment in aggression." In these moments of aggressive entrainment, a group's emotional energy can reach a fever pitch, with the result being an "emotional rush" or, in Vietnam veteran Philip Caputo's words, an "emotional detonation" that tends towards frenzied violence directed at a morally and physically defeated enemy.[88] Collins calls this a "forward panic." Forward panics tend to happen when, after a prolonged period of buildup of fear and tension, one side of the confrontation suddenly gives way in moral collapse and flees or freezes. The other side, in a state of violent euphoria, confidently attacks their demoralized foe. Forward panics are not mere theory – they are an empirically observable form of group behaviour that take place both in civilian life (during riots, for instance, or at the end of police chases) and on the battlefield.[89]

Extraordinary distributions of *gnôle* helped fuel forward panics on the First World War battlefield by first getting men through the bottleneck of fear and tension that characterizes violent confrontations and then providing them with a moral distancing mechanism that excused them from their violent behaviour after they reached the enemy trenches. For instance, once he had received his *gnôle* and gone over the top, Chevallier's protagonist Dartemont – who shows no animus at all towards the Germans for the entirety of the novel *Fear* – joyfully jumps onto the chest of a German, "crush[ing] him like an insect." He sees other French soldiers chase down the outnumbered Germans and kill them from the intimate distance. It is "an instinctive reaction, joyful savagery born of extreme stress," he explained. "Fear has made us cruel," he asserted, and "[w]e need to kill to comfort ourselves and take revenge." In *Fear*, the panicked killing was short-lived – Chevallier did not want his readers disgusted with the heroes of his story, after all – and the French began taking prisoners.[90]

There is evidence in soldiers' personal journals and letters that echoes what Chevallier described in his novel. Pierre Menetrier, for instance, recounted in his war journal that he received at the Third Battle of Artois a "big ration of *eau-de-vie*." Twenty minutes later, just as his blood alcohol level was reaching its peak and he felt most activated and entrained, he left the trenches and attacked. The "surprise was complete," and when Menetrier and his fellows dropped into the German trenches, they found bewildered, demoralized men still in their dugouts, or who ran away in panic. In a bloody, hot emotional moment, the French slaughtered whomever they caught. "What butchery," Menetrier wrote. "No prisoners."[91] But soldiers were understandably hesitant to describe this aspect of the fighting, and so have left only traces of it in the historical record.[92]

The dynamics of the situation itself, Barou's *poilu* Potin strained to explain, absolved soldiers of direct moral responsibility for the frenzied violence that could result when men reached the German trenches, for they got caught up in a hot emotional cascade. He described the sense of intoxicated frenzy the combination of alcohol and attacks could bring:

> We were crazy. When we attacked, we were crazy! We weren't normal, we didn't know what we were doing. Even if we weren't drunk, we were in the fight and became the hammer! We were afraid of nothing! We knew that we could be killed any moment, and so we had to kill![93]

Yet, as Potin himself suggests, many French soldiers drank to intoxication precisely so that they could make this transformation and be able to kill should they need to – many *were* drunk. Antoine Fanget, for instance, asserted that one must be pitiless when one was "clearing the trenches" – and that is why *poilus* drank. The alcohol deranged him such that he would not have known his own father; it separated him from himself and his actions. He insisted his officers made him drink before he attacked so much as to become deranged. "It was the officers who made us drink. They passed along the *bidons*," he recounted, "'Let's go, your *quart*, let's go!'"[94] Alcohol intoxication, in effect, gave men a "time-out" from their ordinary moral world, and this gave them permission to act in ways violent and different, at least for a time. In this way, extraordinary rations of *eau-de-vie* provided men with a moral distancing mechanism that softened the trauma of killing by making them feel transformed into something deranged and different from their ordinary selves.

CONSENT, COERCION, AND BIOPOWER

Not every French soldier drank what was supplied to him and underwent the psychotropic instrumentalization this entailed. For instance, on 9 May 1915, the first day of the Second Battle of Artois, the army distributed extraordinary rations of *eau-de-vie* to soldiers, which Victor Chatenay reported in his journal from that day to be "copious." Chatenay tasted the drink and threw it away – he claimed he did not want the chemical help – but did so subtly, so as to not allow his comrades to see. Chatenay reported that the men who drank did so with enthusiasm, together. Moreover, the *eau-de-vie* distribution worked. It effected a change in the men, and rather than cower, they became "determined and impatient to receive the order and launch the assault."[95] Similarly, Claude Parron reported that on the same day, he and his comrades received *eau-de-vie* to drink right before they attacked, in addition to extra wine. Parron found this shameful, and lamented that "at the front, the soldier is nothing but an instrument of suffering that one sends out as though [he were] a machine."[96]

Louis Barthas described a revealing pre-battle scene near Notre-Dame-de-Lorette that took place sometime soon after, in the early summer of 1915, when the battle system was still young. Just when Barthas and his comrades were receiving their orders to move up and attack, a *gnôle*-carrying rationer arrived in their trench, carrying two cans of the drink to be given out immediately. "Each of us held out our canteens," he recounted, "but many sniffed at the [*gnôle*] with distrust; this unexpected distribution just before an attack appeared suspicious." One of Barthas's comrades, a certain Jordy, claimed that the drink "smelled like a pharmacy," while another named Tort declared, "it's ether." A third, Mondiès, threw his dose to the ground in disgust. "It's poison," he shouted. "They want to make us crazy. But for two sous worth of [*gnôle*], they are not going to make a killer out of me!"[97] These men refused to be transformed and instrumentalized.

Barou's *poilus* reported similar scenes. Ferret, when asked whether he received *gnôle* before attacks, for instance, answered in the affirmative. "Oh yes, yes!" he proclaimed, "we used to drink the *gnôle* to get a little more … a little more determined. We used to drink *gnôle* before we attacked." He denied ever drinking any himself, but insisted that some men – he called them the "bold" ones – availed themselves of *gnôle* precisely to become more violent: "We made them drink *gnôle*: they would have cut the Germans' heads off. We called that a quick attack [*coup de main*]!"[98] Charles Fraty claimed that while soldiers received alcohol before attacks, it was not something that they were supposed to talk about. "Three-quarters" of the men, he maintained, refused to drink it because it made them too unaware of what was happening around them. The ration could be large enough, he suggested, to work against its purposes. "It was crazy, that!" he explained. "It got men half hammered. And then they had no more strength."[99] Similarly, Léon Guichard claimed that the distributions were regular, but that he himself did not drink them. "Because I wanted to keep my cool [*garder mon sang-froid*]," he said, "because when you have a *quart* or two of that crap [*saloperie*], you are halfway crazy!" But he noted that many others consumed enough to get "messed up"; some men *chose* to intoxicate themselves.[100] "It was not normal alcohol," insisted Ernest Pigeron. *Poilus*, he lamented, were treated like dumb beasts needing energy, hardly different from draught animals getting feed: "They took us for animals! They doped us! They doped us to give us a shot of energy! They doped us to give us courage!"[101]

All these men knew that the army was using alcohol to alter them before attacks, to make them less afraid, more murderous, and inured to danger. Many resented it. Some rejected being made instruments, although most still did their duty and attacked. Thus not all needed, and some refused to rely on, alcohol to push them through the bottleneck of fear and tension that came before the attack. Yet, in their denials, those who resisted only highlight the prevalence of the battle system, for even they report that most men, if given the opportunity to drink, took it. Solnon, one of Barou's subjects, claimed that "nobody sent it back, everybody drank it":

[in a very solemn and strong tone] I'm telling you this: without alcohol, we would not have had the victory! I'm telling you this sincerely: without alcohol, we would not have seen the victory ... You were a crazy man with the *gnôle*, you didn't know anything. If we hadn't had it, we wouldn't have won the war ... I'm not afraid to say it often: if we were victorious, it's because we were full of alcohol! Because with alcohol, well, it transforms a man. Alcohol transforms a man![102]

THE POSTLIMINAL PHYSICAL AND EMOTIONAL CRASH

Battle comes with profound physiological changes in the human body, particularly as it concerns the sympathetic nervous system (SNS), whose primary purpose is to regulate the so-called "fight-or-flight" response: combat is itself psychotropic. In particular, the periods immediately before and during combat are accompanied by the release of stress hormones that activate the SNS: adrenaline (which stimulates blood circulation while increasing breathing, pain tolerance, and physical strength), noradrenaline (which increases alertness and arousal), neuropeptide-Y (a strong vasoconstrictor and vigilance enhancer), and cortisol (which directs bodily resources to the flight-or-flight response). This activation of the SNS and release of stress hormones comes with a suite of physiological and cognitive changes, such as vasoconstriction, raised heartbeat, and tremors; restlessness and anxiety; tunnel vision; auditory disturbances; and a subjective feeling of activation. This dump of stress hormones is inevitably followed by a backlash of the "parasympathetic nervous system" (PNS), which regulates bodily homeostasis and serves to reverse the hormonal changes that activate the SNS.[103] This PNS backlash – which, Grossman insists, is well-known to combat veterans – causes an emotional and physical crash characterized by an overwhelming sense of exhaustion and even a need to sleep.

Indeed, after a successful attack that consolidated positions in the German trenches, French soldiers could be overwhelmed by fatigue and sleepiness, even during battle. For instance, in *Under Fire*, Barbusse described this feeling after having taken a trench: "There is a universal slowing down of movements and noises … Exaltation is calmed and there is nothing left except an infinite fatigue that rises up in us, drowning us, and the endless waiting that resumes."[104] Similarly, Chevallier on the rollercoaster of feeling: "Success has given us enormous strength and confidence, which comes from our desire to live and our fierce will to defend ourselves. Our blood is up and right now, in broad daylight, we fear no man … [But o]ur fever diminishes bit by bit, our courage vanishes like a drunkard's stupor, anxiety about the future returns."[105] This could be very dangerous, as the hours after taking a trench were perilous ones for soldiers, who had to work to protect their new positions from German artillery fire and counter-attacks or regroup for another wave of attacks.

Extraordinary distributions of *eau-de-vie* could serve to exaggerate this fatigue and magnify the emotional and behavioural consequences of the after-attack parasympathetic backlash. Recall that alcohol's subjective psychotropic effects are biphasic – it serves as a stimulant while blood alcohol concentration is rising and a depressant while it is declining, which, again, begins to happen approximately half an hour after the last drink. This means that intoxicated *poilus* who successfully took a German trench experienced not only the PNS backlash, but an alcoholic intoxication crash as they worked to consolidate their positions. Put another way, extraordinary distributions could serve as a force multiplier for the fatigue that came inevitably after a successful attack.

Soldiers, as we have already seen, were often reticent in their personal narratives about extraordinary distributions of *eau-de-vie*; they were even more reticent about the potentially disastrous effects of these distributions after successful attacks, when a PNS backlash combined with the depressive effects of alcohol to put men to sleep. Louis Maufrais, a medical doctor at the front, recounted one such event. After an attack that involved extraordinary distributions of *eau-de-vie*, he explained, men could be left vulnerable:

> Just before the attack, they gave a double ration of *eau-de-vie* to the men. We went on to regret it. The next day, early in the morning, the Germans counter-attacked without a sound and took back one of the two trenches we took. The movement was all the easier because our men [*bonhommes*], who drank their *gnôle*, were sleeping deeply. The night['s] attack was thus a half-success.[106]

The result, Maufrais insisted, was "butchery." Moreover, some of Barou's *poilus* who did not drink claimed they avoided *gnôle* precisely because they feared this hormonal and intoxicant crash. Dubuis, for instance, noted that the stimulation the extraordinary rations provided was followed by a heavy fatigue; he drank anyway, as the benefits of doing so were greater than the very real dangers.[107]

The postliminal period of battle was not associated with the initiate's reintegration into society with a new identity – the danger persisted and even the most successful local attack decided nothing in the greater scheme of things. Men were not entirely released from battle, but rather faced the prospect of more extraordinary distributions of *gnôle* and more attacks, as the Delteil quote from earlier in the chapter suggests. In this respect, the micro-situational experience of battle reflects the larger experience of the war as described by Leed, the historian – the rite of passage was never fully complete and the reintegration always at best partial.

It is useful here to return to the historiographical question of consent and coercion discussed in the last chapter and reconsider it in light of the nature of the battle system. And an exercise of psychotropic power it clearly was: it inserted a drug into the bodies of soldiers in order to manipulate and shape their experiences. While *pinard* and the daily system functioned to provide soldiers with a sense of agency, this was not the case with the battle system. As Dubuis explained to Barou, men knew that the *gnôle* was to get men to go over the top by giving them a "boost." "I always understood that," he admitted.[108] The battle system was clearly more coercive than the daily system, in terms of both what it did to the body and human experience; it was precisely for this reason that men were much more resistant to it. Indeed, the battle system provides a paradigmatical example of what we might call "coerced consent" in that it pushed men to do what they believed they had to do to survive and win the war. It points to the complicated nature of consent and coercion in the French army, but leans steeply towards the coercion side of the divide.

Moreover, the battle system has something to teach us about the nature of what philosopher Michel Foucault famously called "biopower." Biopower, of course, has meant many things to many scholars, but can be generally understood as the political power over the processes of life that emerged in the nineteenth century along with the rise of statistics, demography, and biology as fields of knowledge.[109] Its focus is on administrating and optimizing "health, hygiene, birthrate, life-expectancy, and race" and thus growing the productive powers of a population.[110] In bioethicist Catherine Mill's interpretation of Foucault's *oeuvre*, biopower emerged along "two poles": that of the "disciplines," which were new forms of knowledge that treated the individual human body as a machine to be engineered and made docile (Foucault called this the "anatomopolitics of the human body"), and the "population," which focused on the health, hygiene, and productivity of the "species-body" – which is to say, the population as a whole.[111]

The mode of psychotropic power exemplified by French alcohol policy on the Western Front can be thought to serve as a third pole that is orthogonal to the poles of the individual body and of the species-body, one that is simultaneously more personal and more generalized than individual or species: the molecular level, experienced internally and subjectively but based on a biological mechanism shared among all people that is thus elicitable in all people. This, recall, was how France's medical elites conceived of the wine ration: it was a way to optimize both the body of the individual soldier and the health of the army more generally by way of a massive public health intervention. Wine would not just protect a man from the cold and the Germans, but it would also protect the French nation from racial degeneration and biological decay – and it would do this on a molecular level, by recharging and protecting bodily cells. The army's policies suggest it used extraordinary distributions of *eau-de-vie* the same way: they were to make men into brutes and drive them into a forward panic while killing the fear of killing and being killed. The target of both these interventions was not just the body, but more specifically, an organ in the body: the brain.

The point of the interventions was not to discipline or even normalize in the Foucauldian sense – this was not a discursive power to mold – but rather the power to intervene directly in the biochemical processes of life to transform and rearrange them from the inside out. It worked by changing the brain's chemistry, by altering, in the most literal sense, the very tissue of emotion, cognition, and experience.

5

THE PROHIBITION SYSTEM AND THE WORLD-BEHIND-THE-WAR

A TOOL IN THE LINES, A POISON BEHIND THEM

The psychotropic regime created by the daily and battle systems focused on generating emotional experiences and behaviours in the trenches: the one sought to use wine to power, inspire, and energize, while the other sought to use distilled alcohol to derange men and drive them over the parapet and into No-Man's-Land. These two systems, as we have seen, worked, and worked together. The daily system was invaluable in maintaining morale at the front, while the battle system was similarly invaluable in preparing men for combat. Alcohol distributions in the trenches, in short, were a powerful psychotropic tool that the French army widely employed, and to good effect.

Yet there was, too, a whole social world just behind the trenches but still in the army zones. There, in this world-behind-the-war, alcohol consumption – which was very frequent – functioned both as a means of psychotropic control for commanders and as a means of flight for soldiers. There, two conflicting impulses battled one another. On the one hand was the army's desire to surveille and control men's drinking behind the lines to assure that drunkenness, alcoholism, and their inevitable negative consequences did not spread in the army zone's rear areas, which would not only damage discipline, but also corrupt the biological material that was the army. On the other hand was the *poilu*'s understandable desire to find and drink whatever he could once he rotated out of the lines and into the villages and hamlets in which he found his billets.

To protect the *poilu* against himself, the army published a set of anti-alcohol decrees and established surveillance practices at *débits de boissons* that sought to discipline and control his drinking while he was in rest [*en repos*] in the rear areas. This was what I will call the "prohibition system." Crucially, the prohibition system reflected the binary division between bad, unhealthy distilled alcohol and good, healthy wine that characterized French thinking about the two drinks. It was primarily aimed at eliminating the consumption of distilled alcohol, which was considered profoundly and uniquely dangerous for health and discipline. The prohibition system did not extend in any significant way to wine-purchasing and drinking among soldiers, at least not until 1917. As a result, the world-behind-the-war was often wine-sodden.

Prohibition was in Europe's air during the First World War, and the war's emergency opened new vistas for the private French temperance movement in France's civilian zones.[1] As of 1903, grouped together under the umbrella organization the *Ligue nationale contre l'alcoolisme* (LNCA), these earnest men and women believed that distilled alcohol was a racial poison and wine a racial balm, so long as it was taken in moderation. The LNCA's main goal was to pressure the Third Republic's legislature to take up anti-alcoholism by drumming up a groundswell of popular support for prohibitionary measures on distilled alcohol. It grew in the years before the war, with its larger membership allowing it to afford a new office with a prestigious Parisian address in 1911. But the LNCA remained far from popular, and the windows of that new office were promptly smashed.[2]

The LNCA's two major yet modest prewar legislative lobbying efforts – the first to limit the proliferation of *débits de boissons* and the second to ban absinthe – failed.[3] The trench war shifted the terrain in the LNCA's favour, for France's ability to fight was tied tightly to France's ability to produce, and distilled alcohol was thought to be highly destructive to this ability. Suddenly, alcoholism among workers became a pressing issue of national defense, especially in strategic industries. During the emergency of the war, men could not be permitted to drink distilled alcohol as they wished; the dangers for national health and productivity were too great. Thus, on 16 August 1914, just days after the Germans crossed the border, Interior Minister Louis Malvy announced a national ban on the sale of absinthe –

long a goal of France's temperance reformers – and promised that "a complete legislative program against alcoholism" would be forthcoming from the wartime government. Newspapers gave column-inches to the LNCA's propagandists. Patriotic politicians rushed to claim the banner of temperance.[4]

The LNCA sought to put the national emergency to good use in advancing the cause of temperance. It focused in part on education, particularly among workers through an alliance with France's largest union, the *Confédération générale du travail*, and with women's groups, which pledged to fight against distilled alcohol rather than for domestic political causes during the war.[5] It also focused on promoting legislation, first on limiting the number of new *débits*. It was not an easy fight.

A law proposing that no new *débit* be permitted to open in France during the war was submitted for debate in February 1915. When it passed nine months later, it provided numerous loopholes and opportunities for fraud. The LNCA also partnered with Finance Minister Alexandre Ribot in June 1915. Ribot saw the war as a perfect time to reform France's system of taxation and create new revenue by raising taxes on the manufacture of distilled alcohol. He also wanted to surtax certain *apéritifs* and begin to tax the *bouilleurs de cru*, France's home distillers, who had been traditionally exempt. The LNCA supported the effort on the reasonable assumption that increased taxes and thus increased prices would decrease consumption. At the end of the month, the Chamber passed a watered-down version of Ribot's proposal, one whose provisions would sunset at the end of the war. Finally, France had only one law against public drunkenness on the books – the *Loi de 1873*, required to be displayed prominently in every *débit* – that was basically unenforced and unenforceable. The LNCA proposed making the arrest of publicly intoxicated people mandatory and increasing punishments. But reformers had trouble here too. A bill to strengthen the *Loi de 1873* was introduced into the Chamber in July 1915. It passed, again in watered-down form, only in October 1917.[6]

Yet the LNCA succeeded in winning to its cause a portion of the Third Republic's administrative elite (rather than its elected politicians), who tried to exercise prohibitionary powers extra-legislatively. By July 1915, various prefects in the north had decreed a ban on the sale of distilled alcohol dispensed by the glass in *débits* – we have already seen how this policy could create political tension in the case of Bernard Cadenat's comments. In August 1915, Minister of the Interior Louis Malvy attempted by decree to expand this ban to all of France, but immediate popular outcry led to its suspension. He tried again in October and this time managed only to establish that no distilled alcohol could be sold to workers before 11h00.[7] They would, at the very least, arrive at work sober.

The LNCA's wartime successes would have boggled the imagination of *fin-de-siècle* anti-alcohol reformers. Still, they were not particularly profound ones, and they fell far short of what the most ardent anti-alcohol advocates believed necessary for the defense of the French nation and race in a time of existential conflict. Hostility to the LNCA and its prohibitionist program came both from distilled alcohol drinkers and from the powerful lobbying groups that represented the distillers. Moreover, as deputies in the Chamber knew, taxes on distilled alcohol were crucial to the state's finances, and so decreased consumption meant decreased revenue. Thus, bottom-up popular and top-down institutional resistance to prohibition were strong enough to mean that even though the private temperance movement was at the height of its powers during the war, it largely saw its influence checked in the civilian zones.[8]

This frustrated and enraged some of the anti-alcohol community's fire-breathers. "Alcohol," thundered the arch-prohibitionist Jean Finot in the pages of his *Bulletin de l'Alarme*, France's most enthusiastically racist wartime temperance journal, "is the most visible enemy we have to fight." He continued to recapitulate tersely French reformers' understanding of distilled alcohol's effects: "It alters the tissues of our bodies, slowly poisoning and paralyzing our brains, it blunts the highest parts of our souls, our moral senses, [and] corrupts and bastardizes the future generations." Finot did not understand why the government was not taking more energetic action to ban distilled alcohol entirely in France. "The war has shown us the need to regenerate the French race. It is thus a question of life for the nation!" he roared.[9] His group printed perhaps the most fearsome piece of French wartime temperance propaganda. It featured a sinister *Pickelhaube*-capped German lurking behind a glass of poisonous distilled alcohol, with the caption "that which we could not do, alcohol will." But the French race did not seem to want to put the plug in the jug. Even in wartime, social life revolved around cafés and their bars of zinc. Elected representatives were incapable of forcing French civilian society onto the water wagon.

l'ALARME

Ce que nous n'avons pú faire l'Alcool le fera

AUX FRANÇAISES
ET AUX JEUNES FRANÇAIS

L'Alcool est votre ennemi aussi redoutable que l'Allemagne...

Il a coûté à la France depuis 1870, en hommes et en argent, bien plus que la guerre actuelle.

L'Alcool flatte le palais; mais, véritable poison, il détruit l'organisme.

Les buveurs vieillissent vite. Ils perdent la moitié de leur vie normale et sont la proie facile d'infirmités et de maladies multiples.

Les "PETITS VERRES" des parents se transforment en GRANDES TARES héréditaires chez les descendants. La France leur doit environ deux cent mille fous, le double de poitrinaires, sans compter des goutteux, des ramollis avant l'âge et la plupart des criminels.

L'alcoolisme diminue des deux tiers notre production nationale, augmente la cherté de la vie et la misère.

A l'instar du Kaiser criminel, l'alcoolisme décime et ruine la France, à la plus grande joie de l'Allemagne.

Mères, jeunes gens, jeunes filles, épouses, agissez contre l'alcoolisme en souvenir des blessés et des morts glorieux pour la Patrie.

Vous accomplirez ainsi une tâche grandiose, égalant celle de nos héroïques soldats.

l'ALARME, Siège Social : PARIS, 45, rue Jacob

DEVAMBEZ. PARIS

5.1 "That which we couldn't do, alcohol will."

— Voilà un petit marc que les Prussiens n'auront pas !
LE COMBATTANT. — Ah ! s'ils avaient ce vice-là, nous les aurions déjà !

5.2 Untitled Cartoon (1916).

Plus de liqueurs entre les Repas
(Les Journaux)

— Apprends, vulgaire civil, qu'aux tranchées,
les repas manquent quelquefois,. la gnole., jamais !

5.3 "Plus de liqueurs entre les Repas" (1918).

The tension between what reformers behind the lines thought about distilled alcohol and what soldiers in the trenches thought of it can be seen through the contrast of two cartoons. The first, from Finot's *Bulletin de l'Alarme*, shows a *poilu* sitting at a *débit* somewhere in the rear. A waiter opens a bottle of liquor, but the soldier puts up his hand in a "stop" gesture and cries out, "Ah! If they [the Prussians] had this vice, we would have already got them." A small child on the right has less of an objection and guzzles down a glass.[10]

The second, from the trench journal *Le Rire aux éclats*, is nearly identical and thus likely a conscious response to the cartoon from Finot's journal. It features two *poilus* who sit down at a *débit*. One points his finger accusingly at his waiter, who hangs his head in shame. The caption of the image reads, with the words coming from the mouth of the accusatory *poilu*: "Listen here, you vulgar civilian, in the trenches we sometimes don't get meals ... but no *gnôle* ... never!"[11] The difference between the sense of the two cartoons points to the vertiginous gap between the experiences and expectations of civilian reformers in the rear and those of front-line soldiers. In one context distilled alcohol was a poison; in the other, it was an invaluable tool.

Gnôle-lovers in the trenches felt persecuted by the temperance movement in the civilian zones, whose screeching zealots, they feared, might somehow take their *gnôle* away from them. This would be a disaster, as soldiers held that those not in the war could not possibly understand how important and necessary *gnôle* was to those who fight. One noted with an irony that perfectly described the contradiction between *gnôle* rations and prohibition that the properties of the drink were functions of its distance from the trenches. "In the forward zones of the front, it is recommended by the highest medical authorities," he observed. But things were different in the rear areas, where "*gnôle* becomes a noisome substance absolutely prohibited."[12] Another soldier took to verse to defend *gnôle* against its detractors:

Ne le condamnez plus;	[No longer condemn it;
Elle a sa poésie,	it has its poetry]
Cette 'gniole' proscrite	[This *gnôle* prohibited
en milieu civil	in the civilian milieu]
Et je ne trouve point son usage si vil...	[And I do not find its use so vile ...]
...	

On peut la dédaigner;   [We can despise it;
    on ne la maudit plus   we no longer curse it]
Dès qu'on l'a vue,   [Since we have seen it,
    au nerfs héroïques poilus[13]   in the heroic nerves of *poilus*]

A third invited the members of France's temperance organization to come to the front and see the magic of *gnôle* for themselves, begging, "[d]on't take our *gnôle* away from us."[14]

Such language was of course meant to be humorous, but it points to the seriously paradoxical situation in which the army found itself. It had adopted the daily *eau-de-vie* ration as part of a hygiene program but found that morale came to be affected for the better with its distribution; similarly, it had found extraordinary distributions of *gnôle* to be extraordinarily useful in attacks. But uncontrolled *eau-de-vie* drinking ostensibly posed the dangers of drunkenness, alcoholism, and even racial degeneration in the ranks. The army's marriage to distilled alcohol institutionally and culturally was thus contradictory and uncomfortable – what was a tool in the trenches came to be banned in the world-behind-the-war as a poison.

EARLY DRINKING AND THE ORIGINS
OF THE PROHIBITION SYSTEM

During the first terrible winter of 1914–15, soldiers in Corporal Louis Barthas's regiment, impatient at not receiving wine and suffering while sleeping rough, turned to whatever alcoholic drink they could get their hands on to blunt the terror, fatigue, and misery of the front. They were stationed in the *Pas-de-Calais*, one of the northern regions of France that, before the war, was particularly fond of distilled alcohol. The drink was cheap and easy to find, peddled by the civilian alcohol-sellers who appeared wherever there were miserable French soldiers and successfully plied them with their wares.

Barthas recounted that "to do battle with the sleeplessness, the fatigue, the cold, the thirst, the hunger, the men took to drinking poison – the harmful [distilled] alcohol that men brought from Annequin [a village], where the merchants sold it for twenty-five sous per litre."[15] The cost of a litre of distilled alcohol was thus close to that of a litre of wine and packed much more of a punch, especially when taken in the mind-boggling quantities

Barthas describes. "Some got to the point of absorbing a litre a day; the soberest were happy with a quarter or half-litre," he documented ruefully.[16] Barthas's comrades drank this assuredly awful alcohol with purpose. They sought not to socialize nor to recreate some of the comforts of home, but to armour themselves against the war, or to escape it entirely, at least for a while. This form of early, unofficial, and unsupervised distilled alcohol–drinking was in this way was an adaptation to the war's realities; it was men's desperate attempt to remake their internal environments to make the external environment endurable. Drinking was an attempt at agency – the *poilu*'s desire to exert control over the feelings in his own body and mind – amid powerlessness.

The amounts Barthas reported that men consumed went far beyond what the *Intendance*, the army's logistical wing, intended that men receive from the army. Indeed, Barthas's anecdote suggests that the rather infrequent distributions of centrally procured distilled alcohol sent from the *stations-magasins* in the winter of 1914–15 were supplemented generously with distilled alcohol purchased by front-line soldiers or their officers from private sellers near or at the front. Consuming this kind of grey-market *eau-de-vie* in addition to the daily ration (when it was received) to keep up morale seems to have been a common practice in the French army that winter.

For example, the stretcher carrier Ernest Benoist wrote in January 1915 from around Arras that conditions at the front were unimaginably bad. Men were "exhausted," "disgusting and revoltingly filthy," yet morale remained good. "Perhaps it is this alcohol that we drink," he mused; "they give us a lot of it, a few litres per squad each day."[17] And this was the case not only in the north. Élie Vandrand wrote to his parents on 21 January 1915 from Amblény – just west of Soissons, far from the north and its *bouilleurs de cru* – that, to help him and his fellow *poilus* endure the poor weather, the army was "giving them lots of *eau-de-vie*." "I think," he continued regretfully, "I am going to finish by becoming an alcoholic."[18] Vandrand was a peasant from the Auvergne, one of the parts of France that drank very little distilled alcohol.[19] He likely would have had little experience with large doses of the stuff, so it is not surprising that he expressed some unease with the idea that the army was now asking him to drink what it had only just called a poison. Hundreds of thousands of men like Vandrand were introduced to distilled alcohol–drinking during their time below ground in the trenches.

All this effectively made for an unvirtuous circle: conditions in the trenches in the winter of 1914–15 were so bad that soldiers self-medicated more and more with distilled alcohol, often outside of or in addition to their official rations, which posed the threat of the spread of alcoholism within the army. The results were two and reflected French medico-scientific and folk-psychological understandings of distilled alcohol and wine, respectively. On the one hand, men in the trenches were encouraged to drink the distilled alcohol the army supplied them but prohibited from drinking outside of their official rations. On the other hand, men retained easy, virtually unlimited access to supposedly healthy wine when behind the lines, so long as they could pay for it (which was not always easy, for wine sold for a huge markup in the world-behind-the-war). This was the central internal contradiction of the prohibition system.

PROHIBITION OF *EAU-DE-VIE*

Over the winter of 1914–15, commanders in various units closed down *débits* suspected of selling men distilled alcohol and banned men from frequenting them, but there was no army-wide anti–distilled alcohol policy. General Joseph Joffre, the stolid, walrus-mustached Commander-in-Chief of the French army (whom Asquith christened the "Super-Frog"), remedied this on 23 March 1915 when he outlined a new prohibitionary regime that would apply everywhere at the front, rear areas included. "It appears to me necessary," Joffre wrote to his army commanders, "to unify the dispositions already taken and to specify in particular the measures aimed at restricting the circulation of [distilled] alcohol and alcoholic drinks, which should be prohibited in the area of operations." He urged that all those who violated the new rules be disciplined by civil or military authorities.[20]

In an accompanying decree [*arrêté*] that established the new regulations, Joffre used the language of hygiene and public health. Drinking distilled alcohol (including "absinthes, bitters, vermouth, aperitifs, liqueur wines, *eaux-de-vie*, liqueurs, fruits in *eau-de-vie*, and all other alcoholic liquids not listed") outside of the official rations, he held, had become "pernicious, both from the point of view of discipline and that of the health of the men" and "diminished the material and moral strength of [the] army." Civilians who sold distilled alcohol to soldiers committed a "veritable crime against national defense," and such private sales would be henceforth forbidden in the army zones. "In the interest of discipline and health," Joffre's decree contin-ued, soldiers would be permitted to drink only the distilled alcohol that the army supplied for them when they were in the trenches.[21] In other words, drinking distilled alcohol under supervision, in the right dose, and in the right place was fine, even encouraged; drinking it without the official sanc-tion (and surveillance) of the army was the issue. The army's war on distilled alcohol was thus not about stopping the consumption of the drink entirely. It was about controlling it spatially and disciplining it temporally, which is to say, about creating and enforcing a psychotropic regime.

Barthas was one of many ordinary soldiers conscripted into the fight against the circulation of distilled alcohol in 1915. His main job as a guard outside the village of Annequin in May and June was "to prevent the entry of [distilled] alcohol, that poison which the *poilus* unfortunately were cra-zy about." This involved searching all the women coming and going from the town, who were suspected of smuggling the stuff to soldiers. Barthas recalled with disturbing fondness that part of his duties involved "patting down the round and protruding parts" of Annequin's young beauties. But, he insisted, the guard was "useless and ridiculous" because anyone could walk through the fields around their checkpoint. And so, Barthas recalled bitterly, "[distilled] alcohol flowed freely into the gullets of *poilus* and even more into those of the officers who, while lacking in other examples for us to follow, always provided this one."[22]

Yet the prohibition was not entirely ineffective. Lucienne Courouble not-ed on 22 March 1915 – the day before Joffre issued his first prohibitionary circular – that the army announced a new ban on selling and consumption of alcohol.[23] Similarly, Alexandre Robert noted in August 1915 that distilled alcohol became difficult to get after the army's official ban, but that the persistent *poilu* could still find it if he was willing to put in some work. In contrast, Robert noted that it was easy to find wine, but that wine was be-coming increasingly expensive.[24]

Over 1915 and into 1916, the prohibition on the consumption of distilled alcohol in the army zones outside of the rations got stronger and more com-prehensive, a sign both of the army's sense that it was failing to check the spread of alcoholism and of its conviction that more stringent measures would allow it to succeed in doing so. In August 1915, Joffre noted Malvy's attempt to ban the sale of distilled alcohol in the civilian rear and encour-aged his commanders to use their powers to do the same "in all communes in which troops are stationed." In other words, by mid-1915, the army recognized that its generous attempt to allow civilians to continue to drink and sell distilled alcohol in the rear areas of the army zones while preventing it from reaching soldiers had failed; so long as distilled alcohol was circulating among civilians in the world-behind-the-war, it inevitably ended up in *poilus'* bellies. The army's recourse was to ban distilled alcohol entirely in "all cafés, cabarets, estaminets, and *débits de boissons*" in its zones, not only for soldiers, but for everybody.[25] Civilians who lived in the army zones thus lost their right to their *petit verres*. But, again, not their wine: a decree accompanying the letter spelled out clearly that "wine, beer, cider, pear cider, mead, and, should they be less than eighteen percent alcohol, fortified wines" were not subject to prohibition or regulation.[26] The difference between bad distilled alcohol and good wine again made its way into army policy.

In September 1915, the Minister of War granted army commanders the ability to close unilaterally any *débits* deemed to be a "cause of disorder" because of their selling distilled alcohol to soldiers.[27] These measures were expanded again on 1 December 1915 in a long letter from Pellé to army commanders. "It has been brought to my attention by several corps commanders," Pellé began, "that there has been the opening of a considerable number of wine shops and clandestine *débits* in the villages and troop encampments that constitutes a grave menace for the discipline and health of the troops," notably in the forward areas. Independently of what the civilian police might be doing to surveille *débits*, to set and enforce their hours, and to punish drunkenness, the army would be taking additional measures to establish a more robust licensing system and prevent the opening of new *débits*.[28] Soon after, on 3 December, Pellé issued further guidance that echoed what came before: *boissons hygièniques*, fortified wines at less than eighteen per cent alcohol by volume, and liqueurs made with fresh fruit at less than twenty-three per cent alcohol by volume would not fall under the prohibitionary regime.[29]

A December 1915 decree from Joffre reiterated the benefits of prohibition for the troops' health and discipline and again emphasized that the consumption of distilled alcohol must be limited to what men received from the army in the form of rations. The decree contained a section on punishments for those civilians found to have been selling distilled alcohol, which ranged from harsh to harsher. Civilians found to have been selling distilled alcohol would see their *débit* closed upon the first offense, which could be economically devastating to a family that relied on alcohol sales for its survival.[30] In the case of recidivism, the offender would be exiled from the army zones for the remainder of the war.[31] Similar proclamations continued to be issued throughout 1916, further bolstering the prohibition system – one from Pellé early in the year, for example, emphasized that the troops' consumption of distilled alcohol outside of their official rations was a "national danger"; a proclamation from December of that year established unified hours of opening and closing of *débits* in the army zones (10h30 to 13h and 17h30 to 20h) and specified that men on leave could not, in those zones, purchase or drink distilled alcohol.[32]

These directives were not simply promulgated into the ether; the army enforced its policy with an increasingly professionalized system of surveillance and discipline that employed local police, gendarmes, and special army agents. As historian Stéphane Le Bras has recently highlighted, this system of surveillance and discipline marked a "decisive moment in the conceptualization and promotion of temperance" in France, with the "forces of law and order" becoming the "necessary guarantors of a control and repression apparatus process" in the army zones. These agents of law and order were charged not only with recording and disciplining infractions, but also with surveilling and regulating the sale of distilled alcohol in the *débits* themselves. Much of this work, per Le Bras, fell to the gendarmes, the traditional enforcers of laws against drunkenness. While they were overworked, the gendarmes were, in Le Bras's words, "indispensable" in the enforcement of the prohibitionary regime.[33]

The army also created a dedicated surveillance system with its own personnel. For example, in November 1915, Sixth Army established a special detachment charged with the "surveillance of the circulation and sale of distilled alcohol." Led by a certain Lieutenant Mathieu, the group consisted of gendarmes and customs agents on loan from the Ministry of Finance who patrolled the insides of *débits* and the streets around them.[34] They also searched cellars and automobiles for contraband and tested the wine that merchants sold for quality.

Mathieu's was a detachment of detail-oriented men. For instance, a report filed by the agents Felt and Devalez claimed that the two witnessed on "16 July 1916, at 17h30, during surveillance at Amiens, Place Gambetta" a man carrying two bottles of alcohol out of an épicerie, which he placed in automobile number 6879. They intervened and demanded to escort the man back to the épicerie, but he refused, arguing that his own officers had ordered him to bring the alcohol back to them at the Hôtel du Rhin. The agents went with the man to the hotel, where they confronted the officers, who, not surprisingly, denied everything. On 22 November 1916, the customs agent Royer was on his patrol through Breteuil, a town around thirty kilometres from the front, when he discovered the owner of a *débit*, François Vandervauvier, selling a glass of rum to a soldier in uniform. Royer intervened, the soldier refused to identify himself and escaped, but Vandervauvier saw his shop closed.[35] Royer was at it again a few days later, on 5 December, when he discovered a certain Monsieur Guillaume in Saint Just selling a glass of rum to a soldier.[36] Again, the offending soldier escaped and the offending *débitant* was disciplined, which suggests that the army focused less on punishing soldiers and more on regulating the spaces in which they drank.

Royer was one of many assuredly hated agents who combed through the drinking places at the front and filed reports with Mathieu, in the process closing hundreds of *débits*. Yet the front was long and Mathieu's men could not be everywhere, and so their tactics did not focus exclusively on small-time busts. Over 1916, for instance, agents in Beauvais and other towns in the rear areas of the army zone kept tabs on the stocks of distilled alcohol in *débits* and recorded imports down to the litre.[37] When civilians were found to have more distilled alcohol on hand than records of stocks and deliveries would have permitted, agents requisitioned the excess. Similar services were organized in other units, and Mathieu's men soon covered the territory of First, Third, and Tenth Armies.[38]

According to one report, between 18 November 1915 and 23 December 1916, these prohibition cops brought charges 442 times for infractions related to the sale, circulation, or consumption of distilled alcohol outside of the official rations. Only fifty-six soldiers were tried (suggesting, again, that the army's focus was on the alcohol-seller, rather than the consumer), most for trying to resell to other soldiers; some 1,231 litres of distilled alcohol were requisitioned; and "a great number" of *débits* were closed temporarily or permanently.[39] Granted, the system was not perfect and officers could abuse it. Joseph Bousquet, for instance, recalled in May 1916 seeing a group of officers peacefully enjoying their *apéritifs* in a café directly under a sign that read "Drinking is prohibited under threat of disciplinary punishment."[40] Moreover, Mathieu's men could cover but a tiny fraction of the front at any given time. But they did not have to be everywhere – it just had to be possible for them to be anywhere to convince men to police themselves. Revealing here is the testimony of the trench journalist "Trissotin," who, writing in his unit's journal in August 1916, grudgingly tipped his hat to the gendarmes, who he noted ensured "the proper observance of the regulations" regarding the sale and consumption of distilled alcohol.[41] As Le Bras concludes, these forces of law and order played a "fundamental part in the fight against alcohol-related excesses challenging wartime order" in the rear areas.[42]

These regulations and the surveillance system that enforced them were integral to the psychotropic regime at the Western Front, which was bifurcated into the world of the trenches and that behind the war. In the former, drinking was controlled and instrumental. In the latter, men were forbidden from drinking distilled alcohol. And as we have seen, this focus on distilled alcohol was characteristic of French thinking about alcoholism more generally. The drink was viewed as the source not only of drunkenness and indiscipline, but also of degeneration and moral disorder. At the same time, as we will see, men in the world-behind-the-war were given wide latitude to drink wine so long as they could afford it. Wine was seen as a necessary tool to help men recharge after their time in the trenches, and the places where men drank were crucial nodes of soldierly sociability in the world-behind-the-war. This virtually guaranteed that wine-fuelled drunkenness would be a constant problem there.

TOLERATION OF WINE

Pinard was king in the trenches, but it reigned too over the world-behind-the-war, in the villages and hamlets that French soldiers who were rotated out of the lines and *en repos* spent their time and where they found their billets. The march out of the trenches towards the rear could be punishingly long at ten or twenty kilometres, or even more. Men, exhausted from their sleepless nights in their shabby trench shelters, most often departed the labyrinth under the moonlight and arrived at their destination mid-day completely wiped out. Not surprisingly, soldiers reported that drinking *pinard* during these marches helped them endure by giving them energy and raising their morale. François Barge, for instance, claimed to only get through one such twenty-nine-kilometre march because of "big drinks" of the stuff.[43] Once they arrived in the rear areas, men were often responsible for finding their own billets. This, at least, was the situation in before the army erected purpose-built camps with permanent shelters called "Adrian barracks," which it began to do in 1916. This meant that it was often up to soldiers to negotiate their accommodations with the villagers who remained behind and sold lodging, as well as the food and drink with which soldiers augmented their official rations.

These villages varied in condition from damaged to execrable, depending on the season or region, or whether they had been shelled or overrun. Charles Delvert described the typical village of Dommartin-sous-Hans, in which his unit was billeted in December 1915, as "a real cesspit, full of miserable, abandoned hovels. Lurking in the farmyards and behind the barns are pools of liquid manure, dung heap upon dung heap, all drowning in ankle-deep mud."[44] Soldiers' billets were of a quality that reflected the run-down nature of these villages and hamlets. Men often slept in barns and stables, sometimes with the animals, sometimes without even straw to lie on. Georges LaFond described a typical billet in the town of Morcourt. It was a "vile basket, the most modest of huts, ruined and sordid," filled with pests that "descended in closed ranks ... innumerable gargantuan rats" that terrorized him and his friend as they tried to sleep.[45] True to form was one of Barthas's many disappointing billets, the "attic of a tumbling down house" where thirty men lay on bare, "half-rotted away" floorboards without any straw. He made do with a bag of peas as a pillow and was thankful for it.[46] True, a lucky *poilu* could find a billet that was *pépère* [cushy], like one Maurice Genevoix described. It was a big, airy barn with dry straw and a solid roof, close to a butcher's shop, and with a small stream in which men could do their laundry.[47] Even in the best of cases, then, this was rather rough living.

But the real measure of the worth of a village was not the sleeping conditions it offered (which were nearly always bound to be disappointing), but the amount of *pinard* it provided at a good price. As Barge wrote, after eight days or more in the lines the men were eager to "drink a few good glasses of *pinard* to raise morale."[48] And so, after securing somewhere to sleep, men who were *en repos* went on what the soldier Jules Isaac called in a much-cited letter the "*chasse au pinard* [*pinard* hunt]." This, Isaac insisted, was the "principal occupation of the *poilus*" when they were *en repos*. When these eager hunts were successful, men would consume "a formidable quantity" of wine in addition to the "two or three *quarts*" they received from the army every day, for they were still owed and received their daily wine rations when they were out of the trenches.[49] Indeed, it was good to combine what they received with the litre or two they bought, recorded one *poilu* in a trench journal, for only by combining the amounts could a man get enough to really quench his thirst.[50]

Pinard was not cheap in the world-behind-the-war and pay in the French army was generous neither for rankers nor for officers. In 1914, French privates received a remuneration of only .05 francs a day, a piteously small amount; NCOs received more at .22 francs for corporals and .72 francs for sergeants; and commissioned officers got more than that (4.75 francs for a lieutenant, 9.15 for a lieutenant colonel, and 80 for a general). In 1915, the rate of pay for privates was quintupled to .25 francs a day, with similar increases for NCOs and lower commissioned officers. On top of this, each man in uniform received .10 francs for a war bonus and a combat bonus of .50 francs for each day in the front line. Thus, early in the war, a private could receive .65 francs a day; after 1915, this rose to .85 francs, still a rather paltry amount considering the average daily pay for a Parisian worker was a little over seven francs before the war.[51] Thus, after a ten- or twelve-day spell in the firing and support trenches, the ordinary private would expect to have earned between about 8.50 and 10.25 francs. Again, NCOs and officers made more, but in no case did French soldiers earn a lot of money, especially considering the inflated prices at the front. But the pay was adequate to the task facing most *poilus* who were *en repos*, which was purchasing wine.

The price of wine in the world-behind-the-war was a constant source of frustration and discouragement, as wine cost quite substantially more than men had paid for it in their prewar lives. For example, in February of 1917, First Army surveyed the price of wine in its rear areas. For red wine, they ranged from .9 francs per litre on the low end (at Choisy-au-Bac) to 2 francs (at Monchy-Humieres); white wine typically cost .1 francs more than red.[52] This is about an order of magnitude more than wine cost before the war. Thus, and at best, the ordinary private had enough cash in hand after rotating out to purchase around ten or a dozen litres of wine during his spell behind the lines, assuming he spent his pay on nothing else. If he spent the ordinary four or so days *en repos*, the *poilu* would have had access to around of about three litres of wine per day when combined with his rations, which was a substantial amount.

It is hard to quantify exactly how much men could expect to drink when they were behind the front lines, as the amount available to them would have varied with their location, the availability of wine, and their eagerness to drink. There is one study from 1915 that investigated how much, on average, men in the French army drank. Its purpose was not to track consumption for its own sake, but rather to use the army as a population base to investigate arterial hypertension and alcohol consumption's effects thereupon. The work of the cardiac physician Camille Lian, who was a medical Aide-major to the 209è *Régiment d'Infanterie Territoriale*, the paper divides soldiers into four categories of alcohol consumer: those who were "sober" (consuming less than a litre of wine per day and no distilled alcohol, which came to less than six standard drinks a day); those who were "moderate drinkers" (who consumed between one and one and a half litres of wine per day and no distilled alcohol, which came to between six and eight standard drinks); those who were "heavy drinkers" (who consumed between two and three litres of wine a day and "one or two" distilled drinks, which came to a maximum of twenty-four standard drinks); and those who were "very heavy" drinkers (who consumed at least three litres of wine, or a smaller quantity of wine accompanied by between four and six distilled drinks, which came to a maximum of more than thirty standard drinks[!]). Out of a total of 150 soldiers, sixteen (10.7 per cent) were sober; fifty-three (35.3 per cent) were moderate drinkers; fifty-seven (38 per cent) were heavy drinkers; and twenty-four (16 per cent) were very heavy drinkers.[53]

Lian's statistics are highly suggestive but have significant limitations that reduce their applicability to the army at large. The men he interviewed were all territorials in their early forties who spent their time behind the lines, not regular infantrymen who rotated into the trenches themselves. They were thus not typical *poilus*, but rather were rear-echelon support troops who would have had constant access to *débits* and alcohol-sellers. Thus Lian's sample population was not entirely representative of the army or the experience of the front-line soldier, who must have drunk less, particularly while he was in the trenches. Moreover, the study seems to have been conducted early in 1915, before the full elaboration of the prohibition system, and so when men had more ready access to distilled alcohol than they would in the coming years. Indeed, it would have been increasingly hard for men to find the distilled alcohol required to classify them as heavy or very heavy drinkers according to Lian's definitions after mid-1915. Nevertheless, the amounts Lian reported are quite astounding; they reflect not only the ready availability of alcohol in the world-behind-the-war, but the army's alcoholization [*alcoolisation*].

Poilus found and drank *pinard* in the *débits de boissons*, which were (in both licensed and unlicensed form) everywhere in the rear-front and staging areas. In Flanders, one *poilu* maintained, every third house was an *estaminet*, as *débits* were called in the north – and this was a good thing. The places were sites of sociability, where men came together not only to drink, but also "to socialize, to meet up with friends, to learn the news, to play, to sing."[54] Often consisting of only a modestly furnished single room with a table and some chairs, *débits* were places of profound intimacy in which men could find escape from the war into a proxy family hearth. In the best of cases, they could be shelters for soldiers, refuges from command and authority. Émile Morin, for instance, wrote that the *débits* in the villages near the front were "real dens," where men "drank, smoked, and told stories." Inside, there were few arguments because everybody was happy to be "peaceful, out of danger, and free to be themselves a little bit." It was not only the *pinard* that drew men in, but the "familial interior" of these places; they reminded men that there was a world beyond the war and that they might again live in it.[55]

Débits were seldom well-appointed. For example, in one article from his unit's trench journal, a certain "Robinson" described a typical café that sold wine to soldiers. It was different from the well-appointed big city cafés and their less-well but still somewhat-appointed counterparts in towns. The soldier's café was "just another house" in this or that village. "It is not, my God, that it is pretty! Nor pleasant! Nor comfortable!" he testified. Rather, it was a "low room where a sad lamp looks as if it hung from the ceiling in despair," with "trestles for tables" and unsteady stools all around. The only decoration was a picture of Joffre nailed to the wall. The place, Robinson continued, woke up around 18h00, the hour when soldiers were permitted to patronize cafés, with an invasion of hard-drinking and card-crazy gamblers, unit gossips, and men sipping wine while writing to their loved ones at home. "From time to time," he explained regretfully, "solemn people … vituperate against the cafés, [labelling them] scourges of the race, and imperiously demand their closure." But this would be a disaster for morale, for the café was the *poilu*'s most reliable escape from the war and was "all that remains of modern civilization for the modern fighter."[56] They were, in a word, essential.

Le temple du pinard

5.4 "Le temple du pinard" (1915).

In his *L'Ivresse du soldat* (2016), historian Charles Ridel considers these spaces. On the one hand, he argues, they functioned in much the same way as cafés and bars did before the war, as spaces of sociability and relaxation – their function thus marked a continuity with and connection to the world of civilians. On the other, the sorry conditions at the front magnified their attraction, making them of prime importance in the world-behind-the-war as places where the warmth of human contact counteracted the desolation of the front. The bar, the café, the bistro – the last term being, insisted one *poilu*, a "magic word, so voluptuously evocative"[57] – were, Ridel holds, refuges from the war. They were places of "*héterochronie*," meaning spaces in which there was a fundamental rupture with the temporal rhythms of military life set by "reviews, exercises, and roll calls."[58] The rupture that came with entrance into these great good places was experienced as a welcome escape from the war.

Often it was the same people who provided soldiers with their billets who provided them with wine; many civilians at the front made their living from this trade. Delvert recalled one such woman – "a tiny, wrinkled mouse ... eighty or so" – who, after providing his squad with a "hovel" for a billet, came to sell wine at 2.75 francs a litre, which was an outrageous price. "Nice work if you can get it," he observed.[59] Henri Barbusse described a similar scene in his novel *Under Fire*, when the men found their billet's owner – again, an old woman – willing to part with some of what she claimed was her personal supply of wine. Barbusse's men paid what was demanded and would have paid double the inflated price, even knowing as they did that the woman was not in fact dipping into her personal supply at all – Barbusse suggested that she was importing wine in bulk and getting rich off the *poilu*'s thirst. They took the wine and the dinner that their genius cook put together and, using a door as a table, turned their billet into a banquet hall that "overflowed with merriment." Over several bottles, Barbusse insists, men created a "sanctuary" and forgot the war.[60]

Men also frequently purchased wine to go from the windows of homes that had been converted to wine shops. This was, the trench journalist Trissotin claimed, "customary."[61] Such was dramatized in an anonymous short prose piece from a 1916 trench journal titled, appropriately, "The Pinard Hunt." The author describes his hunters coming upon, at the "edge of a devastated village," a "half-opened window and a group of immobile and silent *poilus*." His extraordinary senses activated, the *poilu* knows that *pinard* is near. Soon, he sees the window open farther, and, after a funnel appears, he sees wine poured into the *poilu*'s *bidons*.[62] The hunter had found his quarry. Writing in his unit's trench journal, Jean Ménti described something similar. His *poilus* were too impatient to sit down in a café (Ménti notes that they are "cafés only in name") and instead were served through a window. The men lined up and waited their turn to have their *bidons* filled. Ménti found this to be efficient and appropriate. After all, he noted wryly, there was a glass shortage. And besides, the *poilus* themselves were not too demanding so long as they got their *pinard*.[63]

These wine-sellers – the *mercantis* – were loved and hated, but mostly hated. The market on which they operated was largely unregulated, as citizens were free to import as much wine as they liked and faced few consequences for selling it even without a license. Often they were humble older folk who had nowhere to go and nothing to lose by staying and so remained in their home villages to profit off the war that victimized them. They were loved because they provided an essential service, which was supplying the *poilu* with as much wine as he could buy. Indeed, *mercantis* with wine were everywhere there were soldiers, or almost everywhere. As one soldier noted,

"The mayor sells it, the constable sells it, everybody sells it."[64] The only thing worse than a *mercanti* was a village without one.

Mercantis were hated because they watered down or adulterated their wine, because they committed fraud and misrepresented what they sold, because they charged outrageous prices, and most of all, because they seemed to be benefiting from the war. The *mercanti*, wrote one soldier, meets the "soldier's needs, big and small." He had the "face of a friend, and the soul of a scoundrel," and overcharged by two hundred per cent on everything.[65] Another lamented how the *mercanti* "exploited" the *poilu* and thought him an "abominable monster" who should be placed "in with the murderers."[66] Yet without the legions of *mercantis* selling wine at the front, *poilus'* experience of the war in the rear areas would have been entirely different, and much drier.

GENDER, ALCOHOL, AND THE WORLD-BEHIND-THE-WAR

Normative conceptions of masculinity are historical and thus vary over time and place – what makes for a man in one culture does not necessarily make for a man in another.[67] Yet, as Joshua S. Goldstein argues convincingly in his *War and Gender* (2003), one masculine archetype – the "warrior," who is defined by his physical courage, endurance, strength and skill, honour, and most importantly, his willingness to use violence to defend his community – is largely ahistorical and cross-cultural. This is not, according to Goldstein, because the warrior archetype is linked in some irreducible way to biological differences between the sexes, but rather because all societies need such men for self-defense. In his understanding, norms of martial masculinity are instrumental and coercive, especially in wartime, and especially in conscript armies. These norms threaten men with the shame of cowardice and social death should they not meet masculine expectations of fearlessness, courage, and competent violence in war.[68] Goldstein concludes that normative conceptions of martial masculinity and the behaviours these conceptions engender are essential to military recruitment, discipline, and effectiveness. As he insists, "[c]ultures develop concepts of masculinity that motivate men to fight" precisely because men typically do not want to fight.[69] It is the fear of being "un-manned" and looking the coward in front of one's comrades that drives men forward and into danger on the battlefield, a space that is not only liminal but also profoundly gendered.

Two aspects of martial masculinity were particularly important in pre-war France: physical courage and honour. As Robert A. Nye has demonstrated, in its development over the nineteenth century, French culture imported aristocratic ideals of physical courage and honour into a bourgeois context that already, for its own material reasons, celebrated emotional self-control and asceticism. The result was the creation and lionization of a nationalistic brand of martial masculinity that valorized active heroism and sacrifice for the fatherland. This archetypical image of man had become, by the *fin-de-siècle*, the aspirational and dominant image of masculinity in the country.[70] And, as prewar French military theory, which emphasized the central role of the *offensive à l'outrance* [unlimited offensive], made clear, martial courage meant manful activity – it was always demonstrated in the attack, in movement, in the flight forward.

It was one irony among many in the First World War (albeit a profound one) that the nature of trench-fighting denied men the opportunity to perform the kind of active masculinity that revolved around ideals of physical courage and honour. As historian Jessica Meyer has noted in the case of the British army, soldiers were at first enthusiastic "not simply for the experience of the war as a whole but specifically for the experience of action in warfare through which their soldiering might be defined as heroic."[71] But when the trenches denied men this experience of heroic, masculine action, or at least action that could be defined as heroic in the late-nineteenth-century sense, the result was a gendered anxiety resulting from feelings of impotence and passivity. This was the case in the French army as well.

Demasculization wrote itself upon the *poilu*'s appearance; he did not look the part of the smooth classical warrior. For instance, "Jean G-B" wrote in his unit's trench journal of the filthy, degraded appearance of the "national *poilu*," calling him "an uncultivated being, a kind of dishevelled monkey, with bushy hair and a satyr's goatee"[72] – hardly the stuff of Winckelmann's masculine ideal.[73] More important, though, was the physical immobility the trenches imposed, which trapped men and took from them their sense of masculine agency. Delvert regretted that "a week in [at the front] is a week in a dungeon. It gives you some idea of an *oubliette*" – not places associated with vigorous activity.[74] The *poilu* was a man forced into filth, suffering, and powerlessness: death rushed towards *him*, often from above; he was seldom himself its bringer. He was rendered passive and unmanned by the nature of trench fighting.

Historian Joan Scott has argued that war has the power to "destabilize the stereotypes of masculinity."[75] Such was the case with the *poilu*'s image of himself, which of necessity came to focus less on his skill, strength, and active courage and more on his ability to endure, muddle through [*se débrouiller*], and hold on [*tenir*], with this last concept being of central importance. In effect, there was in soldiers' culture a reformulation of martial masculinity that brought it into alignment with the realities of the trench war. *Poilus* still faced immense pressure to conform to a masculine ideal, but the nature of that ideal shifted. Out went the emphasis on *élan* and aggression; in went an emphasis on fortitude and endurance. One trench poet made the point, contrasting the idealized image of man in the attack with the unglamorous reality of life in the trenches:

Oh! ce n'est pas l'ardeur enthousiaste et fébrile	[Oh! This is not the enthusiastic and fevered ardour]
Quand, grisé par la poudre, on s'élance en avant	[When, exhilarated by the powder, we launch ourselves forwards]
Non, il faut rester là, dans un coin, immobile	[No, we must stay there, in a corner, immobile]
Des jours entiers, des mois, dans un terrain sanglant	[For entire days, for months, on bloody ground]
Respirer une odeur âcre et cadavérique	[Breathing a pungent and cadaverous odor]
Mais, resister à tout, et malgré tout <<tenir>>	[But, resistant to everything, and despite it all, we "hold on"]
Voilà de l'héroïsme obscur, mais magnifique[76]	[This is obscure heroism, but it is magnificent]

In his appropriately titled personal narrative *Tenir!* (1918), Max Buteau wrote something similar. Nothing about the *poilu*'s life, Buteau maintained, was glorious in the traditional sense. Indeed, the *poilu* was nothing more than a "poor man who climbs a long Calvary, and who suffers" through "days and nights that intertwine." But yet, Buteau maintained, the *poilu* continues to climb. That was his brand of masculine glory, to suffer and endure like Sisyphus.[77] Among French soldiers, the ability to *tenir* became the manly trait *par excellence*, the ideal that served as masculine, a glue for behaviour in the trenches.

As we have seen, drinking *pinard* in the trenches was experienced as an expression of masculine agency, a way for men to feel themselves refilled with a vigour and activeness that countered the effects of the front. Men claimed that *pinard* gave men the strength they needed to *tenir* – "We can hold on [*tenir*] so long as we can drink," concluded one trench poet.[78] Similarly, as we have seen, drinking *gnôle* before attacks filled men with the masculine courage they needed to cross No-Man's-Land, face death, and kill. In other words, alcohol served as a tonic for the demasculinized *poilu* in the trenches because it generated manful activity that fought against the femininizing lassitude of *le cafard* and the fear and tension of the attack.

There were, of course, no women in the trenches, but that does not mean that women were not present in the daily lives of *poilus*, who spent hours reading, writing, and sharing letters sent to and received from their sweethearts and wives at home. As historian Frédéric Rousseau has noted, it was a central idea in French war culture that *poilus* were fighting in defense of their home and hearth, and that this gave them motivation to endure. "In this long war, which imposed a separation of exceptional duration, amorous links, no matter how tenuous," he argues, "offered the ultimate reason to *tenir*, a reason to live."[79] In other words, the *idea* of women was a profound motivator for men, who defined themselves as masculine protectors.

But if the means of expressing traditional martial masculinity were constrained and then reformulated in the face of tactical realities in the trenches, an active brand of masculinity could be performed openly in the world-behind-the-war, particularly in *débits* men frequented, where there were real women. Before the war, public drinking in *débits* was of course coded as a masculine activity and the *débits* themselves as masculine spaces.[80] This was even more the case during the war, where *débits* provided men with a space and a female audience for performances of a masculine identity that was less about enduring and more about living hard in the moment and exaggerated expressions of virility.

One ritual of decided importance for morale and masculine primary group identity was singing (often rowdy) drinking songs while in a *débit*, which brought men together in high emotional and physical entrainment and gave them a good dose of emotional energy in Randall Collins's sense of the term.[81] In this way, drinking and singing together served to build morale. Unsurprisingly, drinking songs extolled drinking itself, especially drinking *pinard*. For example, several by the right-winger Theodor Botrel (who was proclaimed the official "*Chansonnier des Armées*" by the Minister of War) involve drinking. This was the case with his popular "Encore un P'tit Coup d'Pinard," whose refrain ran "another little bit of wine / to get going / another little bit of wine / to hunt the *cafard*." It was also the case with his bloody-minded "Rosalie," whose title referred to the *poilu*'s supposed slang term for his bayonet. The song's refrain, which mixed images of drinking wine and drinking the enemy's blood, ran: "Pour the drinks! / She is bright red / So let's pour a drink [*Verser à boire*] / So vermillion and so rosy." Yet "Rosalie" was not entirely appreciated by the men, who saw its valorization of bayonet fighting as but another example of *bourrage de crane*.[82]

The most popular song at the front was Botrel's "Quand Madelon," which historian Charles Rearick has called "*the* hit of the war."[83] The song was written and first performed in spring 1914, so its lyrics do not concern themselves at all with the fighting. Yet it became the soldier's anthem: the *poilu* Lucien Laby called it "our war song [*notre air de guerre*]," while "M. Gagneur" called it the "dear refrain" of the French soldier.[84] The song's subject is the gentle barmaid Madelon, who worked at a soldiers' *cabaret* called *Aux Tourlourous* [For The Infantryman], and who embodied an archetype of femininity against which military men could define themselves: flirty but chaste, tolerant of men's drunken foibles, always there but always out of reach. She refused the favours of any one man, as she claimed to belong to the regiment as a whole. Its refrain ran:

Quand Madelon vient nous servir à boire	[When Madelon comes to serve us a drink]
Sous la tonnelle on frôle son jupon	[Under the arbor, we brush against her petticoats]
Et chacun lui reconte un histoire, une histoire à sa façon	[And each of them tells her a story, a story in his own way]
La Madelon pour nous n'est pas sévère,	[Madelon is not stern with us,]
Quand on lui prend la taille ou le mention,	[When we hug her and grab her waist,]
Elle rit, c'est tout l'mal qu'ell' sait faire	[She laughs, it's all the ill that she does,]
Madelon, Madelon, Madelon[85]	[Madelon, Madelon, Madelon]

5.5 Detail from "Quand Madelon" (1917).

One trench poet reported that "Madelon" was sung with a vigour that was the obverse of the inactivity of the trenches:

Puis, au repos, c'est le réjouissance	[Then, during our rest, we rejoice]
La paix rêvée au doux cantonnement	[The dreamt-of peace of the sweet camp]
Des durs combats il n'a plus souvenance	[He remembers not the hard fights]
Le naturel revient diligemment	[His naturalness returns]
Aves ses amis il chante: "Madelon!"	[With his friends he sings: "Madelon!"]
Et même, "Le moral est bon!"[86]	[And even *"Le moral est bon!"*]

Indeed, *débits* were one of the few places *poilus* at the front could see women (another place was in hospitals), who worked in them as servers and bartenders and were thus inevitably referred to as Madelons. The Madelon as archetype inhabited a special place in the imagination of the *poilu*. She was, one trench journalist recalled after the war, "the Republic incarnated" in "adorable" form," a feminine symbol of the France soldiers protected.[87] She – in her real, rather than her ideal, form – was also a witness and spectator to soldiers' performances of masculinity, for *débits* were frequently run by women whose husbands and sons were at the front. They thus provided men out drinking while *en repos* with an audience of Madelons.

Christian Benoît has noted that the sexlessness of combat means that masculine desire is redoubled when men rotate out of the lines and encounter women.[88] Not surprisingly, Madelons were frequently objects of desire, in both their real and ideal forms. For instance, in a letter home Henri Aimé Gauthé described how, at 17h00, when the cafés opened, men threw themselves upon them. In one such café, a hundred packed themselves in, "most standing, some sitting with an ass-cheek each on the backs of two other drinkers." The place smelled of unwashed men and stale spilled wine. But when a "comely" woman arrived, the scene changed from one of fraternity and fellowship to something ugly. The men began by singing longingly for her, but soon their voices warped themselves into "snarls like a horrible, sexually-charged hymn." Their faces were "congested, sweating alcohol, wine, desire," and they became "drunk, lewd ... a mass, a monstrous mob" falling into a "morass" and "seeing only the pleasure offered to them."[89] Faced with a desirable woman, their restraint collapsed into a performance of a kind of gross sexualized masculinity impossible to express in the chaste if homosocial world of the trenches.

In his surrealist novel *Les Poilus*, Joseph Delteil provides a scene featuring a Madelon that makes this desire clear. While *en repos* behind the Battle of Verdun, where he had just fought and was about to fight again, a nude *poilu* lies in bed with an equally nude Madelon in a room above the *Aux Tourlourous*. The room is typically "hard and poor," with an "indescribable" washroom and grey bed. It is also full of "the sounds of the devil" as *poilus* drink in the *cabaret* below, where "*pinard* is king" and the men "howl with wine." The *poilu* dresses himself. Then suddenly, all falls quiet and the men begin to sing *La Madelon* in a rising crescendo, which overwhelms the *poilu* with "musical vertigo." After giving his own Madelon a final passionate embrace, he turns and goes downstairs, transforming himself from a man back into a soldier, and joins with his comrades to sing heartily the song's refrain.[90] In Delteil's novel, the love made between the *poilu* and the Madelon is allegorical, almost mystical: their union represents the triumph of life over death, of masculine virility over passivity, at least for a time, for the *poilu* must return to Verdun.

There were also clear links between drinking in *débits* and the spread of the *péril venerienne*, the charming French euphemism for syphilis, which became a concern for the French army as of late 1915 and early 1916.[91] On the one hand, inebriated men surely frequented the *bordels de campagne mil-*

itaires, the official, regulated brothels that the army provided for them – those for officers illuminated with a blue light and those for rankers with a red.[92] On the other (and as suggested by Delteil's scene above), *débits* could themselves often be places of unregulated prostitution, and so the word "Madelon" could carry a double meaning. Indeed, the army considered unregulated prostitution to be a significant threat to the *poilus'* health. As of early 1916, to fight the spread of syphilis, the army began registering women suspected of being unofficial prostitutes, particularly those of no fixed address who frequented *débits,* with any *débit* found to be spreading the disease closed to the troops.[93] These kinds of Madelons came thus under various levels of surveillance. Not coincidentally, the same gendarmes charged with regulating the consumption of distilled alcohol were charged with fighting unregulated prostitution. In the army's policies, the two problems were inevitably intertwined – the fight was against the twinned problems of alcoholism *and* the *péril venerienne.*[94] The prohibition system was designed for both objectives.

In the innumerable *débits* that speckled the Western Front like stars in the sky, men could collectively perform and affirm a kind of masculine agency, both because these drinking-spaces provided men with an escape from the constraints of the war and because they provided audiences of women. This is not to say that men's masculinity, frustrated while in the trenches, was forced out into the world-behind-the-war in some crude pneumatic sense upon women who were rendered objects of desire – or at least, it is not only to say that. Rather, it is to say that *débits* provided men with physical and psychological shelters from the war that provided them with stages upon which they could perform for a female audience they valorized and mythologized in ways that compensated for their emasculating experience in the trenches. *Poilus* availed themselves of the opportunity, especially after a few glasses of *pinard.*

Moreover, it is impossible to separate these masculine performances from the psychotropic effects of alcohol – these men who frequented *débits* were, after all, drinking together, usually quite heavily. As they entrained themselves bodily and emotionally while in the space of the *débit,* the head-change that came with drinking in this context came to mean not only bodily and emotional release from the prison of the trenches, but also an affirmation of a besieged masculine identity. Put another way, drinking in the world-behind-the-war could allow men to feel their masculinity restored and flowing through their bodies. The interoceptive and affective sensations that came with wine consumption were read and experienced as a restoration of manly vigour. The *poilu*'s desire for escape, for the ability to feel himself an active man rather than a passive victim, and for the Madelons who served him: all were inextricably tied to the physical sensations of intoxication.

But, as we have seen, that intoxication was necessarily of a specific type: it was the intoxication that came with drinking wine rather than that which came with drinking distilled alcohol, with the former being considered healthy, even necessary, and the latter profoundly dangerous and threatening not only to the health of the French army, but to the perpetuation of the French race. In this sense, the French army imposed a psychotropic regime at the front that was characterized by a bifurcation distinguishing between two types of alcoholic intoxication, which reflected prewar conceptions of the difference between the two drinks. The intoxication produced by wine was deemed acceptable while that produced by distilled alcohol was deemed unacceptable, at least in those circumstances in which the army was not the distributor. But the rub is that despite what French medical science and folk-psychology held, unsupervised wine-drinking was not somehow more benign than unsupervised distilled alcohol-drinking in either the biological or social sense. This would be made clear during the French army mutinies of 1917, which were fuelled by wine.

6

WINE AND THE FRENCH ARMY MUTINIES

INTRODUCTION TO THE FRENCH ARMY MUTINIES

On 2 June 1917, at around 10h00, a group of a dozen soldiers from the 59è *Régiment d'Artillerie* (RA) arrived in Trépail, a small village about thirty kilometres southeast of Reims, on foot. The men, described in a report as displaying a conspicuous "poor appearance [*manque de tenue*]" and freely employing "bad language," were *en repos* and had come from their nearby camp on a *pinard* hunt. They were frustrated to find the local *débits* closed at that hour, per the army's rules. Nevertheless, they persisted and over the course of the day managed to find plenty of wine from local sellers. By the early evening, the report held, the men were quite drunk. The "commotion turned into a scandal," it continued, as intoxicated men roamed Trépail's streets, "singing the Internationale and shouting 'Down with the army', 'Long live Russia', and 'Long live the Revolution', etc." Patrols were sent to restore calm. Encounters between the troops and forces of order became violent, with one artilleryman brandishing a knife and another a revolver towards the patrolmen, who then struck out with the butts of their rifles. This succeeded in dispersing the "demonstrators," as the report referred to the men, who fled anonymously into the woods in the direction of the village of Villers-Marmery.[1]

Similar events unfolded that same day in the evening in Mourmelon-le-Petit, a village about a dozen kilometres east of Trépail. At about 21h00, a group of around forty soldiers from the 221è *Régiment d'Infanterie* (RI) took over the village's Grande Rue, where, according to one report, they "[sang] the Internationale and [shouted] seditious cries, such as 'Long live Russia', 'Down with the army', 'Long live the Socialist International', etc." They then assaulted the "Café de la Gare," which had earlier refused to sell wine to soldiers – one report described the men as a "drunken band" that "ransacked [*saccagé*]" the *débit*.[2] While officers present attempted to establish order, they failed, and again the demonstrators dispersed into the night. "From the information gathered on the spot," the report concluded, "it appears that the leaders of the demonstration were drunk."[3]

A third anti-war demonstration broke out that same evening of 2 June in the village of Camelin, about 110 kilometres northwest of Trépail and thirty northwest of Soissons. As the colonel in command of the 3è *Brigade de Dragons* (BD) entered the town at around 18h00, he was met with "shouts, hooting, and insults" from men of the 360è RI, who were quartered in Camelin – some of the shouts included "kill him!" According to the colonel's report, drunk infantrymen filled all the windows and doors of the buildings in the village. He approached them and threatened them with being brought before military tribunals for their indiscipline but got nowhere. He retreated and surrounded the town with his dragoons overnight. The next morning, with the men sobered up, calm restored itself. As for the inebriation of the demonstrators: Camelin had received on 2 June a substantial resupply of wine, of which the infantrymen availed themselves at the steep price of 1.60 francs per litre. This, the colonel held, helped in explaining the "overexcitement of the men, a large number of whom were taken by wine." He concluded that it would be in the best interest of discipline to prohibit civilian sales of wine to soldiers from that point forward, a radical recommendation to expand the prohibition system.[4] Another corroborating report noted that the men were "taken by drink."[5]

These acts of collective indiscipline share certain key characteristics, even though there were no contacts among the different groups of men involved. First, they all took place in the Chemin-des-Dames region, which stretched from Soissons to Reims; second, those involved were all *en repos*, and they all sang the same anti-war songs and shouted the same anti-war slogans; third, many, if not most, of the men who demonstrated were intoxicated with wine. The demonstrations seem, in short, to have followed the same script; the demonstrators certainly engaged in the same type of performance. And these were not the only soldiers' anti-war demonstrations that took place on 2 June in the Chemin-des-Dames region: there were also events at the villages of Chacrise, Louppy-le-Petit, Coeuvres, Ferme Panthéon, Fresnes-en-Tardenois, Beuvardes, Blérancourt, Ostel (twice), and Leury, involving, all told, well over a thousand men.[6] And these, in turn, were but a small portion of some 120 acts of collective indiscipline involving around 40,000 men that took place in the world-behind-the-war around the Chemin-des-Dames between late April and early June 1917.[7]

Not all these mutinies – and there is some debate about whether they should even be called such, rather than demonstrations [*manifestations*] or strikes [*grèves*] – were alike.[8] Indeed, even those from just 2 June show variation: at Ferme-Panthéon the fifty men who demonstrated were not violent and the indiscipline was resolved by officers, while in nearby Fresnes-en-Tardenois, some among the twenty who mutinied fired shots. Among the many differences, though, there are clear similarities. At Chacrise, sixty men refused to mount the line when ordered, sang the "Internationale," and demanded more rest and leave; at Coeuvres, 400 refused to mount the line, also sang the "Internationale," and ambitiously sought to commandeer a train and ride it to Paris in order to bring an end to the war; at Beuvardes, 150 men who were "taken by drink" threw stones, lit things on fire, and called out "Long live peace, long live Russia, down with Poincaré."[9] All drew elements from the same performative repertoire with some local improvisation. In this sense, they represented a single movement – the French army mutinies of summer 1917.

The first archive-based study of the mutinies was Guy Pedroncini's *Les Mutineries de 1917* (1967).[10] Pedroncini influentially argued that the mutinies were the result of a crisis of discipline that began slowly but immediately after the failure of the Nivelle Offensive, which is to say, by the third week of April 1917. By the second week of May, the indiscipline spread rapidly like a "contagion" moving through a morally vulnerable host. The protests grew more frequent and violent. Pedroncini held that the mutinies ended with the promotion of Henri-Philippe Pétain to Commander-in-Chief. Over June, Pétain re-earned the trust of the average soldier through a mix of repression and concession. It was his unique empathy and "noble firmness" that restored the army's confidence and fighting power. Pedroncini concluded that the protestors did not want so much to end the war as to change the way it was fought.[11]

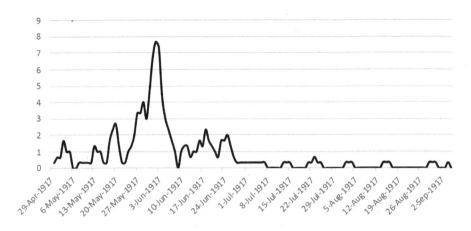

6.1 Frequency of acts of collective indiscipline at the front.

Subsequent major works on the mutinies have not substantially undermined Pedroncini's chronology or the general outlines of his interpretation. They have, however, challenged or re-interpreted specific elements of it, such as how many mutinies took place (Pedroncini claimed some 240, but recent archival research has put the number closer to 120), how important Pétain's role was, whether the mutinies were truly anti-war or just against a certain way of conducting it, the relative balance of sticks and carrots used on the mutineers to restore order, and most importantly, whether the army's return to discipline was the result of *consentement patriotique* or *contrainte*.

Important here is Leonard V. Smith's *Between Mutiny and Obedience* (1994), a case study of the experience of the 5è *Division d'Infanterie* (DI) over the course of the war that investigated the nature of the power relations between commanders and their men from the bottom up. In late May 1917 at the Chemin-des-Dames, hundreds of men from the division mutinied. Smith's interpretation of the events hinges upon his Foucauldian understanding of power as a constant negotiation. He argues that the crisis of morale was a crisis also in military power relations, a moment when French soldiers, schooled in the republican tradition, found themselves "essentially free political actors" with the power to renegotiate the extent and nature of command authority. The men wanted better living conditions, more leave, and an end to wasteful offensives. When they got these things, they re-consented to fighting the war, albeit a war more on their terms.[12] Smith's thesis, which essentially turns Pedroncini's on its head but comes to a similar conclusion, is the outstanding example of the *consentement patriotique* school.

Denis Rolland's *La Grève des tranchées* (2005) is a survey of the mutinies from start to finish that seeks to highlight their similarities and differences. For Rolland, the mutinies were a complex social movement against the war in which men did not so much renegotiate power relations as reject them in a highly charged but relatively short-lived emotional outburst. "If troops mutinied in 1917," he writes, it was because they believed that "the political context [after the Nivelle Offensive] allowed them to end the war." Rolland concludes that the mutinies were not only a reaction to the failure of the Nivelle Offensive, but also a "sort of outlet for the collected resentments of the men built up since the start of the war."[13] In his view, resentments burned themselves off though their expression.

André Loez's magisterial *14–18. Les Refus de la guerre: Une Histoire des mutins* (2010) is the outstanding example of the *contrainte* school. Like Rolland, Loez seeks to provide a comprehensive view of the mutinies; unlike Rolland, he does not see them as akin to strikes, but as a genuine popular movement against the war from within the army. "[T]he mutinies really were a refusal of war that was massive and multiformed," he writes, a refusal that failed because of the repressive disciplinary and social environment of the army, the institutional inertia of the war, and the practical difficulties of organizing a mass anti-war movement from within the army, which were too great.[14] The mutinies were, in this sense, predestined to fail in their goal of ending the war, but this does not mean that such was not the mutineers' true purpose. For Loez, the men did not choose to come back under discipline voluntarily but were rather forced to do so through repression and an immense pressure to conform.

Allegations of drunkenness among those who demonstrated are a constant in commanders' contemporaneous reports of the events. Indeed, the army's official history – the monumental *Les Armées françaises dans la grande guerre* (AFGG) – estimates that more than half of the men involved in these acts of what it euphemized as "collective indiscipline" were drunk.[15] Granted, some commanders may have seen what they wanted to see or reported men as drunk to escape culpability. They may have overstated the prevalence of intoxicated men in their reports to transfer blame from them to drink. But the volume of the evidence from the archives, where there are hundreds of reports involving drunkenness, suggests that if the AFGG is exaggerating, it is not exaggerating by much.[16]

Nevertheless, recent historical interpretations of the mutinies have not ascribed much causal robustness to the widespread inebriation among the mutineers. It is not a factor for Smith at all, for his mutineers in the 5è DI – for reasons discussed below – were aggressively and uniquely sober. For Rolland, the men's drunkenness served to disinhibit a pneumatic drive to protest that, once released, returned to equilibrium. Loez's interpretation is like Rolland's, with men's alcohol consumption playing an adjunct role in a larger social context in which drink helped in creating an environment conducive to "a liberation of speech that saw soldiers contest, alone or in a group, the continuation of the war and the dominant discourse."[17]

In contrast, the interpretation of the mutinies provided below puts the inebriation of men at centre stage – it argues that the mutinies were not only a crisis in morale, but also a crisis in the psychotropic regime the French army had created at the front. I begin with a review of the Nivelle Offensive and the first events before moving to a series of short case studies of the mutinies of the 162è RI, the 18è RI, the 82è *Brigade d'Infanterie* (BI), and the 10è BI. The central argument is that men's drinking was central to the mutinies because it was generative of the emotional energy and sense of moral purpose that *poilus* required to overcome the barrier of fear and tension that lay between them and outright indiscipline. The ready availability of wine in the world-behind-the-war where the mutinies took place provided a psychotropic predicate for a powerful group experience and enabled a set of collective performances based on a common repertoire. Moreover, the spaces in which men drank together, and most particularly the *débits* that dotted the rear areas, served as incubators of indiscipline and nodes in a rumour network that disseminated information about the mutinies throughout the army, thus making collective action possible.

Put another way, men did not mutiny because they were drunk – this is, in a sense, to get things backwards. Rather, men drank intentionally and instrumentally, precisely because they *wanted* to mutiny and believed that wine, their source of inspiration and power in the trenches, would give them the courage and initiative they needed to face down their commanders. Alcohol consumption, with the rituals and performances it enabled, brought men together, filling them with a common purpose, moral unity, and a sense of permission that gave them the ability to defy orders, at least for a time, and at least while they were intoxicated. In this sense, the mutinies represent a breakdown or even reversal of the French army's system of emotional and behavioural control at the front. Men took wine's power to energize and drive behaviour and turned it against their officers in a massive, sodden protest against the war.

THE NIVELLE OFFENSIVE AND EARLY EVENTS

On 17 December 1916, General Robert Nivelle was promoted to Commander-in-Chief of the French army. He proposed an aggressive, massive offensive for the spring of 1917. Nivelle's battle concept had two stages. In the first stage, he would launch a two-pronged attack aimed at either side of the German salient that projected out towards Noyon, with the British attacking southeast from around Arras and the French northeast from around Soissons. In the second stage, and once the Germans were engaged on the salient's sides, the French would slash through the weakened centre and push "a maneuver force" through the breach, forcing a decisive battle in the German rear. The plan was bold and, other commanders thought, wildly over-optimistic.[18]

In early February 1917, the French began to prepare, moving masses of men and materiel. The enemy refused to comply with their plans. Beginning in mid-March, the Germans withdrew from the Noyon salient to a set of extensive and hardened fortifications called the "Hindenburg Line," removing the very bulge that the French sought to pinch off in the first stage of the battle. The Germans decimated the land they left behind, even, in an act of cruelty that brought tears to Frenchmen's eyes, chopping down the region's ancient apple orchards.[19]

By shortening their lines by some forty kilometres, the Germans increased the density of infantry and artillery around the Chemin-des-Dames region by around a dozen divisions.[20] The Chemin-des-Dames, in short, became a much harder target. Nivelle's concept seemed obsolete.

Whether the offensive should continue in these circumstances was hotly contested on 6 April in a Cabinet meeting at which the entire French high command was present. Nivelle argued that France should attack with the whole of its effort directly north on a front between Soissons and Reims in two massive waves. He reasoned that the British had committed to the offensive. Not to attack would be to betray them. Moreover, French materiel and men were already present and ready. It was too late to go back. Finally, Nivelle lectured, "[t]he offensive alone can give victory; the defensive brings only defeat and shame."[21] Nivelle then offered his resignation. He thus forced a choice between a risky offensive and the certainty of having the commander-in-chief resign in a scandalous public protest. To sweeten the deal, Nivelle pledged to relinquish his command immediately if the offensive failed. His threat and promise won the day, and the revised Nivelle Offensive was greenlit for mid-April.

For the battle, Nivelle amassed the largest concentration of firepower in the war so far. Between 9 April and 16 April, a dense bombardment of millions of shells pounded German defensive and artillery positions in preparation for the attack, although the effectiveness of this fire was limited.[22] In his personal narrative *La Guerre sans galon* (1920), Georges Cuvier wrote of his anticipation for the offensive, which he was convinced would be the last. "As the day of the attack approached, so dreaded and so hoped for," he recounted, "there arose in us a strong feeling; made of a desire to finish with this nightmare, made of confidence also, in a victorious result."[23] Another soldier, this one in a machine-gun detachment, in a letter from 15 April: "I have never heard such an uproar before ... The *boches* will never be able to resist this deluge. The ridge in front where the *boches* are is all on fire."[24] Or another, from the same machine-gun unit and on the same day, as he witnessed the preparatory barrage:

It's always banging around here, it's the real land of the *marmites* [a slang term for shells]. Over there, nothing exists, the shells raze everything. On the ridge in front of us, constant smoke, the *boches* are seriously taking it and it's not over. Will this plan force them out quickly? I don't know, but willingly or by force, they will give it back, all we need is good weather.[25]

The army's postal censorship records are full of such misplaced optimism.

Tens of thousands of men threw themselves into German fire on the morning of 16 April, thinking themselves playing a part in the war's final act, risking themselves to bring it to a conclusion. When they went over the top, most ran directly into German fire. The French bombardment largely failed to destroy the fortified strong points in the first and second German lines, and the attack's rolling barrage moved too fast, leaving thousands of men trapped helpless in No-Man's-Land, where they were ripped apart.[26] The offensive, along nearly all its length, stalled within the first couple of hours, with few units achieving their objectives and most failing to penetrate more than a few hundred metres into German positions. By 20 April, the battle had devolved into a series of disconnected local fights over territorial features. Nivelle was soon sacked, and on 29 April, General Henri-Philippe Pétain took command of the French armies on the Western Front. On 15 May, he was named commander-in-chief.

The Nivelle Offensive cost France around 30,000 men killed, 100,000 wounded, and 4,000 captured between 16 April and 25 April. This was nowhere near the level of casualties of Joffre's big offensives in 1915 and 1916, but the destruction was concentrated over a short timeframe: April 1917 was the worst single month for the French army since November 1914.[27] Moreover, these casualties came at an unpropitious time. Army intelligence reports suggested in the winter and early spring of 1917 that morale was dangerously low both in the army and in the rear.[28] Soldiers were frustrated with a backlog of leave and rest and generally unhappy about conditions in the trenches. Just as importantly, the harsh winter had made men resentful that the war was keeping them from their families and farms. It is precisely because French soldiers in early 1917 did not have much to believe in or look forward to that Nivelle's promise was so electrifying. This helps in explaining why the collapse in morale after its failure was so sudden and severe.

One concept useful in explaining the acts of indiscipline that followed is that of "moral injury," which was first explored in psychiatrist Jonathan Shaw's influential *Achilles in Vietnam* (1994). Shaw argues that encounters with mass violence – which is to say, encounters with the core reality of war – are morally corrosive for those who experience them. This reality, Shaw argues, can and does cause traumatic psychological wounds by challenging combatants' deepest-held beliefs about "what's right [*thémis*]."[29] Moral injury can be the result of seeing a battle-buddy maimed or killed; or of killing the enemy; or of killing non-combatants intentionally or unintentionally; or, most importantly, of feeling betrayed by commanders. In particular, when soldiers feel that their existence as moral beings has been devalued, instrumentalized, and sold cheaply to war – which is to say, when they believe their suffering has been for naught – a profound moral injury may result.[30] This is what happened in the French army after the collapse of the 1917 Nivelle Offensive: the mutinies that followed were an expression of rage at the fact of being betrayed and morally injured. The expression of this rage was often enabled by men's drinking.

The first mutiny took place on 29 April in the 20è RI's camp in Châlons, when approximately two hundred men failed to show up while the regiment was assembling in preparation for its tour in the trenches the next day. The men, who had been drinking, sobered up and ended their protest of their own accord.[31] Next, between 2 May and 5 May, the 321è RI saw desertions among soldiers ordered to mount the trenches and attack. These men also voluntarily came back to their regiment within a few days.[32] Between 3 May and 19 May, there were around fifteen similar events involving several thousand men, most of which were peaceful on their face, with men refusing orders to mount the trenches and calling for more rest and leave. This was the case with the events in the 121è RI on 14 May; with the events in the 32è RI on 17 May; and with those in the 152è RI on 19 May.[33]

On 20 May, there were four events, the most serious of which took place in the 128è RI. After they learned that they were going to return to the battle, some 400 intoxicated men from the unit formed what one officer called a "drunken mob" that shouted out anti-war slogans and refused to disperse.[34] The men protested that their leave was in arrears and that they were due rest. Their rights as citizen-soldiers were being violated, they claimed, and they were seeking to redress this, through revolution if necessary. As one of the demonstrators declared, "we are in a republican army, [and] we want republicanism."[35] They explained that they would not fight until their complaints were addressed. Their immediate superiors did not know what to do and decided to wait, according to one report, for "the drunkards to sober up."[36]

It is not easy to get at the motivations of the early mutineers in these "precursor incidents," as Pedroncini has called them.[37] Yet some men involved wrote letters that discussed their mutinies, which means there are traces of their thinking in the postal censorship records. Granted, these records must be read critically, for they represent less an objective survey of soldiers' sentiments than a curated one.[38] Still, they offer crucial insight into the mindset of those who rebelled.

Extracts of letters from several witnesses to the mutiny in the 20è RI (the very first) exist in one censorship report that has fortunately been preserved in the French military archives. Some men lionized the sacrifices their comrades made in the battle, while others lamented them, as did one *poilu* who regretted that "[a]ll this suffering, all the cruel losses that we submitted to will be in vain."[39] Two letters explicitly addressed the indiscipline in the regiment. According to the first, which reported that several hundred men had confronted their officers, things were bound to get ugly between soldiers and commanders: "It's only just starting, but when it starts, it will be bad."[40] According to the second, "funny things are going to happen" because "all the *poilus* are like me, nobody will go up there because we all did our duty and if we didn't reach the goal, it wasn't our fault." Command's goal, its author claimed, was to achieve victory only by "ruining [*esquinter*]" the *poilus*; commanders and politicians were but a bunch of "bandits"; men refused to mount the trenches and were confronted by their colonel, who had "tears in his eyes." He ended with a prediction: "If the war keeps going, bad things are going to happen because everyone has had enough."[41] Here the language of moral injury is clear, as is the sense among these men that they were witnesses to the birth of a larger movement against the war.

Indeed, letters transcribed by the army's postal censors in early and mid-May are full of such sentiments, as well as of a desire to revolt. This is true even in some regiments not directly involved in the indiscipline, which suggests both that rumours of the collective acts spread quickly and that the acts themselves were tacitly supported by those who heard the rumours, even if they themselves did not participate. "For our part," wrote "An Old Peasant *Poilu*" from the 56è RI (which did not mutiny) in a letter from 2 May, "our sole desire is to see the end of the war, and as you have seen the way it ends is not important to us." He did not care about the conditions of the peace – he just wanted the war to end, to "get out of this slavery, to see our wives, our little ones, to raise them up as we want, to work freely as before and *voilà*." He thought of the moment as explicitly revolutionary. "You talk about revolution," he predicted; "it is coming fast … There is nothing to do now but wait."[42] Once again, the letter was shot through with the bitter language of betrayal and moral injury, along with the hope and threat that *poilus* might act collectively to end the war.

THE CONTENTIOUS PERFORMANCE OF THE 162È RI

A helpful way to view the mutinies is as a cluster of what sociologists Charles Tilly and Sidney Tarrow have called "contentious performances," which they define as "standardized" ways by which one set of actors makes collective claims on another. Contentious performances draw upon "repertoires of contention" for their form, with such repertoires being established routines of claims-making and improvisations with them (within limits). According to Tilly and Tarrow, contentious performances are modular, meaning they can be "adopted and adapted" by different sets of political claimants for different ends.[43] This is what took place during the French army mutinies, where *poilus* came together in contentious performances to make emotionally charged claims to redress moral injury – rest, leave, no more wasteful offensives, an end to the war, and so on. Alcohol consumption was central to enabling this type of contentious performance because it helped men overcome the barrier of fear and tension that held back indiscipline. In short, it lowered the threshold for collective action.

Many of the mutinies after that of the 128è RI roughly followed the same script. Men first heard news that they were to be placed in the trenches along the Chemin-des-Dames for further attacks. They then drank together through the day and into the evening, often in *débits* that provided them with both a shelter from command surveillance and a social environment in which they could rile themselves up to a high state of emotional energy. In these spaces, men spread rumours about the mutinies, boisterously sang anti-war songs, and, in some cases, resolved to face down their commanders. Next came the contentious performance proper, during which intoxicated men confronted their officers with their demands, which again varied widely from better food to world peace. Depending on how officers responded and how riled up soldiers were, the performance could turn ugly, and although most mutineers refrained from outright violence towards their superiors, the threat of such was always present. Commanders would then depart the scene, set up a perimeter around the intoxicated men, and wait for them to sober up before transporting them further to the rear for quarantine and investigation.

For example, on 21 May, there was a serious act of collective indiscipline in the 162è RI, whose contentious performance influenced and shaped many of the mutinies that followed. The unit had been part of the first wave of the attack on 16 April and suffered heavily. After the attack, the regiment was placed *en repos* in the village of Coulonges, in the Fère-en-Tardenois region. When, on 21 May, its men received unwelcome orders to return to the trenches for another attack, they were furious. That evening, a group of inebriated soldiers overran an ostensibly morale-building theatre performance. This inspired more spontaneous indiscipline. Men caroused and sang the

"Internationale" – always a troubling development – calling out "Down with the war! We want rest and leave! Death to shirkers! Death to officers! To Paris!"[44] The demonstration grew, and men from the 267è RI, which was stationed nearby, came to see what the noise was about, with some of its members deciding to join in the protest. At its height, the demonstration involved some five or six hundred men, which provided safety in numbers: soldiers knew that the army could not possibly punish *all* of them.

Yet for all the tough talk, the demonstrators' violence was mostly symbolic. A few shots were fired into the air, and there was one tense stand-off between a guard and some demonstrators, but nobody was seriously hurt.[45] One man who participated in the events wrote home about them in a letter captured by the postal censors. He described an effervescent atmosphere: "Sing the Internationale. Shoot at the cops and the autos that have come to take us back to the lines with machine-guns. There is nothing else to do, we have had enough. It is peace that we want."[46] The regiment's officers were vastly outnumbered and allowed the demonstration to go on through the night, presuming that the indiscipline would burn itself up as the alcohol burned off.

Yet the contentious performance continued into the following day, when a small group of men from the 162è RI left camp and headed south to the village of Ronchères, where men from the 267è RI were stationed. Men from both regiments made their way to a local *débit* called *La Folie*, which was run by the Assailly family women. There, they drank together and swapped stories. In a case of propitious luck, Monsieur Assailly, who was a member of the 267è RI, was himself there with the group as they drank.[47] In addition, according to one report, Mme Assailly had just received an "important resupply of wine," so there was much to go around.[48] As a result, the drinks flowed easily and cheaply, and the men "heated themselves up," as another report put it, over innumerable glasses of *pinard*.[49] The *débit* thus served as a node of information-sharing about the mutinies and an incubator of emotional energy. After all, mutiny was hard to do. It involved considerable risks, physical and social. But as the men in *La Folie* talked and bonded over drinks and a common disgust with the war, they became more committed to engaging in a contentious performance of the type pioneered by the 128è RI – drinking together unified them and strengthened their resolve.

In the evening, the inebriated men took to the streets and, chanting for war's end, set off to confront their commander.[50] They found him and made three complaints that were clear expressions of moral injury and demands for redress: they lamented that they had not been on leave in seven months; they wanted a period of rest; and they claimed that their unit deserved to receive the *fourragère*, a unit-wide designation for valour, for its courage on 16 April. Their commander described the men as being in a state of drunken "madness," fitting after having imbibed at *La Folie*.[51]

The contentious performance had inertia: as more men joined in, more men joined in. Even those with no intention to demonstrate, who were initially bystanders or rubberneckers, were swept up in the emotional effervescence of the moment. In effect, a core of inebriated demonstrators attracted a following once their protest went public. The demonstration swelled in size as men saw and heard others saying and doing what they wanted to say and do publicly and getting away with it. And not all who agreed with the demonstrators joined in – even non-participating soldiers could be sympathetic to the mutineers and their goals. Cuvier, an eyewitness to the events, recalled he too had had "enough of the war, and demanded only one thing: peace." He did not join the demonstration and could not condone the outright revolt he was seeing, which offended his sense of patriotism, but he appreciated and shared the sentiments of those protesting.[52]

Commanders fought back on 24 May, once the men had sobered up. Eleven soldiers were arrested and sentenced to terms between three years in prison and ten years of public works.[53] The 162è RI was transported to the rear, where it was quarantined and the events investigated. On 25 May, the unit's commander reported that the men's morale was improving through a mix of repression and indulgence on the part of commanders. He punished some supposed ringleaders while promising the remaining men that he and other commanders would address their grievances, especially regarding unit citations and leave. The combination mollified the men some.[54] On 27 May, after several days of enforced sobriety, this same commander reported that things were "perfectly calm," adding that his men were eager to get back into the fight so as to prove themselves brave and willing to do their duty.[55] Purged of alleged troublemakers and ostensible alcoholics, the unit got its opportunity on 9 June, when the Germans launched a large counterattack and the 162è RI was called to the lines for emergency service. The men reportedly performed admirably.[56]

MUTINY IN THE 18È RI

The example of the mutineers from the 162è RI opened the floodgates, with knowledge of their actions and of their repertoire of contention quickly spreading through the units stationed behind the Chemin-des-Dames. Consider: in the month between 29 April and 26 May, there were but twenty-four events, including that of the 162è RI. Between just 27 and 31 May, there were a further eighteen, and between 1 and 7 June, when the mutinies reached what Pedroncini called their "paroxysm," there were thirty-five. These events tended to be more violent and disorderly than the precursor incidents. They threw French commanders, who found themselves doubting the reliability of entire divisions, into a panic.

The mutiny in the 18è RI at the end of May clearly shows how alcohol consumption could inspire and then direct the course of collective indiscipline, as well as the crucial role of *débits* in spreading knowledge of the mode of contentious performance that defined the mutinies. The 18è RI was designated part of the second wave of attackers on 16 April, but because the first wave failed to crack the German positions and the attack stalled, the 18è RI did not immediately enter the fight. Its men passed the Nivelle Offensive's first day watching thousands of casualties flow backwards, a scene horrific and dismaying. The army's sanitary planning had, predictably, failed to prepare for the casualties sustained.[57] The roads and villages around the battle were saturated with dying and screaming men. It was an unpropitious omen, and not one that was good for the 18è RI's morale.

The 18è RI was ordered into the lines at the Chemin-des-Dames for the first time on 23 April. On 4 May, the unit attacked and, surprisingly, took its objective – the dreaded *Plateau de Californie*, where today a monument stands in its honour – although at high cost. The regiment was relieved on 8 May, but only after suffering a horrible toll: 1,155 casualties. On 12 May, it was put into rest near the village of Villers-sur-Fère, within walking distance of Coulonges and Ronchères. The men were given real time off with limited fatigues and inspections and spent their time carousing and drinking "more than was reasonable"[58] – trying, no doubt, to forget what they had just seen or to make sense of it. As reinforcements replenished the 18è RI's numbers, its men began to fret that they might be ordered back into the same trenches from which they had just been evacuated and ordered to attack again.

Fear of being fed to the battle was on the minds of the men on Sunday 27 May. The day was brilliant and hot, as were most in late May through July.[59] Some of the men elected to drink away their sorrows and quench their thirst at the local bar, which was, once again, *La Folie*.[60] And once again, Assailly himself seems to have been there.[61] This time, the Assaillys reportedly let the men from the 18è RI drink for free, partially out of a sense of humanitarian pity, but also because Mme Assailly allegedly had strong anti-war views and wanted to encourage indiscipline.[62] Over innumerable glasses of wine, men from the 18è RI learned the story of the 162è RI's mutiny: what happened, what the men chanted, and how commanders reacted. They learned, in short, how to perform indiscipline collectively. Moreover, Assailly's crew shared some additional scuttlebutt: the 18è RI was going into the lines precisely because the 162è RI had mutinied.[63] This was maddening enough, but there was even more. Rumour was that the Germans were savaging the very stretch of trench into which the 18è RI was to be placed with terrifying "Big Bertha" guns.[64]

The rumours were false, but no matter: the men from the 18è RI, rendered excited and in a state of high emotional and physical entrainment by drink, reeling from moral injury, and having little faith in their commanders, believed the rumours enough to act. It was the combination and contextual convergence of many things – fatigue with the war, the disillusionment and moral injury that resulted from the Nivelle Offensive's failure, the fear and anger that came with the injury, the rumours and fake news, the widespread and heavy intoxication, and a shrinking window of opportunity to resist – that came together to drive the contentious performance forward. The men from the 18è RI concluded that they were being asked to suffer all over again, and for another unit's cowardice; this was a serious betrayal of trust. They decided to follow the example set by the 162è RI and resist before it was too late and they were already in battle.

At 18h30, about fifty men left *La Folie* and marched to their encampment at Villers-sur-Fère, calling out for peace. The regiment's commander, Colonel Decherf, came out to head them off. Decherf assured the men that the rumours they had heard were false. One report stated that the short-lived protest was broken up "fairly easily."[65] The men then returned to *La Folie* and the consolation of the Assaillys' *pinard*, of which they continued to avail themselves. There, hidden from view, they drank more and worked themselves up further, generating a high level of emotional energy. Decherf arrived again in person three hours later at *La Folie*, having come to find and gather up the intoxicated men for transport to the front lines. He brought with him half a dozen officers, with whom he confronted about 150 soldiers, who refused to leave *La Folie* when ordered. It is unclear how, but there was a scuffle and the officers were driven from *La Folie* under a hail of fists and curses.[66]

Fortified by wine and driven by a sense of injustice and fear of the front, the men spilled out from *La Folie* intent on making war on the war. The officers fled to regroup. The mutineers took over Villers-sur-Fère's streets, where they sang the "Internationale," fired revolvers into the air, and violently destroyed the transports that were supposed to take them to the front with machine-guns, grenades, and even bayonets. They tore up the streets and built barricades in preparation for a fight with the forces of order. But this only happened, it is imperative to emphasize, during their second attempt at collective indiscipline, when they were more inebriated and their emotional energy higher than earlier. Mutiny was an iterative process.

What were these men thinking? The official reports penned by officers give few answers. Although many men would be arrested, interrogated, and tried for their participation in the events at Villers-sur-Fère, the judicial records for their cases are mostly unilluminating. Soldiers either denied taking part or claimed to be mere drunken spectators. But immediately before he was executed, one of the mutineers from the unit who was sentenced to death – the report does not provide his name – was interviewed and asked about his motives and goals. The man, who was going to be shot and had no reason to lie, explained himself simply. He was "motivated by hatred for the war," trapped and constrained by the social pressure to fight. He acted violently to resist out of a sense of desperation, claiming that "in order to stop this butchery [those are his exact words], he could find no other method to bring it about." He considered himself a "martyr for the cause" and did not regret his actions. He was confident that his example would be followed.[67] Granted, this soldier likely felt these things more strongly than his fellow mutineers, which is how he ended up in his unenviable position. He may not be entirely representative. But there is no reason to think that his belief that he was acting as part of a much larger movement was not widely shared among his fellow demonstrators, or that he was not serious about ending the war.

The French army's postal censorship service also intercepted a candid and disjointed letter written by another participant in the events. The letter's author, a certain Désiré Collas, was not a member of the 18è RI. Rather, he was a member of the 413è RI, which was transported to Villers-sur-Fère for its own rest on 27–28 May.[68] Indeed, the vehicles that had carried the 413è into the town were the very ones in which the men from the 18è were supposed to be carried out. Collas, fresh from the trenches and their evils, stepped off his lorry into the middle of the mutiny.

Collas began a letter to a friend by proclaiming, with perplexing guilelessness (as he should have known his letter would likely be read), that he deserved "twelve bullets in his hide" for what he did next, but "had no regrets." He explained that soon after he disembarked from his lorry, he witnessed mutineers from the 18è RI fire machine-guns at the vehicles, exhausting their supply of cartridges. They then "threw grenades in the officers' faces." Collas, who was not at all surprised by the events – he and his fellows were *expecting* a "Revolution" with a capital "R" – threw himself in with no small enthusiasm, something even more remarkable considering he would have known neither the men from the 18è RI with whom he was mutinying nor even for what they were mutinying. The contentious performance itself drew him in and he went with the script. Collas wrote breathlessly:

> We guessed that this was the Revolution and everybody was in a rage, we chugged down *pinard* and off we went. We stop the commander and we would like to (you know what I want to say here) … I jump up in a bound and get my pistol. Then I head towards the officers crying out "To the death!" They got out of there. It was great to see.[69]

First he drank, then he revolted: his drinking activated his indiscipline, with the feeling of intoxication providing a sense of moral permission and a lowering of his threshold for collective action. And while Collas was likely exaggerating his own role, he was not exaggerating or mischaracterizing the events, as his testimony is corroborated by officers' reports. Collas's "Revolution" was not some airy idea: it was a concrete movement against the war, and he was taking part in it.[70]

The army prepared its response in the early morning on 28 May, when the forces of order surrounded Villers-sur-Fère.[71] The mutineers refused repeated exhortations to put down their weapons and depart from the town. A single shot was fired, but into the air, and it is unclear who was responsible. But things remained tense and the stand-off lasted two hours. Eventually, the men agreed to march themselves – under escort – to the nearby town of Fère-en-Tardenois. They had vague aspirations to commandeer and ride a train to Paris and bring their protest to the government.[72] For their part, the gendarmes were content to allow the mutineers to walk themselves to the station, for that is where the transports that would whisk them away for quarantine and punishment were waiting. At 7h30, the group arrived in front of the station at Fère-en-Tardenois to find it empty of trains but full of lorries.

The men, who still outnumbered the gendarmes, discussed for half an hour what to do next.[73] After an animated debate, and over the very strenuous objections of some, they elected – as a group – to mount the transports. The mutineers, to the last man, climbed aboard by 8h30.[74] The question of why they did so is a difficult one. Why did they, after making such a dramatic statement, return to some semblance of order and walk themselves into transports that they should have known would take them to the rear for interrogation and punishment? And this is a question pertinent not only to the mutiny in the 18è RI, but to the mutinies more generally, as they nearly all ended in this same way, with men – seemingly of their own accord – ending their protests.

Men had various reasons for doing so. Some probably regretted and were ashamed of their behaviour and wanted to show good faith; others trusted the officers present, who disingenuously assured the men that they were going back into rest, not quarantine; and yet others feared what would happen if their group were to splinter, leaving them without the armour of numbers. But, I would argue, the most important factor was that dawn had broken and brought with it physical and emotional sobriety. It had been fourteen hours since the mutiny began, enough time for the men to sober up. Without alcohol to help prop it up, the emotional energy of the mutineers and thus their will to revolt collapsed.

In other words, the men's grandiose pretentions to revolution, death to officers, and an end to the war – so robust in the smoky environment of *La Folie* the night before – seemed wan in the hard, honest light of morning. The powerful emotional links that bound them together during their act of collective indiscipline were fragile, held together by liquid ropes of *pinard* that evaporated with the dawn. In this way, the collapse of the mutineers' morale is evidence less of their decision to come back under discipline and more of how hard it was to mutiny, as well as of the array of constraints placed upon men's actions, which felt loosened for a moment with their intoxication but snapped back into place in the morning. Moving from mutiny-in-the-abstract to mutiny-in-the-flesh required overcoming significant fear and tension, as well as risking the shame of cowardice and severe punishment, which was hard enough. But so too was *sustaining* the powerful emotions that underwrote the mutinies.[75] Without alcohol to act as an emotional accelerant and fuel, indiscipline became harder and harder to perform.

130 men from the unit – meaning virtually all of those who participated in the events – were arrested and punished. Most received a month or two of prison time. Twelve went before a military tribunal, of whom five were sentenced to death. All claimed in their defense to have been drunk and incapable of understanding their actions. Four were executed. One, the legendary Vincent Moulia, escaped his sentence when a bombardment came down on the village in which he was held, allowing him to make a run for it and escape to Spain. The men involved in the mutiny of the 18è RI were not, contra Smith's interpretation, interested in debating their duties as citizen-soldiers or trying to explain themselves to their commanders. They simply no longer wanted to fight and were willing – at least for a short time – to risk their skins to end the war. Yet if their emotions burned hot, they did not burn for long. The cohesion that held the group together and gave it the resolve to demonstrate was fragile and exceptional, attached as it was to their mutual state of intoxication. Time and sobriety were its enemies. When sobriety returned, the men returned to a semblance of order.

MUTINY IN THE 82è BI

Soon thereafter came the positively bacchanalian mutiny of the 82è BI, which took place on 1–2 June in the town of Ville-en-Tardenois – not far from where the 162è RI and 18è RI mutinied. The 82è BI's mutiny clearly shows how alcohol consumption could change the nature of an act of collective indiscipline from a relatively peaceful demonstration into an orgy of nihilistic violence. The 82è BI formed the very tip of the spear when it attacked on 16 April. After leaping from their trenches with, one report held, an "élan irrésistible," its two constituent regiments – the 23è RI and the 133è RI – saw some initially encouraging results. But their attack stalled by around 11h00 in front of the fearsomely gunned Fort Brimont, which remained in German possession.[76] The cost was high. The 23è RI suffered

87 killed, 513 injured, and 41 missing; the 133è RI suffered 125 killed, 366 injured, and 30 missing on just this first day of the offensive.[77] Nevertheless, the day of attack was declared a "great success."[78]

What came next was less so. The brigade remained in the trenches for eight days, only rotating out on the night of 24–25 April.[79] During this time, the big German guns at Fort Brimont savaged the brigade and machine-gun fire pinned men down in No-Man's-Land. There was little or no resupply of ammunition or food, with men forced to drink the evil water they found in shell-holes. As early as 20 April, the brigade's commander, General Mignot, demanded it be relieved before it was "completely destroyed."[80] It was nearly so by the time it rotated out. Between 16 and 24 April, the 82è BI suffered an astounding 1,646 casualties.[81] But the brigade's trial was not over. Between 25 and 29 April its manpower was replenished. On 4 May, it moved back into the same positions it had evacuated just days earlier. The tactical situation had not improved and the brigade gained no new ground. The men suffered more of the same: days of thirst, hunger, fear, and anguish in one of the hottest corners of the battle. By the time the brigade was again rotated out on the evening of 11–12 May, it had taken another 101 casualties. On 18 May, the brigade was ceremonially presented to the Army Corps commander and received the *fourragère*. The 82è BI thus had as good as a claim as any other unit to drape itself in what passed for glory on the Chemin-des-Dames.

On 24 May, the brigade was moved to the town of Ville-en-Tardenois, just south of Reims, and put *en repos*. There, a week later, a familiar pattern asserted itself. At 13h00 on 1 June, the men from the brigade received expected but unwelcome news: at midnight, they were to move toward the Chemin-des-Dames once again. About 100 men from the 133è RI decided to follow the script that the 162è RI and 18è RI had laid out. Forming a group outside their billets, they called for an end to the war and declared that they would not fight. Several dozen men from the 23è RI joined in shortly thereafter. The group formed up in a column and began a march on the town. Lieutenant-Colonel Brindel, the commander of the 23è RI, rushed to the scene. Unexpectedly, rather than engage with the men, he raged at them, roughing up a soldier named Antoine Hartmann, who was waving a red flag. Brindel trampled the flag in the dirt and ordered his men back to their billets. They were intimidated and complied. Brindel, thinking the affair settled, departed.[82]

At 14h30, like drops of mercury flowing together, the group of protestors re-formed. 100 men, defiantly headed by Hartmann, the recently abused leader of the last demonstration (who would later be executed for his involvement in the events), marched in a column on Ville-en-Tardenois, shouting the usual slogans and threats. They were headed off by Generals Mignot and Bulot, commanders of the 41è DI and 82è BI, respectively. The stars on these men's shoulders had an effect and the protestors quieted themselves. The generals strode through a parting lake of horizon blue and arrested Hartmann. Nobody came to his defense and he did not resist. They again ordered the men to return to their billets and prepare to move out. Bulot even marched at their head back to camp.[83] Mignot had an optimistic read on the situation. He described the men as wearing "very reasonable expressions." Neither he nor Bulot felt threatened at any time.[84]

Commanders must have been surprised when they learned at 18h30 that the men had, for the third time, formed a column, marched on the town, and were making the by-now-standard imprecations. Bulot came out and headed off the column at the entrance to Ville-en-Tardenois, intent on assuring that this third attempt at mutiny would not be charmed. But alas, it was: the crowd was much larger – Bulot estimated its size at between 600 and 800 men – and this time they did not listen to him. Many were "particularly drunk."[85] Mignot reported that the men had spent the hours between their last confrontation and this one "getting themselves really worked up," drinking together and building up one another's resolve. The men, he concluded, were no longer soldiers: they had become "drunken apaches."[86]

Bulot commanded, then asked, and then begged his men to return to order. He called out to them about the 82è BI's past and future glories and praised their valour and bravery. He appealed to their patriotism and manliness – to that deep sense of having been violated and ruined by Germany and its armies – and evoked the "necessity of holding on [*tenir*] in order to punish that nation of murderers [and] prevent [France] from becoming the *boche*'s slave."[87] All to no avail. "The over-heated minds of the over-excited men," as he described them, were on something else. They argued and accused in slurred, heavy syllables.

This went on for more than an hour, over which the crowd grew to more than 2,000 men. It is understandable why men came to watch, if not to participate, as it appeared on its face to be a topsy-turvy scene from a carnival: the just-lately-so-proud Bulot, his morale shattered at the indiscipline of his men, weeping openly in front of them in shame and frustration. Bulot remembered, his bitterness failing to cover his humiliation: "I had before me the complete spectacle of an unchained mob." The men surrounded him on three sides, his back to Ville-en-Tardenois's townhall, where the divisional headquarters were located. That is when the first piece of wood was thrown in his general direction. More followed, and then stones, as the men changed their cries. "Murderer!" they cried out feverishly. "Blood-drinker!"[88]

At this point, nearly all the unit's commanders came out of the townhall. One of them, Piebourg, reported that he felt "absolutely powerless" to do anything considering the men's anger and the size of their group.[89] Mignot did not like what he saw. "General Bulot seemed to be their specific target," he wrote in a debriefing report. "It appeared that the situation would turn tragic any minute, and we were afraid that the General, squeezed in and shoved around, found himself in a rather tight spot."[90] The officers shielded Bulot and brought him into the building while Mignot remained outside and attempted to restore some semblance of order. Mignot was well-liked and held in high regard, but this was of little help. He promised the men more rest and more leave. He assured them that he would do all he could to keep them out of the lines. In short, he misjudged the situation and treated a confrontation like a negotiation. Moreover, even if Mignot's accession to their demands pleased the men, they would not be satisfied without some flesh. They continued to shout and demand blood. The increasingly violent mutineers grabbed now at Mignot, hitting him with their fists and feet. He too had to be rescued and pulled into the townhall.

Everyone was now in unscripted territory – this contentious performance had gone further than any other. The mutineers placed the townhall under effective siege, surrounding it with makeshift barricades. As night fell, they called out, over and over: "Murderer! Blood-drinker! Death to Bulot!"[91] At 22h30, the men attacked the building, trying to beat down its front door with a makeshift battering ram, but were repulsed. Bulot wisely refused to accede to their demand that he come out. As midnight approached, a group of men broke off and set out for nearby Romigny, where two other regiments were camped, to spread their mutiny. They were turned away by rifle fire. Most others wandered off in small groups of vandals. They pelted buildings with stones and pieces of wood, tore up the village's *pavé* streets, overturned ammunition and baggage trains, and harassed residents. A hard-core group of eighty or so men maintained the siege until around

3h00 on 2 June. At that point, fatigued from all the calling for blood, the men wandered off and passed out. Mignot reported that, once "the last drunkard had disappeared," Bulot was spirited out of Ville-en-Tardenois with a recommendation – which he followed – to never show his face in front of the brigade again.[92] In any case, he could not have retained his command even should he have wanted to, as the brigade was soon to be broken up and its men redistributed into other units.

Most men in the brigade took part in the mutiny, either as participants or as witnesses, and assuredly, by dawn's light, every man knew about what had taken place. Which is why the next morning's events were so strange: the men answered their roll call and acted as if nothing at all had happened the night before. Company commander Libaud, for one, reported that his men showed "the most perfect calm, excellent manoeuvres," and concluded that his men "had regained their normal appearance," indirectly highlighting how abnormal this all was. He ended the day confident that his men would follow him into the trenches.[93] Mignot too thought morale had miraculously recovered. He ascribed this to his tremendous negotiating skills, offering that the men "seemed satisfied with the provisory solution offered, a few days' extra rest in the rear, with transport to begin the day after tomorrow."[94]

Mignot's promise was of course made in bad faith, and he had not the least intention to make good on it. His goal was to quarantine the unit, interrogate its men, and punish them. Some men may have been fooled by his gambit, but it is unlikely that was the case for many. They must have known that whatever was coming next would not be particularly desirable given the outrageousness of their actions the night before. After all, some of them had called for the murder of their own commanding officers. What is most probable is that the men sobered up in both a literal and a metaphorical sense. The period that elapsed between when the men began their protest and when it ended – about nine hours – is just about the amount of time it would have taken drunk men to regain their senses. This is not a coincidence.

During 2–3 June, the brigade was transported to its division depot in Bassu, far south of the Chemin-des-Dames. The investigation began the following day and continued for about a week. Morale was not so good, for there was a further demonstration on 4–5 June, this one involving around fifty inebriated demonstrators and a hundred curious observers. The demonstrators not only called out for the usual things – rest, better food, leave, and an end to the war – but also claimed they "did not want to do anything but drink to our fantasies" and attacked an officer.[95] Rather shockingly, even while in quarantine, the men had access to enough alcohol to reignite their indiscipline, which effectively continued so long as they could drink. But this situation would soon end with dryness.

One inspector reported by 6 June that the men were contrite. He was encouraged that they were "reasoning coolly" and many allowed themselves to admit what was plainly obvious, "that they had gone too far."[96] Morale was improving, the report continued, mainly because most of the "trouble-makers" had already been arrested. The 82è BI was punished more harshly than any other mutinous unit in the French army. On 5 June, investigators brought charges against 164 men for the events of 1–2 June and an additional sixty-nine for those of 4–5 June. Military tribunals found twenty-eight soldiers guilty of serious crimes, five of whom were sentenced to death and four executed. The brigade's field-grade officers all lost their commands and the brigade itself was completely dissolved, with its men integrated into other units. In a certain way, the mutiny succeeded: the brigade never entered the trenches again.

The mutiny of the 82è BI provides a natural experiment clearly showing the importance of alcohol in shaping its events. The men from the brigade attempted to mutiny three times, twice when they were sober and once when they were drunk; mutiny was again an iterative process. In the two former cases, they were unable or unwilling to overcome the fear and tension that marked the line between mutiny and obedience. Both times they were cowed by their commanders. It was only after they drank together that they gained the courage to commit entirely to their contentious performance. This is because drinking brought men together in a common task; it dulled fear and heightened their aggression; it filled them with courage, resolve, and rage; and it prepared them to sacrifice themselves for the greater good. In short, drinking did exactly what it was supposed to do on the Western Front. Only this time, the men from the 82è BI directed alcohol's effects at their commanders rather than at the Germans.

The events in the 82è BI were the high-water mark of the mutinies and their midpoint chronologically. There were forty-eight acts of collective indiscipline between 29 April and 1 June and sixty-three between 2 June and 5 September, although after 15 June, the events become relatively infrequent. It also represented their high-water mark in a different sense: no subsequent mutiny would be as ugly or vicious, as large or as violent. This does not mean that they would all be peaceful. The 42è RI's mutiny at Ville-en-Tardenois on 7 June was resolved only when the mutineers came under fire from a machine-gun, and 120 men from the 85è RI "rioted all night long" on 25 June.[97] And while no other mutiny reached 2,000 men, as did that of the 82è BI, subsequent events could be large. 1,400 men from the 221è RI demonstrated at Mourmelon on 4 June, and 1,000 from the 298è RI did the same between 19 and 26 June at Corcieux.[98]

THE STRANGELY SOBER MUTINY OF THE 10È BI

The mutiny in the 5è DI, which took place in the Soissons region on 28–30 May, was of a different kind from what came before – more deliberate, measured, and entirely sober – and provides a useful contrast with other acts of collective indiscipline. This mutiny is the best documented in the French military archives and served as Leonard V. Smith's case study in his *Between Mutiny and Obedience*. My intention below is not so much to dispute Smith's interpretation of these events, but to focus on the role that the conspicuous *lack* of alcohol consumption played in this demonstration, and particularly in the events that took place in the 10è BI (one of the 5è DI's two brigades; it consisted of the 129è RI and the 36è RI).

Between 16 April and 28 May, the 10è BI was stationed behind the battle in the Chemin-des-Dames region, but never entered the trenches or saw action.[99] On 27 May the troops learned they would soon mount the trenches. This upset and alarmed them because it meant that, soon enough, they would be thrown into a losing battle which, up to this point, their unit had avoided. To make things worse, many soldiers' families had come to the brigade's camp around Nogent to spend the Pentecost holiday with their husbands and fathers. The order to depart meant that these joyful little family reunions were cut short. The men were bitter and considered this a "deception" on the part of their commanders.[100]

The division arrived at new billets near Soissons on 28 May, with men from the 10è BI expecting to mount the trenches the following day. Wasting little time, a group of around 150 thirsty *poilus* from the brigade left camp and headed to the nearby hamlet of Léchelle in search of its comforting wine.[101] There, they encountered some engineers from another division who had just returned from leave and carried an unwelcome rumour from the rear: Indochinese labour battalions were machine-gunning women strikers in Paris. The rumour was not true – women were striking but they were not being abused and murdered in the streets – but that mattered little. The men from the brigade were willing to believe the rumour out of a combination of racial prejudice, gendered anxieties about their place in the rear, distrust of their own leaders, and alcohol myopia.[102] As the men drank with the engineers for several hours and learned about the mutinies that were taking place, they resolved to launch their own. Again, an alcohol shop served as an incubator of collective indiscipline and as a node in the rumour network through which knowledge of the contentious performance spread.[103]

When the intoxicated men returned to camp at around 20h00, they began to call out for an end to the war. They were met by their battalion commander, Aubergé, who listened as they said they had "had enough of the war and wanted the government to know it."[104] These demonstrators explicitly claimed to be following the example of the other regiments who had refused to mount their trenches.[105] Aubergé assured the men that no-one was being slaughtered in Paris's streets, and the men returned to their billets for the night of their own accord, but not before letting him know that they intended to continue their protest the following morning at 8h00.[106] Aubergé headed to headquarters and reported the events. He was ordered to give instructions that the brigade's officers were to "act with gentleness" during confrontations with their men to avoid escalation.[107]

The next morning, when the men were assembling themselves in the pre-dawn light, some of their officers came to convince them not to hold their demonstration. The men held firm and insisted that following orders would make them "suckers." At the same time, they assured their officers that they bore them no ill will. After breakfast, one hundred of Aubergé's men set out to find more recruits for the demonstration.[108] Once they learned of the protest, men in other battalions got over their shock quickly and threw themselves in. In every infantry battalion from the 10è BI that the mutineers visited, around two-thirds of the men joined the demonstration. Even cooks contributed in their way, staying behind to make a hearty lunch for the growing group. By 15h00, a significant part of the brigade was in open revolt. Reports estimated the size of the crowd at around 700–850 men.

But this was a revolt of a special sort. The mutineers from the 10è BI were polite and respectful towards their officers, who were well-liked and respected. There were no recriminations, no threats of violence, and no hostility.[109] The demonstrators followed rules of self-presentation for their iteration of the contentious performance: "all the protestors carried a walking stick [*canne*], some of them had a flower in their *boutonnière*, and many had unbuttoned their coats to give themselves the appearance of strikers."[110] But they maintained internal military discipline of a sort. The men marched themselves around in ordered, smart columns and continued to demonstrate the outward signs of respect towards their officers, addressing them "correctly and with deference."[111] At the same time, *poilus* became orators, filling the streets, climbing buildings' steps and using them as pulpits from which they proclaimed their desire for an "immediate peace."[112] All this took place in front of the brigade's collected officers, including de Roig, the divisional commander, Martenet, the commander of the divisional depot, and Lebrun, the commander of the army corps. Each of these men at different points in the afternoon attempted to convince the men to come back under military discipline, but all failed.[113]

The men of the brigade decided upon and presented their commanders with a set of demands that they claimed must be addressed before they would go back into the trenches and fight. They demanded nothing new or different from earlier mutineers. Concrete complaints about the quality of food and the availability of leave were paired with vague but lofty aspirations for universal peace and justice. A soldier from the 36è RI, Alfred Combray, listed six negotiating points: "1. Peace and the right to backlogged leave; 2. No more butchery. We want freedom; 3. Regarding food, it is disgraceful; 4. No more injustice; 5. We wish that the blacks and other foreigners do not mistreat our women. 6. We want peace to feed our wives and children and to be able to give bread to women and orphans." This was very similar to a list provided by Menager, one of the brigade's commanders, in a 29 May report. He listed five points: "1. We no longer want to attack. We were brainwashed with the last one and it was too costly; 2. We demand peace … 3. We no longer accept that we are killed while in the rear, shirkers ride in automobiles with women, while the profiteers enrich themselves in a shameful fashion, and while factory workers earn up to 25 francs a day; 4. We want our right to leave to be respected and that we are not and not be mocked and put to work when we are in rest; 5. We don't want Annamites employed to police and kill our women. We want to be better fed, etc., etc."[114]

What was important was the tone and tenor of their demands, which were formal and respectful. Commanders explained what the unfortunate consequences of the men's behaviour was likely to be. They begged their men to stop, to save themselves from shame and punishment. They failed, and all wept openly at this humiliation.[115] The mutineers simply held out their empty hands, palms turned upward to the sky in a non-threatening gesture [*les mains retournées*].[116] In these moments at least, the spectres of shame and punishment had little power to constrain their actions. As one of them wrote home in a moving letter to his lover: "I know that I am risking my skin [by mutinying], but I can through this way save it, and that is what I want. Beloved, say it with me: down with the war that separates us, and long live the revolution that will bring the peace that will reunite us. I love you and do not want to die."[117]

In the moment, with generals weeping and rebellious *poilus* ascendant, mutineers from the brigade were remarkably confident that they could end the war. Indeed, they believed that their demonstration gave them power and agency. This is what soldier Provoste from the 36è RI thought. He recounted in a letter home that, very soon, "there will be a little change, *entirely thanks to us*, because we have had enough of all this." He saw himself as part of a vanguard: "Thus there needs to be someone to provide an example and it is we who have started it, and you will see the whole world will approve."[118] A soldier named Henri Mille from the 129è, who was sentenced to death and executed, wrote something similar in a letter on 16 June – well over two weeks after the mutiny, after the indiscipline had supposedly burned itself out – in which he predicted that mutineers would "be recognized in the near future" as having done "good work."[119] He was confident that the judgment of history would vindicate him.

As evening fell on 29 May, the men retired to their billets for the night. They informed their officers that they intended to hold a "monster" protest the following morning at 8h00, with their goal being to travel to Paris and confront the Chamber of Deputies directly.[120] But neither the projected meeting nor the march on Paris took place. Commanders moved quickly during the night of 29–30 May. They planned to surprise the men, rouse them from their sleep, and herd them onto transports before the men could organize a collective response. The required transports arrived at 3h00, which Smith calls the "moment of decision" for the mutineers: would they follow their officers and mount the transports or would they risk it all and try to march to Paris right then?[121] Their resolve faltered, and per one report, "the exhortations of the officers finished by overcoming the resistance opposed by the most resolute troublemakers and the convoy set off without a violent incident."[122] In short, they agreed to get on the transports without putting up a fight.[123] The men were subsequently placed under guard in the town of Revigny and interrogated by a certain Colonel Boucher, who then relayed detailed reports.

The repression in the nonviolent 10è BI was comparable to that in the violent 18è RI and 82è BI. While it was impossible to punish everyone involved, some examples had to be made *pour encourager les autres*. In the 129è RI, twenty-two men were brought before a military tribunal, of whom four were condemned to death. All were executed, and all but one, Smith argues, were chosen at near-random from the crowd of demonstrators.[124] In the 36è RI, thirty-six men were brought before a military tribunal, of whom thirteen were sentenced to death. None were executed. The 10è BI was then dissolved.

The mutiny in the 10è BI was unusual in many respects, making it dangerous to draw broad conclusions about the nature of the mutinies from it.[125] For example, the men's exaggerated demonstrations of respect for their officers, as well as their peacefulness and lack of aggression, were not the norm.[126] Their internal discipline was unusual. But what was most unique about the mutiny in the 10è BI was that the men were stone-cold sober. "Not a single case of drunkenness was observed," noted the investigator Boucher, and it was a rule among the demonstrators that it was "forbidden" among them to have any "wine in *bidons*."[127] Indeed, the mutineers made and enforced abstinence as the central internal rule governing their demonstration. One soldier, for instance, recounted draconian internal discipline regarding drink, writing in a letter that the rule that must be followed was a "complete prohibition on having a single mouthful of wine in the *bidons*." He continued, rather shockingly, to declare that any man who did not follow this rule should be "immediately shot by his comrades." Such is how the men in his brigade assured that "everything happened in the greatest calm and coolness."[128] The men's sobriety, in effect, was a conscious tactic of self-presentation, a means of presenting themselves as rational actors with agency rather than as a drunken mob.

Moreover, men from the 10è BI consciously tried to inspire others to make the rejection of the bottle the central fact of their mutinies to come. "Follow [our] example," one soldier demanded in a letter to a friend. "Do not hesitate, it is the moment to act." "*Pinard*," he wrote, "is dead. No more *pinard.* [It is] revolt. The officers are no longer our masters. It is our turn. They will not react."[129] Crucially, this soldier tied what he considered the servitude of militarism to drinking *pinard*, making the latter a function of the former. To drink was to be a slave to the army, to embed oneself in a system of restraint and control. For him, sobriety was a way that he might relieve himself of his enslavement and become his own master. Indeed, by rejecting drink, the men from the 10è BI consciously and effectively rejected the entire psychotropic regime at the front; by putting down the *bidon de pinard*, they declared that they were no longer willing to hold on or sacrifice themselves for their commanders.

During the first week of June, copies of an anti-war tract that mentioned the 10è BI and its sobriety circulated around Soissons. It proclaimed that the 10è BI "refused to mount [the trenches] and demonstrated in silence with not a single man drunk." This was the winning formula, the tract proclaimed: "Do the same when it is your turn to mount, and we will surely have peace."[130] In short, the men from the brigade wanted their sober version of the repertoire of contention to spread. Yet their formula was largely ignored. Thousands of men in the Soissons region were directly inspired to mutiny by the 10è BI, but they were not sober like those from the 10è BI — they found alcohol intoxication to be extremely useful in overcoming the barrier of fear and tension that prevented collective indiscipline.[131] Indeed, it seems that only one other unit, the 57è *Batallion de Chasseurs à Pied*, followed the sober advice of the men from the 10è BI when it demonstrated on 1 June in the Braine region.[132] That so few men — only hundreds out of tens of thousands, and in only two units — chose to make sobriety a conspicuous part of their demonstration is powerful evidence of how important intoxication was in the other cases. In effect, the strangely sober mutiny of the 10è BI is the exception that proves the rule.

THE NATURE OF THE EVENTS

It is tempting to view the mutinies as a ritual of expurgation analogous to a medieval or early modern carnival. Scholars of ritual have argued that carnival, with its excessive drinking, eating, and promiscuity, as well as (most importantly) its temporary inversion of normal power relations characterized by the mocking denigration of both secular and religious authority figures, serves as a safety valve for the expression of social resentments.[133] The mutinies certainly resembled a carnival superficially with their widespread drinking and temporary inversion of normal power relations. But this is to misinterpret them. Carnivals, after all, are planned. Indeed, the mutinies were not rituals, let alone rituals whose bounds were known by both sides and established by tradition. Their function and intent were not to burn off energy so that command authority could be re-established along stronger lines. They were improvised contentious performances that challenged the very basis of military authority.

The mutinies thus represent not only a crisis in morale, but also a crisis in the psychotropic regime that shaped and, in some circumstances, drove French soldiers' experiences and behaviour along the Western Front. As we have seen, the prohibition system's central internal contradiction was that it allowed men to drink wine *à volonté* in the world-behind-the-war if they could pay for it. This reflected the French scientific and folk-psychological distinction between healthy wine and dangerous distilled alcohol. It also assured that, in the late spring and early summer of 1917, *poilus* would be able to drink and then work themselves into a state of what commanders' reports frequently termed "over-excitation [*suréxcitation*]." Men in the 18è RI were described this way (a report related how officers tried to save the unfortunate Decherf from the "overexcited men"), as were those from the 82è BI (Bulot held that the "overexcited men" were "impossible to reason with").[134]

Generating this sense of overexcitation through drinking wine was entirely the point. To be sure, it is important to note that the case of the 10è BI shows clearly that drinking was neither a necessary nor a sufficient cause of the mutinies. Yet drinking *was* clearly central to the contentious performance that characterized many of them. In these acts of collective indiscipline, *poilus* intentionally mobilized their intoxicated overexcitation to help them overcome the fear and tension that lay between them and revolt. Moreover, they used the space of the *débit* to spread information, rumours, and inspiration to disobey. They thus took the very psychotropic drug that the army was using to shape their emotional experiences and turned it against their commanders. The irony was that the very unchecked wine-drinking that the prohibition system permitted as a release valve in the world-behind-the-war fuelled, in the context of the moral injury experienced after the Chemin-des-Dames offensive, precisely the kind of deviant behaviour the system was intended to avoid.

It is for this reason that, beginning in early June 1917, the French army under Pétain launched a war on wine that was of the utmost importance in the process by which the army regained control over soldiers in the summer of 1917. As we will see, Pétain's crackdown on wine sales and drinking in the world-behind-the-war did not end the acts of collective indiscipline right away. They continued to spread to the rear, along the railways that connected the Chemin-des-Dames to the front and over which men travelled while going on and coming back from leave, where wine sales were not banned or regulated in any way. In dozens of train stations, tens of thousands of largely inebriated men demonstrated against the war in more than 240 instances of collective indiscipline that took place over the month of June and July – the repertoire of contention spread west along the rail lines. Pétain's war against wine and these understudied events in train stations are the subject of the next chapter.

7

WINE AND THE REVOLT OF THE *PERMISSIONNAIRES*

INTRODUCTION TO THE *PERMISSIONAIRES'* REVOLT

At 18h37 on 3 July 1917, *train de permissionaires* RM bis – a special train carrying men who were returning from leave, which was known as going *en permission* – pulled into the station at Château-Thierry. It was *en route* to the Chemin-des-Dames sector, having departed from Paris. Captain Schniegans, the head of station security, met the train warily. Earlier, he had received two messages about RM bis from stations upstream. The first, from Meaux, warned that the soldiers in the train were "a little bit rowdy." The second, from Nogent l'Artaud, reported that the rowdy men had thrown a colonial soldier [*zouave*] off the moving train. The *permissionnaires* (as men on leave were called) were inebriated, having drunk both in Paris before starting their journey and during the train ride. Schniegans mounted the train to quiet them. He was supported by ninety men from the 8th company of the 43è *Batallion de Chasseurs à Pied* (8/43è BCP), an elite unit, under the command of a certain Lieutenant George.[1]

As Schniegans moved through the train, George's men deployed in three groups of equal size. They approached cautiously – there had been, by early July, dozens of confrontations between *permissionnaires* and the forces of order in train stations. While George reported that there was at first "nothing out of the ordinary," Schniegans noted worriedly that RM bis had no police detachment aboard, which meant that the men had been without any supervision for the length of their journey.[2] He learned too that the *zouave* had not been thrown from the train but rather had fallen off while scrambling from car to car in an attempt to rile up the men and get them to refuse to return to the front.[3]

Schniegans gave RM bis's conductor clearance for departure, but as the train pulled out, some of the *permissionnaires* began to harass George's men. They called out "[you] sons of bitches, down with the cops!" "Death to the pigs!" and "Long live liberty!"[4] Schniegans signalled the conductor to stop the train and George ordered his men to surround it and restore order. George himself was then, in his words, "surrounded by a loud and rowdy mob" of *permissionnaires*, one of whom (a corporal) shouted "we have had enough [of the war]!" in his face. George grabbed the man, pulled him from the crowd, and threw him to the *chasseurs*, who arrested him.[5]

Upon seeing this, two of the *permissionnaires* called out "we will not let you take him!" and fought to pull the corporal back. According to Schniegans, the *chasseurs* "intervened energetically," and this produced a "huge scrum" during which the *permissionnaires* and the *chasseurs* fought over the corporal. More *chasseurs* joined the fray and more *permissionnaires* descended from their cars. The *permissionnaires* recaptured the corporal and beat up several *chasseurs*. Schniegans described the scene (with a telling word) as "a mutiny of at least 800 *permissionnaires*."[6] At 19h30 – about an hour after the train had pulled in – George retreated outside the station with his men. Schniegans reported: "Estimating that my detachment was incapable of controlling the situation, and in order to prevent the general over-excitement from leading to even more serious events, I left the mutinous train isolated on the tracks and surrounded it with the 43è BCP."[7] The *permissionnaires* took over and occupied the station.

Schniegans telephoned his superiors, apprising them of the situation and asking for reinforcements. The military commissioner at Noisy-le-Sec offered a detachment of army bakers, but Schniegans demurred, guessing that they would be "rather unsuited for energetic action." As evening fell, Schniegans and George had no choice but simply to stop the train from leaving and wait for reinforcements. They settled into a siege. Reinforcements arrived at 4h40 the next morning, consisting of two well-armed companies of the 14è *Batallion de Chasseurs Alpins* (BCA), about three hundred men. Schniegans now had around four hundred at his disposal. He decoupled the train into its component cars and pulled them one at a time to the far end of the station. This allowed the 8/43è BCP, 14è BCA, and *gendarmes* to gain local superiority of numbers. Under armed guard, the cars were emptied one man at a time. The *gendarmes* identified the alleged ringleaders, who were arrested. Thirteen *permissionaires*, including the corporal who started the whole thing, were identified as the "principal agents of the incidents."[8]

The *permissionnaires*, much like their brother mutineers at the front, offered little resistance with morning's arrival. Schniegans reasoned that "the reflections over the course of the restless night and the presence of the police contingent had their effect."[9] To be sure, but just as importantly, the demonstrators had spent eleven dry hours in the station, and during this time the men had sobered up. They were then confronted with overwhelming force, which brought them back to order. At 8h00 on 4 July, almost twelve hours behind schedule, a quiet Train RM bis left Château-Thierry and made the uneventful trip to Epernay. Later that morning, the *zouave* who had fallen off the train the afternoon before found his way into the station. He came directly to Schniegans's office, where he was arrested.

The familial resemblance between the revolt of the *permissionnaires* at Château-Thierry and the mutinies at the front is clear: the former is the mirror image of the latter.[10] The men who revolted at Château-Thierry drew from the same repertoire of contention as those at the front. They called for liberty and an end to the war, and they had a tense confrontation with officers. Again, drinking among the men was central to their overcoming the fear and tension that prevented outright indiscipline – they turned to the power of wine to mobilize and unify against their commanders. Again, the collective intoxication of the men was instrumental in raising their emotional energy over the threshold for collective action. And again, when they sobered up, their emotional energy crashed.

Rebellions in train stations were commonplace in between late May and the end of July, with similar events happening nearly every day, and most often multiple times a day. All the major stations on the lines connecting the Chemin-des-Dames with Paris saw similar *permissionnaire* rebellions, with Châlons, Creil, and Meaux seeing dozens of events each over a short period of a few weeks. Archival evidence suggests that there were at least 240 such rebellions in train stations between the end of May and early August 1917, with a steep increase as of the first week of June and a similarly steep decrease at the month's end. At first, they were concentrated in the Aisne and Marne, but they quickly spread as far back into the rear as Dunkerque, Le Havre,

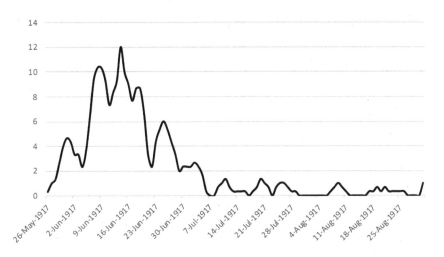

7.1 Frequency of acts of collective indiscipline in train stations.

and even Bordeaux. The available data put their average size at about 150 men, suggesting that at least 36,000 soldiers returning from leave in June and July of 1917 revolted, which is about as many men as mutinied at the front.

Historians have long been aware of these events in train stations but have not investigated them closely, describing them as, in historian André Loez's words, an "echo of" or "halo around" the mutinies at the front, which were the real indiscipline.[11] The problem is not one of documentation: there are hundreds of reports about these events in the French military archives. Nor does it reflect any distinction commanders made at the time. They considered the events at the front and those in train stations to be part of the same anti-war movement.[12] Part of this historical lacuna is the result of a lack of quantification of the events, which has led to their extent, size, and seriousness being underestimated.[13] Part of this is because alcohol played so great a role in the events that it is tempting to dismiss them as mindless drunken hooliganism. Historian of the mutinies Denis Rolland sums up the established wisdom well: revolts in train stations, he contends, "have no other signification than the liberation of unconscious drives by the absorption of alcohol."[14] The interpretation of the revolts provided below again puts the inebriation of men at centre stage. It argues that the rebellions represented not the liberation of unconscious drives, but a conscious extension of the movement against the war begun at the front – they were an act of agency aided by alcohol.

PÉTAIN'S WAR ON WINE AT THE FRONT

To understand how and why the movement against the war migrated west from the Chemin-des-Dames along the rail lines that attached the army zones to the rear, it is necessary to place the revolts in train stations in the context of the early decisions Commander-in-Chief Henri-Philippe Pétain took to address the collapse in morale at the front. As we have seen, part of Pétain's strategy to end the mutinies involved concessions to the demands of the mutineers. These were the carrots, such as better food, more leave (which had important unforeseen consequences that are described below), and an end to wasteful offensives.[15] And indeed, *poilus* welcomed all these changes heartily. For Pedroncini, this was evidence of Pétain's intuitive understanding of his troops. For those of the *consentement patrotique* school of historiography, this was evidence that soldiers largely considered the mutinies to be a successful negotiation for carrots. That school's leading members conclude that, "in the end, the mutinies of 1917 were more about consenting to the war than about rejecting it."[16]

In contrast, those from the *contrainte* school emphasize Pétain's repressive measures, which included the spectacular punishment of alleged ringleaders and disciplining officers for a lack of energy in repression. Moreover, as both Rolland and Loez argue, mutiny was hard to do, and there were only so many men willing to risk themselves and openly defy officers for even a short time. Indeed, by the first week of June, most of the men along the Chemin-des-Dames who were desperate, courageous, or inebriated enough to mutiny had probably already done so. Thus, the *contrainte* school holds, Pétain's repression combined with this exhaustion of human and moral resources to bring the mutinies to an end.

However, because historians have underemphasized the role of wine consumption in the mutinies at the front, they have also missed an important element of Pétain's repressive program there, which was his war on wine in the world-behind-the-war. Beginning in early June, right at the height of the mutinies, Pétain thoroughly reformed the French army's wine policy at the front. Indeed, central to Pétain's ability to bring the army back under control was his establishment of a highly prohibitionary psychotropic regime in the world-behind-the-war, one that would now extend to wine. He attacked on three fronts.

First, Pétain required that the army requisition wine imported to *débits* and so limit the amount imported to a stringent and ungenerous interpretation of military and civilian needs.[17] In his words, from a 30 May note to his commanders: "Experience has demonstrated that if we want – and the need is absolutely essential – to eliminate the abuse [of wine] we must avoid the arrival of wine in excessive quantities in the areas occupied by the army. It is the circulation of wine that we must limit."[18] Pétain also decried the professional and "part-time" wine-sellers who prowled the front. He maintained that eliminating their influence was "one of the most essential and pressing needs" of the army. Military authorities were given the power to requisition wine and close wine shops suspected of being staging grounds for indiscipline.[19]

Second, Pétain changed the way men in the army were paid. As of June 1917, instead of receiving remuneration in cash when they left the trenches, they saw their pay go into a special savings account from which they were permitted to make withdrawals only to purchase items from army-run cooperatives or to send money home.[20] Thus, even if they found wine in *débits*, men would have had trouble purchasing it. At the same time, Pétain *expanded* the system of army cooperatives that sold wine to soldiers, which the postal censorship records suggest was a popular move, as the cooperatives sold good wine at relatively good prices. "We now have a cooperative in the regiment," approvingly reported one soldier in a letter from 11 June, "where we can get anything and above all at a good price, wine for 1.2 f a bottle."[21] But the spread of cooperatives had a dual purpose: it also gave the army the power to better control men's drinking by taking it out of the space of the *débit* and surveilling it in camps. Moreover, soldiers *en repos* were prohibited from leaving their camps for most reasons, and many of the camps were soon surrounded by fencing, which prevented men from going into town on their *pinard* hunts.[22] The result was that if *poilus* wanted to drink, they had to buy from the army and consume under its panoptical supervision.

Third, Pétain purged the army of some of its worst drinkers. He tasked officers at the divisional level with identifying habitual troublemakers and forming them into a "group of incorrigibles" to be "made an example of."[23] Most of the men so identified had numerous infractions related to, as the French code of military justice termed it, "public and manifest drunkenness." Their disciplinary records frequently contained phrases such as "inveterate drunkard," "very bad attitude: this soldier is frequently in a complete state of inebriation," and "an alcoholic with terrible habits."[24] They were sent to the colonies for the rest of the war to dry out. There were not a lot of them – the number is probably less than two thousand[25] – but the point was to discourage future bad behaviour, not purge the army of heavy drinkers, which would have been, after all, catastrophic for French manpower.

But – and this is crucial – Pétain did not want or envision an army of teetotallers. Indeed, Pétain refused to eliminate *eau-de-vie* rations, which he considered a "necessary stimulant," even after his chief medical officer and the Minister of War pressured him to do so. The problem, he explained in a familiar argument, was not that men were drinking *eau-de-vie*. The problem came when they drank it unsupervised in contexts not beneficial to the war effort.[26] Similarly, Pétain did not want soldiers to go without wine; hence the expansion of the cooperative system. This, as we have seen, had the benefit of allowing an accounting of how much men were drinking.[27] Finally, Pétain – to the great acclaim of his troops – increased the daily wine ration to three-quarters of a litre, its highest point during the war.[28] All these actions together meant that men became more dependent upon the army for the wine they desired and required.

This is not to say that reducing or even eliminating men's ability to drink without supervision was the only reason the mutinies ended. Such would grossly overstate the case. But it was undoubtedly a crucial reason, as it increased the difficulty of the contentious performances that characterized so many of the mutinies. As Pétain himself later wrote, "[m]utineers, drunk with slogans and alcohol, must be forced back to their obedience, and every means must be used to reduce to impotence the criminals [i.e. wine-sellers] who had exploited the distress of the fighting troops."[29] Pétain's comprehensive, extended prohibitionary regime worked quickly and in concert with his carrots and sticks. It cannot be a coincidence that the frequency of acts of collective indiscipline at the front plummeted precisely when the new prohibitionary regime was put in place.

But as of early June 1917, there were still places where there was little or no surveillance and control of drinking and plenty of wine to go around, where military authorities had little repressive power, and where thousands upon thousands of men from all over the army mixed in a great human churn. Those places were the train stations that connected the front with the rear, which soldiers travelled through when they went *en permission*. Beginning in late May, the contentious performance that characterized the mutinies spread to the rear along the rail lines the *permissionnaires* rode.

THE IMPORTANCE OF *PERMISSION*

When the French army took the field in 1914, commanders assumed that the war would be short and made no arrangements for soldiers to go on leave. In the war's first months, Commander-in-Chief Joseph Joffre resisted calls to establish a system of rotating leave, arguing that France required every able man to remain on the battlefield.[30] After the war of movement ended, the situation changed. In June 1915, Joffre accepted that regular bouts of *permission* would have benefits for the French economy and the army's morale. Beginning in early July 1915, commanders began to send men on regular leave. The goal was to have around three to four per cent of a unit's effective strength on leave at any given time, with men qualifying for an eight-day leave every six months. By late 1915, *permission* had come to be considered a right among both French politicians and soldiers.[31] There was a further elaboration of the system and its rules in late September 1916, when Joffre issued a circular that became known as the "*Permissionnaires'* Charter," which formally allocated to each *poilu* seven days of leave triannually.[32]

The system of *permission* functioned well enough in between battles, but was put under considerable strain during offensives, when rail traffic was clogged with munitions and the proportion of soldiers on leave was slashed. For example, in early February 1917, before the Nivelle Offensive, the army set its level of leave to five per cent for all units at the front. It then further lowered the level to two per cent on 29 March. The average level of leave across the army hit its lowest point since the *permission* regime was put in place – 3.84 per cent – on 20 April. Four days later, Nivelle removed the restrictions on leave, raising it back to a nominal thirteen per cent.[33] But by that point, the damage was already done: tens of thousands of men along the Chemin-des-Dames were owed leave in the late winter and early spring of 1917. When they did not get it, they felt as though their rights as Frenchmen had been violated.[34]

It was Pétain's generous leave policy that inadvertently set the stage for the rapid spread of revolts in train stations. On 2 June 1917, he issued a new set of instructions regarding leave, broadening it substantially. He also affirmed the army's continued commitment to providing seven days of leave for every four months at the front, with a direct reference to the "*Permissionnaires*' Charter." Leave levels were set at a minimum of thirteen per cent across the army and at twenty-five per cent where possible. And for the units involved in the fighting along the Chemin-des-Dames, the level would be raised to an astounding forty or fifty per cent.[35]

This led to a steep increase in the number of soldiers who travelled through France's train stations in June and July. More than 450,000 were *en permission* by 1 July, coming to 16.35 per cent of the effective strength of the army, with the increase localized in the Aisne and Marne sectors. Thus, the trains that connected the battle along the Chemin-des-Dames to the rear were packed full of *permissionnaires* who were recent witnesses to the indiscipline at the front (or at least privy to rumours about it), disillusioned with command, and unsupervised by officers whom they knew. The effect of Pétain's expansive leave policy, then, was to evacuate from the front thousands of men who either had never had the opportunity to demonstrate or who were, considering Pétain's repressive measures at the front, unwilling to run the risk of mutiny in June or July, and to then throw them into a wine-sodden environment in which indiscipline was temptingly easy.

The presence of civilians, particularly at the debarkation point in Paris at the Gare de l'Est, was of critical importance in these events. In late May and early June, the station was a scene of chaos, and not only because so many *permissionnaires* were travelling through it. At the time, Paris was experiencing its first significant labour unrest since the war's outset, and between mid-May and late August 1917, the city was rocked by around 200 strikes involving around 130,000 women strikers. Demonstrating at the station, they demanded an end to the fighting, calling out "*Vive le paix!*" and "Down with the war!" The women carried red flags, sang the "Internationale," and harangued *permisionnaires* who were departing for the front, encouraging them to revolt. They mixed labour demands with cries for their husbands' return.[36]

In letters picked up by the postal censors, soldiers described the Gare de l'Est as a scene of great disorder. One machine-gunner, for instance, wrote of the "rebellious women" in Paris's stations who were "stopping the *permissionnaires* from coming back before getting satisfaction." The women, he suggested, were part of a large movement against the war that was convulsing all of France, and the troops were serving as the spearhead. "The People" were in revolt against the war, he concluded, noting that "*le poilu, c'est le peuple*."[37] A soldier from the 20è RI – which, recall, was the first unit to demonstrate at the front – wrote on 22 June that "[t]here are on the one hand the demonstrations in the stations by the *poilus*, and on the other it's the women who place themselves in front of and block trains ... This is the beginning of the end."[38] Not all soldiers who witnessed the events in Paris were approbatory, but many saw a mass movement that would link soldiers to civilians and unify French society in protest against the war. As one from the 73è *Régiment de Genie* (RG) reported:

> The *permissionnaires* say that it is a shambles everywhere, I think that if the war does not end soon a revolution will break out, because in Paris there are strikes with women carrying the red flag, I have a friend who while coming back [from *permission*] saw some really worked-up *permissionnaires*, they broke all the windows in the train, they got in the gendarmes' faces, it is becoming ugly.[39]

THE NATURE OF THE EVENTS

The first reported act of collective indiscipline in a train station took place at Saint Simeon, a tiny village on the Paris–Saint Dizier line, at 18h10 on 26 May. *Train de permissionnaires* RV was not supposed to stop in Saint Simeon, but the train in front of it, Commercial 41077, had some mechanical problems and came in for a quick repair, temporarily blocking RV. Soon, as one report recounted, a "quantity" of men, "drunken and over-excited," descended from the train and confronted the station chief. They demanded he provide them with wine, and then surrounded and attacked him. The men continued by assaulting a signaller, taking his flag and beating him with it. After finding that there was no wine to be had, they then climbed back onto the train, which departed at 18h15, making the confrontation a quick five minutes.[40]

In the following days, there were a handful of acts of spontaneous acts of collective indiscipline in the train stations: two on 28 May, one at Damery and the other at Noisy-le-Sec; two again on 29 May, this time at Meaux and Troyes; then four on 30 May and six on 31 May. These events followed the general pattern set at Saint Simeon in that they involved intoxicated men descending from their trains and confronting officers. Events on 30 and 31 May at Dormans are indicative of the general pattern. On both evenings, soldiers, according to one report, "protested loudly" during their passage through the station on the way back to the front. "Down with the war," they called out on 30 May; "We have had enough! We want peace! Long live the revolution! Down with the officers! Off with the officers' heads!" On 31 May soldiers waved red flags that they allegedly obtained from women at the Gare de l'Est. No arrests were made either night because the forces of order were greatly outnumbered.[41]

Documents in the French military archives allow for a detailed construction of one revolt, which took place at Château-Thierry on 7 June 1917. At 1900h on that day, in the haze of the golden hour, *train de permissionaires* RS Ter pulled into the station. It had departed from Paris's Gare de l'Est that afternoon and was scheduled to terminate at Bar-le-Duc at midnight. The train made slow progress, covering about thirty kilometres an hour. This was typical, but that was little consolation for the men, who were stuffed into uncomfortable and soiled third-class accommodations. Many had been travelling and sleeping rough for several days. All had spent boring and frustrating hours kicking around in train stations, with little to do other than drink in *débits*, swap stories, and wait to return to the battle. And all had passed through the radicalizing environment of Paris. Indeed, RS Ter was the last *train de permissionaires* to leave the city that evening, meaning its riders were the last to leave the station's cafés and bars.[42] The weather was unseasonably hot and a little wet, and the men were tired, sweaty, and unkempt. Some were visibly drunk.[43]

When the train pulled in, a small group of *permissionnaires* exploded in protest. The men were dishevelled, "in shirt-sleeves and with heads uncovered," according to one report, which hid the unit designations marked on their caps and jackets and so made them anonymous.[44] Some had collected and packed stones in their haversacks, suggesting they had plans to act out. The rowdy men threw these stones out from the train's windows, smashing streetlights and signs. They cried out, just as did the mutineers at the front, "Down with the war! Long live the revolution! Long live peace!" Seeing the disorder, the agent charged with station security came out to investigate and make arrests. He was wary and on edge. In the past few days there had been dozens of cases of drunken *permissionnaires* demonstrating against the war, destroying materiel, and attacking officers.[45]

The *permissionnaires* harassed a fifty-year-old employee of the rail company on the quay, first calling him a shirker and then jumping down from the train and threatening him. The small police contingent at the station interposed itself between the *permissionnaires* and their victim, only to be attacked itself, with the head of the detachment seriously injured and taken to the hospital. The train's conductor decided to pull out, hoping to force the soldiers back on. All but two got back aboard, seeking safety and anonymity in numbers. The *gendarmes* arrested one of the two refractories while employees of the railway subdued the other, this second described as being "in a state of drunkenness."[46]

The arrest of the latter man precipitated a fresh outbreak of stone-throwing as *permissionnaires* responded with outrage to what they considered the mistreatment of one of their own. The bandwagon grew: seeing the arrests and rough treatment of their comrades spurred men who had until that point been bystanders into becoming active agents of disorder. What was a scuffle became a riot, as hundreds of "fanatics," as one officer described them, blocked the train from leaving and attacked and injured the face of a general named Montbeliard, who happened to be in the station. They then, another report continued, "stampeded through the station in order to free their arrested comrades, adding that they would not leave without them."[47]

Soon came a further step in escalation. A quick-reaction force in the form of a fully armed company of the 120è BCP, an elite unit, arrived after being called from ready status in the immediate area. The men from the 120è BCP fixed their bayonets, loaded their rifles, formed up, and took aim at the *permissionnaires*, who, being without rifles themselves, lost their nerve. They threw their hands up and called out "No bayonets! No bayonets!"[48] Montbeliard, his broken face in his hands, placed himself between the protestors and the forces of order, commanding that the arrested men be released and the 120è BCP stand down. The 120è BCP complied, and this quelled the commotion. The rebellious *permissionaires* remounted their train, keeping with them their two liberated comrades.[49] Once these men climbed back aboard, and at 20h00 – after an hour of tense confrontation and standoff – the train departed. The stone-throwing and shouted imprecations began again. One threat made a particular impact on eyewitnesses. "We will be back soon," the soldiers cried out, "and we will be bringing grenades."[50]

This scene was played out with some variation several more times as RS Ter continued down the line and towards the front, with further reports of disorder coming from the stations at Mézy, Dormans, and Epernay.[51] There are no records of arrests during the rest of the journey, suggesting that most, if not all, of those involved were not punished. The indiscipline ended when the men and their train reached their terminus. At that point the countdown for the return to the carceral world-behind-the-war ended and the gates snapped shut. Gone was the *permissionnaires'* short-lived identity as a group, as whatever bonds they had formed were broken apart when men separated to rejoin their units. Gone too was the window of opportunity presented by the intoxicating anonymity of the train journey itself. Up farther, near the battle, in the closely surveilled world-behind-the-war, men were known to their officers and the consequences of indiscipline were high. And, perhaps most importantly, there was no more wine to be found.

Captain Henri Désagneaux's diary illuminates the difficult situation in which the security forces found themselves during this time. It also provides more evidence that the men who revolted were largely inebriated. Désagneaux was given command of station security at Meaux in the second week of June. He arrived at the station at 9h30 on 7 June and immediately began to organize his men. His travails began just hours later, at 15h00, when the day's first *train de permissionnaires* arrived. As soon as it came to a halt he witnessed "a horde of savages, all the doors opening on both sides [of the train] and the men flooding out on the platforms." The men called out for "death to shirkers" and an end to the war. Luckily, this first group of protestors was loud but not violent. It departed noisily. Another *train de permissionnaires* pulled in at 16h00. This second load of *permissionnaires* "invaded a garden" in a "mad rush" during which "everything was destroyed." They also attacked a house, all the while shouting anti-war slogans. Désagneaux was unable to restore discipline.[52]

The last train of the day arrived at 17h00. These men were the worst of the bunch: they were from RS Ter, the very same who later demonstrated downstream at Château-Thierry, Mézy, Dormans, and Epernay. "As soon as [the train] stops, the troops surge out menacingly," Désagneaux recounted. The men wasted no time before vandalizing trains, which were, he observed, "in a lamentable state; the doors are wrenched off and thrown on the track during the journey; all the windows are broken, and the seats slashed to ribbons."[53] He was helpless to do anything about it. "My men are well-disciplined and will be ready to act at the first signal," he wrote proudly. But they were too few and the protestors too many: "how can I intervene should the need arise," he demanded in his journal, "with thirty or forty men, against a frenzied horde of a thousand individuals, the majority of them in a state of intoxication?"[54] Unhappily, the week to come was much the same for Désagneaux, with analogous events repeating themselves over and over. Every day, he wrote, passed with "the usual cries of down with the war." Some of the protests turned violent, but Désagneaux made only one arrest. He was happy when he and his contingent were replaced on 15 June and ordered to the Chemin-des-Dames.[55] He preferred the front and its Germans to the "hordes" of *poilus* he confronted at Meaux.

But what of the ordinary soldiers who were detailed to station security? What did they think about these rebellions? The French military archives contain, in a happy coincidence, a 9 June postal censorship report from the 120è BCP, the very unit charged with station security at Château-Thierry on 7 June. The disorder the men referenced in their letter extracts undoubtedly referred to the event described above involving RS Ter. These men disliked their assignment. One soldier wrote home that being tasked with "re-establishing order" was "dirty work that could perhaps engender a catastrophe," surely meaning the spectacle of French soldiers firing on French soldiers.[56] He was echoed by a second, who cried out, "Oh! What a dirty job! When will this be over?"[57] Like Désagneaux, the men from the 120è BCP preferred the drudgery and terrors of the trenches to the job of enforcing order in train stations.

Many men from the 120è BCP had little love for the *permissionnaires*, whose movement they feared would continue to build and cascade out of control, subsuming the army in a rising tide of indiscipline. One noted with distaste and a healthy dollop of pessimism that "a General [e.g. Montbeliard] wanted to intervene [and was] beaten, injured, and struck in the face." It was pandemonium, with "scenes of complete anarchy." The security forces – other than the men from the 120è BCP, that is – were "non-existent." Everyone was depressed, with "morale declining from all corners." It was all shameful and alarming: "I don't want to say any more, but if this movement isn't blocked with force like it must be, I foresee a catastrophe."[58] Another described the *permissionnaires* as making a "shocking scandal; they break everything and don't want to go back to the front ... I think that this will go bad and finish one way or another."[59] A third was even more distraught, writing that "there was a big battle in the station, many were injured." He continued: "it seems [an issue] with *permissionnaires* who revolt and break everything; now, the orders are to shoot without hesitation on anyone who makes a tumult."[60] Yet a minority found something to like in the *permissionnaires'* demands, if not the nature of their contentious performance. One soldier from the unit wrote that he "was like everyone else" in that he too "had had it up to here": all the men – the protestors and security forces included – were full of resentment, discord, and moral injury.[61]

What happened at Château-Thierry was very much like the mutinies at the front that were, at that very same moment, amid a steep decline. The *permissionnaires* were driven by the same powerful emotions as the mutineers: fear of returning to the battle at the Chemin-des-Dames and indignation at having to, hatred of the war and what it did to men, and resentment towards those who commanded, which is to say, toward those who inflicted moral injury. The two groups of men shouted the same slogans and called for the death of the same kinds of people – officers, shirkers, and cops, all symbols of military authority and its perversions and absurdities. They sang the "Internationale" and waved the red flag. The forms of contentious collective action were analogous.

At the same time, the indiscipline at Château-Thierry and the mutinies at the front had several crucial differences. In the former, those who protested and those who sought to restore order were strangers to one another, while in the latter, commanders knew exactly who was mutinying. This made *permissionnaires* extra bold and aggressive, and more willing to use force, for commanders could not rely on pre-existing relationships or mutually held respect to bring men back to order. The *permissionnaires* themselves too were strangers to one another, all coming from different units, different regions, and having different experiences. There were no pre-existing primary groups among them, which makes it even more incredible that they came together in a contentious performance to defy their superiors. Yet the bonds they formed and the collective sense of purpose that resulted were terribly fragile and could exist only while the men were intoxicated on the train together. But when they arrived at their destination, they found all the wine shops closed. They must have been disappointed to find that the revolution at the front was already over.

There is scattered archival evidence in the postal censorship records that sheds light upon the experience and motivations of the *permissionnaires*, both witnesses to and participants in the indiscipline.[62] Again, these postal censorship records must be treated critically, as censors were tempted to pull extracts from letters that agreed with their pre-existing beliefs. Moreover, soldiers' letters generally tended to avoid discussions of dramatic events at the front for fear of being caught by the censors. Yet this was not always the case regarding indiscipline in train stations in the late spring and early summer of 1917. Some soldiers wrote about the events at length and confidently, sometimes implicating themselves in the events. They also frequently discuss the role of inebriation therein.

For example, the censorship records contain a complete transcription of a remarkable letter sent by a soldier from the 73è RG that describes his journey from Paris to his terminus in the Aisne on 5 June.[63] His experience can stand in for that of hundreds of thousands of men in the early summer of 1917. The voyage was eventful from the very beginning. At the Gare de l'Est there were scuffles and shouting matches between soldiers and station security. Indeed, *poilus* were eager to denounce the war and demonstrate. They caroused, insulted station agents, and sang the "Internationale" while crying out for the war's end, and this all before their train had even left Paris. At Châtillon-sur-Morin, the men expanded their repertoire, trying to delay the train's departure by descending and refusing to get back on. At Esternay and Sezanne, the men became "very hot," with each station acting as a rung on a ladder leading up to a more spectacular and violent revolt. At each stop the fear that prevented some men from joining in lessened as they saw others demonstrate unmolested and increasingly vocally. As the crowd grew, more and more men became comfortable joining it.

This soldier from the 73è RG emphasized that the men who revolted were drinking and inebriated. Indeed, he observed that what they had drunk before in Paris was not enough. Neither were the bottles they brought with them on the train. At one of the stations, he recounted, "the *poilus* pierced two casks of wine" so they might refill their *bidons*. "The affair got more interesting," he continued, at Sezanne, when the tension broke out into outright violence and near tragedy. Sezanne had a contingent of about fifty *gendarmes* as its station security that came out to confront the intoxicated *permissionnaires*. The latter insulted the former, and during a scuffle, one of the "more zealous" *gendarmes* pulled out a revolver and made threats. The *permissionaires* set upon this man and disarmed him. They proceeded to unhook the train's cars and demanded to return to Paris. The letter's author concluded that "one senses here that there is a hatred for the government, for the *gendarmes*, and above all for the capitalists who fatten themselves to the detriment of our children." "I think," he wrote, "it is time to make peace."[64]

Indeed, if the postal censorship records are any guide, these events in train stations made a large impact on morale. Some who observed them became fatalistically resigned to the army's impending collapse, such as a semi-literate soldier from the 168è RI named Gaston, who wrote in broken French on 31 May:

> But I really believe that [t]his cannot go on much longer like this, because after all the *permissionnaires* who are coming back these days ... they tell us that everyone is in revolt it hasn't ended, in the newspapers they don't tell us what is really happening ... Let this end quickly, I am sick of it.[65]

Others were enthusiastic about the events, such as a soldier from the 70è BCA who wrote home on 30 May that "there arrives a train decorated in red flags on the doors, after having pierced seven or eight casks of the *bon pinard*, it is pillage; then we start to move around a little bit; all the same our patience is about out."[66] His effortless slipping between the third and first person – "there arrives" becomes "we start," and it is "our patience" that is in question – highlights how these protests worked. The man was swept up by the effervescent, intoxicating atmosphere and threw himself in once it reached a critical mass.

Moreover, in the postal censorship records, there are a few letters written by men who admit to being involved directly in rebellions in train stations. One such is from a man involved at events at Meaux on 30 May and deserves to be quoted at length:

> I have never seen a *train de permissionnaires* so excited singing revolutionary songs and crying out down with the war, peace, long live the revolution and other such things and more at every stop descending from the train and broke open the barrels of wine that were on the platform we drank wine cheaply I took the opportunity to fill my *bidon* after what I saw in Paris I believe that the end of the war is near the Parisians want the war to be over by winter and decided as soon as possible.[67]

The prose is breathless, grammar broken, and the passage reads as if the author's hands were still trembling with adrenaline and head still spinning with *pinard* as he wrote it down. But he ties it all together: the drinking, the radicalizing environment of Paris, and the conviction that he is playing a vital role in a larger movement against the war.

THE SPREAD OF THE *PERMISSIONAIRES*' REVOLT

Most threateningly for the French army in early June, the movement against the war broke free of the shackles of the Aisne and Marne. Stations in provincial France began to see rebellions. For instance, Angoulême, in the Charente (far from the Paris and Chemin-des-Dames lines), saw several serious and large acts of collective indiscipline between 3 and 5 June. On 3 June, men harassed station workers and civilians who happened to be nearby. On 4 June, the next group added vandalism to imprecations, breaking streetlamps and windows. They were, according to a report, "for the most part unfortunately taken by drink." For the time being, the station chief theorized, the *permissionnaires* were content to "make a ruckus," but the trend was clear: the destruction of materiel and "words that can injure French sentiments" were only the beginning.[68]

The disorder in the station on 5 June was serious, involving hundreds of men. Second-Lieutenant Beausoleil, an eyewitness to the events, reported that men from two successive trains demonstrated. In front of a sympathetic crowd of civilians, men from the first train shouted out the usual slogans and performed the standard gesticulations. They remounted the train when the time came, and their protest rolled down the line. Just five minutes later, the second rolled in, and the scenes replayed themselves, only more violently. The noise was, Beausoleil insisted, "infernal." Again, the men remounted the train when the time came, and no arrests were made. Unsurprisingly, a large enough portion of them "appeared taken by drink."

Beausoleil was shaken by what he saw. He wrote to his superiors of his "fear that the authorities do not dare try to prevent or calm these protests, [and] attempt to dismiss their importance in their reports," and felt it his duty to report just how bad things were. "The fact that such a protest can take place in two different reprises in an important station like Angoulême, with no intervening authority," he wrote, "permits the men who have taken part to believe and to repeat to their comrades that everything is permitted when they are outside the army zones and more importantly that their be-haviours are approved by the [civilian] population, which comes as though to a theatre to watch these sad and demoralizing scenes."[69]

Events like those in the Charente also took place in Brittany – about as far away as one could get from the Aisne and remain in France – around the same time. On 11 June, men who, according to one report, had "profit-ed" from the alcohol sold in and around train stations turned their *train de permissionnaires*, which had left Quimper at 10h45, into a day-long mobile demonstration. One of them was arrested and subsequently sentenced to five years in prison. On 12 June, *permissionnaires* on the same line demon-strated in a similar fashion, these ones throwing pacifist flyers from their cars. On 15 June, there were violent incidents at Redon, where a civilian was arrested for haranguing and encouraging the *permissionnaires*.[70] The indis-cipline even spread to Dunkerque, where men demonstrated on 11 June.[71]

The army responded with a three-pronged strategy. First, it sought to significantly increase the size and aggressiveness of station security detach-ments and assure that the forces of order would not be so grossly outnum-bered. Second, it sought to identify and punish individual "troublemakers" and "mutineers" and make an example of them. Third, it sought to reduce or eliminate soldiers' drinking in and around train stations by closing alcohol shops, patrolling stations looking for wine-sellers or inebriated men, and closely controlling soldiers' behaviours and movements. The point was to erect a panoptical system of surveillance and control to reduce and control soldiers' drinking and thus re-establish the army's psychotropic power over alcohol. Working together, these three prongs served prevent the men from crossing the threshold of collective action, both by increasing the conse-quences of getting caught and by making men less likely to act out in the first place by keeping them sober.

THE REPRESSION

The army's instinctual reaction to the revolts was to send more forces of order to train stations. On 1 June, in response to the scattered reports of indiscipline that were coming in, it increased the size of security details in train stations throughout the rear-front. For instance, Vic-sur-Aine, whose security was provided by only one officer and four soldiers during May, received an additional detail consisting of one officer and fifteen soldiers, quadrupling the number of men dedicated to station security. At La-Ferté-Milon and Villers-Cotterets both, the detail went from one officer and four men to two officers and thirty-four men. At Crépy-en-Valois, the single officer and thirteen men received an entire company – four sections of around forty or so men – as reinforcements. GQG also assigned elite infantry and *chasseurs* detachments, as well as non-combat territorial and *prévôté* units, to be quick-reaction forces in the event of indiscipline. It reserved automobiles and trains for this purpose.[72]

Pétain's goal was to allow these forces of order to deploy to any train station in the rear-front within three hours of being alerted. When called up, they were to prepare to engage the enemy. According to the orders, "dress will be that of campaign, with arms, cartridges, and haversacs."[73] The men were told too that the enemy might be the alcohol-seller. Patrols were to be tasked specifically with surveilling cafés and *débits* around the train station. Standing orders were to arrest any man "in a state of intoxication" immediately and escort him under armed guard to a prison away from the station.[74]

By 14 June, one officer and twenty men from the second cavalry corps were at the disposition of the station chief at Sezanne. The same arrangements were made at Esternay. These men were armed with Browning semi-automatic pistols.[75] The arrangements seem to have had an immediate effect, as Sezanne experienced no indiscipline after 14 June and Esternay saw but one event. Connantre saw its security detachment increased on 16 June to three officers, six subalterns, ten NCOs, and forty-four men, all of whom would be armed with revolvers.[76] Increases notwithstanding, Connantre's forces could not stop a monster demonstration in the station on 19 June, when the men who composed the security details were "drowned in the flood of *permissionnaires*."[77] On 26 June, even more men were made available, over and above the dedicated detachments in stations for immediate deployment: a minimum of three hundred men and sixty-six gendarmes were designated as a rapid-reaction force in the region.[78] The upshot is that by the end of June, the French army had made significant manpower available to restore order in train stations. Some stations that had previously had security details of five men now had fifty times that number.

This expansion in the security services was paired with another important security measure: the trains themselves received security detachments. Debeney, Pétain's aide, formalized this in an instruction from 28 June 1917, after which date every *train de permissionnaires* would have its own special guard drawn from territorial regiments.[79] Consider, for instance, the 29 June report of *Inspecteur de Police* Hourbette, who rode and patrolled dozens of *trains de permissionnaires* in June, July, and August. In late June, Hourbette noted seeing a soldier call out when he got on the train, warning his comrades, "Attention my friends! The trains are full of police now!"[80] Hourbette did not report seeing any indiscipline, either on his train or in any of the stations at which it stopped, in this or his other reports filed at the end of June and beginning of July. Indeed, the reports from Hourbette and those like him show that as the month neared its end, negative sentiments and observations of disorder became more infrequent on trains.

Moreover, over the month of June, the forces of order became aggressive in making arrests and commanders encouraged energy and initiative. General Émile Fayolle, the commander of Army Group Centre, was adamant about this point in a 5 June note. "Acts of indiscipline," he held, "must be countered with the greatest energy and the man who is culpable must be brought before a military tribunal every time it is possible."[81] Pétain was of the same mind, lamenting that some officers "have not demonstrated repression, initiative, or the necessary energy." "Inertia is complicity," he declared.[82] As he put it in an 11 June note to his commanders: "it is imperative that the punishment follow the fault as closely as possible to strike the imagination of those for whom the sentiment of duty is not strong enough to keep them on the right path."[83]

The army began in mid-June putting soldiers involved in acts of indiscipline in train stations directly in front of special military tribunals.[84] Some of these convicted soldiers for relatively minor charges that resulted in a month or two of jail time. Others convicted soldiers on more serious charges of revolt or rebellion and gave *permissionnaires* up to five years of hard time in prison. Consider, for instance, the case of events at the station of Clermont on 16 June, when, in a familiar pattern, a soldier cried out anti-war slogans, the security forces arrested him, and there followed a brawl on the quay and arrests.[85] Four men were charged, all with "violence against superiors, outrages, and attempting to facilitate evasion."[86] These were serious charges that could lead to years of imprisonment.

Crucially, as of the second week of June 1917, the army began to punish members of security forces involved in suppressing acts of rebellion in train stations when they failed to show the requisite "energy" in confronting protestors. This was what happened to Sous-Lieutenant Goviller, the *chef* of the security forces at Créil, on 11 June, who was punished with fifteen days in prison for "not knowing how to maintain discipline and repress the offences committed" when train HZ came through his station on 8 June.[87] Georges Louis Humbert, the commander of Third Army, was particularly vigilant in punishing the forces of order for failing to use force to restore order. On 17 June, he wrote to all the commanders under him that "certain officers charged with maintaining order, either in the stations, or on the *trains de permissionnaires,* have not shown the necessary energy in the course of these latest incidents."[88] Officers, he thundered, were acting as if "afraid of their men," and "far from intervening, they pretend not to see anything and do not report the facts about what they have witnessed."[89] If they did not show more energy, they would be made an example of. Humbert's word was good. He intervened in individual cases to increase punishments and prison sentences, a startling kind of micro-management for a commander of his rank.[90]

Just as important as increasing the size of the security forces and energetic repression was a serious crackdown on drinking. As of mid-June, the highest levels of the army had concluded that excessive wine consumption in train stations was a primary cause of indiscipline, as men on trains and lingering around stations were, according to one report, "pressed to drink in excess and [followed] bad advice."[91] A report from the Minister of War mid-month requested special patrols dedicated to preventing drinking be put in place in the stations through which *permissionnaires* travelled. The cabinet demanded: "We ask that you immediately begin to surveille the stations in the strictest fashion, and to rigorously apply the laws upon alcohol-sellers involving public drunkenness, and to find and arrest individual suspects."[92] On 19 June, one such inspecting agent of order, Guillemin, wrote of how "it is essential to prevent men drunk men from getting on trains back to the front and to eliminate their ability to purchase wine during the trip"; another, Jacqot, wrote that "drunkards must be isolated at special trains and sent on only after the end of their intoxication"; and a third, Roussel, wrote that *all* the indiscipline was due to "men who were abominably drunk."[93] As long as drunkenness was endemic in train stations, commanders believed, so too would be rebellion.

Indeed, central to Pétain's strategy to fight indiscipline in train stations was establishing tight control over men's drinking there. Pétain made this plain on 10 July 1917, when he issued specific guidelines for how different kinds of train stations were to accommodate their *permissionnaires*. He identified three kinds of stations through which *permissionnaires* flowed, all of which would be reconfigured spatially to allow for the prevention and surveillance of drinking.

First were the "Assembly Stations," major nodes in the network such as Château-Thierry, Troyes, and Bar-le-Duc that handled thousands of *permissionnaires*. In these stations, large camps that served as massive waiting rooms were constructed. According to official instructions, the camps were to be "seriously closed – chain link fence topped with barbed-wire."[94] They had guarded entrances and exits with their own bathrooms, some beds, tables for card and board games, reading rooms, and a cooperative selling wine. While in camp, each soldier would be given the option of purchasing one token [*jeton*] redeemable for a single litre of wine.[95] This effectively capped the amount of wine that could be distributed to a manageable level. It would no longer flow *à volonté*, and men could no longer drink in the shelter of the *débit*. The point was not to eliminate men's drinking entirely but rather to discipline it and bring it back under the army's control.

The second kind of station, the "Bifurcation Stations," handled many fewer men, but still could see hundreds of *permissionnaires* getting on and off during a day. These stations were also to have specific enclosed waiting areas [*camps d'attente*] for *permissionnaires* with some latrines, beds, a tobacco shop, some writing desks, and a cooperative that sold only beer, not wine.[96] The reasoning was that soldiers had to drink something in the summer heat, and it would be much harder to get drunk on fizzy beer than on wine. There was also to be an anti-alcohol blitz out of the dreams of the prohibitionists of the *fin-de-siècle*: "All along the quay," Pétain's *Instruction* demanded, there would be small stations distributing non-alcoholic drinks such as coffee and tea to soldiers.[97]

The third kind of stations were designated "Embarkment and Debarkment Stations." These were the biggest of France's regional rail stations, including Dunkerque, Lyon, Bordeaux, and Paris. They were too large and too built into urban spaces to make dedicated, isolated waiting camps possible. Instead, the surveillance of *permissionnaires* was conducted by police agents on the ground, who circulated in the crowd. These agents made sure that no large groups of *permissionnaires* formed and that there were no men lingering about.[98] Even then, the army was to set up open-air "reduced installations" of the services provided in the waiting camps, meaning tables providing non-alcoholic drinks and giving out soup and water for free (nobly described as protecting soldiers from the "rapacity of the merchants," but in reality restricting their access to alcohol), tables and chairs, and lavatories.[99] The main purpose of all this was, according to the *Instruction*, "to regulariz[e] and limit the amount of wine sold."[100]

By early July, the effectiveness of the security forces' focus on keeping *permissionnaires* away from civilians and drink was clear. Consider, for example, the following, from a 21 June report authored by a police inspector detailed to *trains de permissionnaires* based out of Crépy-en-Valois, just while security forces were in the midst of being pumped up and police detachments placed on trains. He describes the nightmare situation in which the security forces could find themselves mid-month:

> It can be estimated to happen several hundred times a day. The already almost sloshed *permissionnaires* manage to slip into town, despite the surveillance, and they go to the cafés, and when closing time comes, they get the civilians to top off their *bidons*. They head back in small groups, in a complete state of drunkenness, and it is at this time that the sometimes violent mixing happens, that seditious cries are uttered, cries of drunkards who had never cared for propaganda. The streets around the station are stuffed full of drunken soldiers, laying on the sidewalks, talking or drinking their wine.[101]

Less than three weeks later, things were entirely different, as evidenced by the reports filed again by the police officer Hourbette, who was detailed to ride amongst the *permissionnaires*. In the early afternoon on 10 July, Hourbette boarded a *train de permissionnaires* leaving Paris and heading to Jonchery, just outside of Reims. He was on the train when it pulled into Crépy-en-Valois, where its riders were scheduled to switch trains. Hourbette reported that, immediately upon their arrival, the "soldiers were directed towards the waiting area [*camp d'attente*], close to the station's entry, where the trains stop."[102] During the wait, the station's security services prohibited all soldiers from leaving the waiting area and heading into town in search of wine. Per regulations, special army canteens installed in the waiting area served soldiers "the food and drink necessary," but no more – presumably only beer and non-alcoholic drinks.[103] The men were thus prevented from contacting civilians, denied the opportunity to purchase wine, and placed under close surveillance to prevent their drinking excessively. The most important effect of the extension of the prohibition system to wine was the dramatic reduction in the consumption of alcohol among *permissionnaires* returning to the front.

Much of what the French forces of order learned about the nature of acts of indiscipline in train stations, as well as what it had done to combat them, can be gleaned from a reading of a long synoptic report from 10 July 1917. The author identified several causes of indiscipline in train stations. There was first the fear men experienced when returning from *permission*, as they got closer to the front and thus closer to again coming under fire along the Aisne. There was then the lack of surveillance in stations throughout June, where just about anyone was ostensibly able to enter, exit, and circulate. There also was the bad influence of Paris itself, whose Gare de l'Est was "infested with streetwalkers and shady people who incite the soldiers to refuse to rejoin their corps."[104] And finally, there was, above all, alcohol:

> In a general sense, the most serious acts [of collective indiscipline] are always committed by men taken with drink, their drunkenness provoked by the abuse of wine ... It is always easy for men to procure *pinard* for themselves.[105]

The report concluded that "the spirits and morale of the troops [are] improving gradually from day to day. Drunkenness is the one problem to combat with the most energy."[106]

Such was the conclusion of the army. Indeed, it was controlling, reducing, or eliminating *permissionnaires'* ability to drink that proved most important in bringing about the precipitous decline in acts of collective indiscipline in train stations witnessed in first week of July. Without wine and its social effects, men found the barrier of fear and tension that came with outright indiscipline too high to cross. As of mid-July 1917, the French security forces in train stations had erected a sophisticated apparatus of surveillance and control focused on restricting and limiting men's access to wine. And this new, more robust prohibition system worked. As of late summer 1917, soldiers found it difficult to find alcohol of any kind outside of what the army supplied. Denying men wine helped keep their thresholds for collective action high, high enough to make this form of demonstration too difficult to participate in.

RECONSIDERING THE CHRONOLOGY OF THE MUTINIES

Rebellions in train stations were an irreducible part of the movement against the war launched by the mutineers at the front. Soldiers disillusioned with the Aisne offensive, fearing the return to battle and distraught at what they had seen in the rear, adapted the repertoire of protest developed by the mutineers and deployed it in a new context. Thinking about the mutinies and the revolts in train stations as part of the same movement against the war implies that historians' understanding of the chronology of the crisis of indiscipline in the French army in 1917 needs revision.

As we have seen, historians have typically dated the end of the movement to mid-June, after which men at the front all but stopped demonstrating. But this was precisely the time that acts of collective indiscipline began to spread through the rear, not the time the crisis ended, which is clear when the difference between the number of mutinies at the front and revolts in train stations are graphed chronologically. If we combine the number of mutinies at the front with the number of rebellions in train stations, we can see that indiscipline in the French army plateaued through the entire month of June.

A better chronology of the indiscipline would include rebellions in train stations alongside mutinies at the front. Demonstrations against the war endured through the entire month of June at roughly equal severity, with around ten events each day, and this implies that whatever brought an end to the indiscipline did so in early July, not early June. The standard explanations of the indiscipline's end – which focus on what Pétain did to fight mutinies at the front – are in this sense inadequate, as they cannot account for the beginning, duration, or end of the demonstrations that spread through the train stations. This is not to say that Pétain's changes in strategy, granting more leave, pledging to improve conditions, and repression were irrelevant in bringing the indiscipline to a close. Rather, it is to say that the effects of these changes were not the proximal cause of the indiscipline's end, for it continued to spread for nearly another month. Indeed, as we have seen, in the case of expanding *permission*, Pétain's changes inadvertently contributed to the disorder.

This movement was an expression of a deep hatred for the war and of the feelings – fear, resentment, existential panic – that men ordinarily drank to escape or overcome. But in the context of both the mutinies at the front

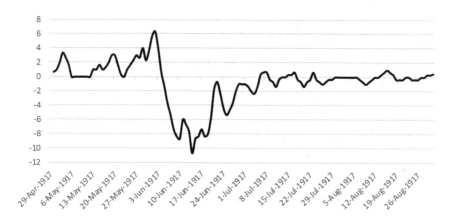

7.2 Difference between indiscipline at the front and indiscipline in train stations.

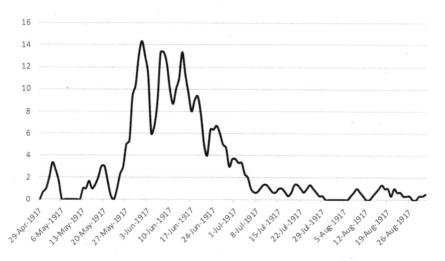

7.3 Frequency of acts of collective indiscipline at the front and in train stations.

and the rebellions in train stations, men drank to help them in translating the fear and rage that came with moral injury into collective action. In both cases they *drank to disobey*. Indeed, drinking lowered the threshold for collective action among both those who drank intending to revolt *and* those who drank intending no such thing. Those who rebelled seized a fleeting and unique opportunity to be as their own masters and lash out at symbols of command. And again, cafés and bars served as the nodes in an informal

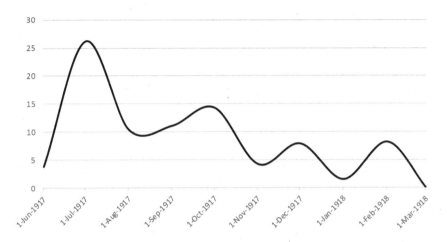

7.4 Percentage of military tribunals in the GAN related to drunkenness, July 1917–March 1918.

communication network through which information and rumours about the indiscipline spread, and as shelters in which men drank and plotted together. It was during their search for *pinard* that they found one another, and over drinks when they talked and told stories that they recognized one another as like-minded. And it was by fighting against alcohol and in the process vigorously asserting the army's power over soldiers' drinking that Pétain bought the time he needed for the army to heal. The indiscipline ended with the extension of the prohibition system to wine and the re-establishment of emotional and behavioural control over soldiers.

The clearest evidence that Pétain's newly robust prohibitionary regime – one that now, it is imperative to emphasize, included *eau-de-vie* and wine – re-established psychotropic control over the army is the rapid decline of acts of collective indiscipline at the front and in train stations in the summer of 1917. But this is not the only evidence. The postal censorship records from that summer suggest two things: first that *poilus* found the *mercantis'* wine increasingly expensive and harder to find, and second that they appreciated the cooperatives that sold good wine at a reasonable price. This strongly indicates that the army's program of driving up the cost of wine outside of that supplied by the army and making it harder to find, as well as the program of surveilling men's alcohol consumption in camps, were effective.

But perhaps the strongest evidence of the robustness of the army's post-mutinies psychotropic regime comes from disciplinary records. Military tribunals from the Army of the North between June 1917 and March 1918 tell a clear story. Of 646 convictions over this period, 11.3 per cent related to drunkenness. The data show a clear decline over this period, with convictions for drunkenness as a percentage of total tribunals at its highest point in July 1917 (when they consisted of 26.2 per cent of all convictions) and its lowest in March 1918 (when they consisted of 0 per cent of convictions).

The French military archives, unfortunately, contain virtually no information on the army's alcohol rations after late 1917, so it is difficult to chart the functioning of the daily, battle, and prohibition systems from that point onward. I would speculate that they continued to function as Pétain intended until March 1918, when the Germans' spring offensive broke through the British and French lines and restored movement to the battlefield. In their personal narratives, men report that they continued to drink during the battle of movement and the Hundred Days offensive – the psychotropic program functioned until the war's end on 11 November 1918.

EPILOGUE

LE PÈRE PINARD AFTER THE WAR

After the war, the cult of *pinard* was celebrated as a patriotic expression of French identity. The drink itself was, along with France's famously belligerent Prime Minister Georges Clemenceau and the ever-cool Henri-Philippe Pétain, hailed as one of the fathers of victory.[1] Wine, just as French doctors and commanders intended, raised emotional energy and gave *poilus* the physical feeling of patriotism, and this, they claimed, helped them endure to the end. Unsurprisingly, in their personal narratives published after the war, soldiers lionized the drink. So did those trench journals that continued to publish into 1919. The cult was still vigorous as late as 1938, when Jules Laurent edited and published a memorial compendium of *pinard* lore, *Le Maréchal Pinard*.[2] In his "Preface" to the volume, the future Nazi collaborator Paul Chack explained:

> And here is a work dedicated to the *Pinard* that gave heart to so many chests. Soldiers named it the marshal [*maréchal*]. They were right. This Marshal of France greatly helped to win the war.[3]

The collection began with a "Hymn to *Pinard*" ("You make us forget the sorrows that plague us," etc.).[4] It then moved to a short play featuring a similar hymn to *gnôle*:

À ceux qui sont crevés, fourbus,	[Those who are tired, exhausted,]
Quand, martelés par les obus,	[When, hammered by the shells,]
Le coeur flageole	[The heart trembles]

> *À tous ceux qui n'en peuvent plus,*   [For those who can't take it anymore]
> *Verse la gnôle*[5]   [Pour the *gnôle*]

It continued through more poems, songs, and short stories in much the same vein. The veteran Charles Delvert, in one such story, declared:

> *Pinard!* Beneficent *pinard!* You replaced for all the need to sleep. We felt the heat that you give, as they say, from the heart to the stomach, to be able to persuade the *boches* that one does not violate with impunity the soil of our France, from which the magnificent grapes spring forth.[6]

The language clearly echoes that of the war's trench journals. It was certain to warm the hearts and inspire reminiscences among the veterans who gathered and drank in their clubs.

Yet, despite the fulsome reverence of *pinard* the nation over, the French wine industry faced several challenges in the interwar period: many vineyards had been destroyed through firepower and neglect during the fighting; export markets had collapsed; and the casualties of war meant that the viticultural labour force was reduced and demand for wine slackened. Indeed, French doctors' plan to use the ration to train men to drink wine was only half successful: those soldiers who lived through the war likely drank more, but many men of prime drinking age did not live or were horribly injured. As historian Rod Phillips notes wryly, "[t]he belief that a *pinard*-drinking army would become a large wine-drinking population was predicated upon the soldiers' surviving the war."[7]

Despite these depressing factors, the interwar French wine industry produced an over-abundance because of large harvests throughout the 1920s and 1930s. The result was, according to Phillips, a "serious oversupply" of the drink by the late 1920s.[8] In the 1930s, the French state intervened to protect the wine industry from overproduction. On the one hand, it introduced complicated new taxation and classification systems intended to regulate wine production and assure quality.[9] On the other, it sought to boost demand by associating wine-drinking with health and patriotism through a public-relations campaign via posters and billboards, sensational flashing neon signs, radio broadcasts, strategic placement in films, and pedagogical materials for schoolchildren.[10]

E.1 "Now for you, a cork" (1919).

The effect of these government interventions was modest. Consumption statistics provided by historian Sarah Howard show a slight increase in total wine consumption among adults between 1920 and 1939. While the numbers can vary widely from year to year, they were still quite high vis-à-vis prewar statistics. The French drank a maximum of 283 litres of wine per adult in

1922 (followed closely by 1934 with 272 litres) and a minimum of 152 litres in 1936. The average was 214 litres.[11] This was forty-six per cent more than civilian adults had consumed during the war, and about twenty per cent more than they had consumed between 1900 and 1913. Historian Charles Ridel concludes that, when consumption of distilled alcohol – which also grew, despite the permanent ban on absinthe – is considered alongside that of wine, the 1930s were the "most alcoholic [alcoolisée]" in France's history.[12] Increasing numbers of French temperance reformers began even to discourage wine consumption.[13]

The army's daily wine ration survived after the war, with French soldiers in the interwar period due half a litre per man per day – although this meant a reduction from wartime rations, which, recall, were set at .75 litres. There seem, again, to have been no plans for the mass distribution of alcohol in the event of a conflict. The army was to march on water and plenty of coffee, although there was an official wine ration on the books.[14] It once again became an advocate of the French style of temperance, one harsh on distilled alcohol and soft on wine. Military handbooks specified explicitly that soldiers on campaign were to abstain from "alcoholic beverages [boissons alcoolisées]" to "preserve [their] physical strength and resistance to fatigue." Consuming such beverages, it held, "predisposes [men] to the most serious accidents."[15] The division between good, healthy wine and bad, unhealthy distilled alcohol remained powerful in army culture and practice.

One military handbook, for example, warned that the distilled alcohol drinker suffered from, among other unenviable symptoms, "nightmares with visions of ferocious animals ... 'alcoholic cynicism' ... [and] moral degradation."[16] But this sentiment was tempered when it came to healthy wine, with the same manual proclaiming it to be "an excellent drink when consumed in moderate doses." It reviewed some of the recent science on the matter: "wine, by way of its organoleptic [organoleptique] properties, is an agreeable stimulant for the nervous system; thus it is recommended for bodies a little weakened by excess work." Even the alcohol contained in wine was of a different quality from that in the distilled stuff. Rather than poisoning the body, it "acts as a stimulant, as a tonic for the nervous system, and it raises hemoglobin levels in the blood."[17] In other words, wine makes blood redder and more energetic on a cellular level and so drives activity in the name of the nation and race – a clear hearkening back to the patriotic biomedical language and logic of the French doctors who justified the wine ration in 1915.

So it is unsurprising that in the fall of 1939, at the beginning of the "Phoney War [*drôle de guerre*]," *pinard* was again mobilized as a weapon in French war culture. As early as mid-September, just days after the declaration of war, wine's evangelists began demanding that French soldiers receive a daily ration while on campaign. "*Pinard* won the war-to-end-all-wars [*la der des ders*]," wrote Émile Condroyer in *Le Journal*, "[and] *pinard* will win this one." The drink, he concluded, would once again "beat the *boches*."[18] Edouard Barthe, a lawmaker from the Hérault who was known among colleagues as the "wine deputy," emphasized that *pinard* had a dual action that would be beneficial for military effectiveness: "it is at the same time a strengthener during the hard days of winter that provides calories to the body and a comfort through the optimistic euphoria that it gives men."[19] And so the cult of *pinard*, perhaps inevitably, was remobilized.

In a reprise of the First World War's *vin aux soldats* campaign, Barthe launched the "soldier's mulled wine campaign [*oeuvre du vin chaud du soldat*]," which again sought to drum up public support for wine for its special hygienic, nervine, and moral properties.[20] A campaign for wine donations began in October 1939 and garnered wide praise in the press. Wine was necessary for the "joy and comfort of the soldier," *Le Matin* held in November. It reported happily that "fountains of *pinard*" were beginning to be distributed to soldiers at the Gare de l'Est.[21] Other journals printed doggerel in *pinard*'s honour. Consider this poem from the right-wing *Je suis partout*:

Celui qui chasse le cafard:	[It's what hunts the *cafard*:]
C'est l'général Pinard!	[It's General *Pinard*!]
Celui qui rend l'poilu gaillard:	[It's what makes the *poilu* strong:]
C'est l'général Pinard!	[It's General *Pinard*!]
Celui qu'aura l'boche en peinard:	[It's what will defeat the *boche*:]
C'est l'général Pinard!	[It's General *Pinard*!]
Et lui foutra son pied quelqu'part:	[It will put its foot somewhere:]
C'est l'général Pinard![22]	[It's General *Pinard*!]

Or this one from the local paper *Le Grand écho de l'Aisne*:

Pour vous protéger du cafard	[To protect you from the *cafard*]
Pour éviter les traquenards,	[To avoid the traps,]
Vive le Pinard!	[Long live *pinard*!]
Pour trouver les temps toujours beau	[To find the weather always beautiful]
Pour avoir le moral bien haut	[To keep your spirits high]
Vive le vin chaud![23]	[Long live mulled wine!]

And once again, Pierre Viala – who was, recall, perhaps the greatest supporter of wine for soldiers during the First World War – extolled wine's benefits in his *Revue de viticulture*, even going so far in 1940 as to reprint parts of his 1916 essay in support of the wine ration.[24]

Thus the entire world of suffering, courage, and triumph that was encapsulated in the condensed symbol *pinard* was excavated and mobilized at the beginning of the Second World War: we hear the powerfully patriotic language of the First World War repurposed. Again, there is the *cafard*, the *poilus*, the *boches*, and the promise of victory. Again, *le Père Pinard* would fuel the French army and help the French soldier put the invading Germans in their place. Wine's mythological place in France's war culture was revived.

But, of course, it was not to be. Instead of a glorious victory in the late spring of 1940, when the Phoney War turned real, France experienced the wholesale collapse of its armed forces within a matter of weeks. Rather than fight a cataclysmic battle on the Dyle in Belgium as the French had predicted, the German army pushed through the under-guarded Ardennes, sweeping around behind the French in a reverse Schlieffen Plan and pinning them in the north against the Channel. The war in France was seemingly over before it even began, with the armistice signed on 20 June 1940. Pétain, the hero of the First World War, became the head of the rightfully maligned collaborationist "French State" based in the spa town of Vichy.

THE PSYCHOTROPIC LANDSCAPE OF MODERN WAR

In late 1915, a rumour circulated among the French regarding the German army's use of a novel stimulant drug that increased combat effectiveness. Strange *pilules* [little pills], the rumour held, had been found on the bodies of German soldiers, although it is not clear who found them, or where, or when. In October 1915, several French newspapers reported that, per prisoner testimonies reported in the Russian press, German soldiers were provided with "two of these *pilules* each day, primarily before attacks or during particularly hard times in the trenches," and had to swallow them in the presence of their officers. The pills made them feel fearless and powerful.[25] A follow-up article, reprinted several times, provided more detail: the *pilules* supposedly, again according to the testimonies of German prisoners, gave men a "mild sense of drunkenness" that made them feel brave and a "flood of energy" that stimulated them "for a short time."[26]

The rumour is fascinating as a projected fantasy of the very brand of psychotropic power France was exercising over its soldiers at the time. In truth, such *pilules* did not exist during the First World War, for the Germans had not yet invented them. But they had by the Second. In the late 1930s, German scientists tested methamphetamine (first commercially synthesized in 1929 for use as an asthma medication) for its properties as a vigilance and energy enhancer and obtained good results. In 1939 – just in time for the *Blitzkrieg* – the German army adopted a ration of the drug, which was intended to increase combat effectiveness.

Historians Nicolas Rasmussen and Lukasz Kamienski argue that the speed of the German advances in Poland and France in 1939 and 1940, respectively, is inextricable from the Nazis' use of methamphetamine on the battlefield. The drug, they claim, helped adapt men pharmacologically to the invasions' frenetic pace and thus allowed for complete success. "The German *Blitzkrieg*," holds Rasmussen, "was powered by amphetamines as much as it was powered by machines."[27] This is, however, to overstate the case. Poland's defeat was due more to the country's paucity in men, armour, and aircraft than to German operational brilliance, however chemically fuelled. And France's fall was due more to the spectacular overconfidence and operational incompetence of the country's high command than to the indefatigableness and tactical virtuosity of German super-soldiers hopped up on methamphetamine.

German soldiers on the Eastern Front also received methamphetamine, which they called "Tank Chocolate" or "Hermann-Göring-Pills," after the legendarily over-dressed and inevitably drug-addled high-ranking Nazi. According to Kamienski, there was a racial and ideological basis to methamphetamine distributions, which were to make soldiers into the very image of the *Übermench*. As he writes, "[methamphetamine] was hoped to turn the Luftwaffe pilots, Wehrmacht soldiers, and Kriegsmarine sailors into superhuman warriors, or, in a word, to produce an army of true Aryan *heroes*."[28] Yet the power of methamphetamine to raise morale and pharmacologically construct super-soldiers was tempered by its negative qualities, for the drug proved to be highly addictive and led to compulsive redosing. The threats of physiological dependence and methamphetamine psychosis meant that consumption had to be regulated, however imperfectly this was done in practice.[29] Moreover, the number of pills distributed was not particularly excessive given the size of the German armed forces, and the dosages were restrained.[30]

The logic of the methamphetamine ration thus tracks with the logic of the French army's alcohol rations during the First World War: both were mechanisms of emotional and behavioural conditioning via the exercise of psychotropic power, and both served to create a certain type of psychotropic regime at their respective fronts. This is not, though, to say that the latter inspired the former directly. Rather, it is to say that the conditions of modern warfare provide both the need for, and the opportunity to conduct, experiments in the strategic mass distribution of psychotropic drugs to generate and sustain fighting power under highly adverse conditions.

Indeed, the Germans went even further than methamphetamine in their quest to create super-soldiers. In 1944, they began to test a drug called D-IX, a daring mix of cocaine, methamphetamine, and Eukodal, a powerful synthetic opioid. D-IX produced a high level of euphoria, energy, and imperviousness to pain. Early tests involving concentration camp inmates were evilly promising: prisoners marched around the clock until they literally dropped dead from exhaustion, sometimes covering up to ninety kilometres in a day. Fortunately, the drug – a pharmaceutical super-weapon to accompany the V1 and V2 programs – never went into mass production.[31]

Indeed, the Second World War was generally speedy.[32] Britain's Royal Air Force explicitly copied the Luftwaffe's psychotropic practices after finding methamphetamine pills on captured German pilots. In 1941 it ran a series of experiments to see whether amphetamine or methamphetamine was a better drug to increase combat effectiveness. It settled on the former and distributed it to its own pilots, navigators, and gunners. British ground forces in North Africa also received tablets of Benzedrine-brand amphetamine.[33] American airmen, soldiers, and marines from Dunkerque to Tawara received the same drug. Kamienski cites one study that claims some eighty-five per cent of American GIs took the drug regularly, although this seems like an exaggeration.[34] He also notes how the Japanese broke a long cultural aversion to psychotropic drugs to provide methamphetamine to the Emperor's suicidally courageous pilots and soldiers. In the Japanese military, the drug was distributed in a ritualistic manner.[35] The interoceptive and affective sensations it produced – which is to say, a rush of energy, focus, and vigilance – thus raised emotional energy and provided a psychotropic preparation for the dead-end liminal experience to come. In this way, Japanese practices mirrored the logic of the French battle system of the First World War. Indeed, according to Rasmussen, the Japanese referred to methamphetamine as the "drug to inspire the fighting spirits."[36] It was psychotropic power in a pill.

Indeed, of all the major belligerents in the Second World War, only the Soviet army did not employ stimulants as a source of psychotropic power. The Soviets employed the same strategy as did the French in the First World War, which is to say, they distributed large rations of alcohol. The official vodka ration in the Red Army was .1 litres per man per day, about twice what the *poilus* got in their daily *eau-de-vie* ration during the First World War. But, among the "Ivans," the amount was routinely exceeded in practice. As Kamienski shows, Soviet soldiers developed a unique heavy drinking culture: they drank not only their rations and more, but whatever they could that contained ethanol, including "solvent, brake fluid, or antifreeze" – which suggests that the vodka rations were insufficient and irregular.[37] Moreover, as historian Edward B. Westermann has recently argued, despite harsh penalties for drunkenness on the books, frequent and liberal consumption of alcohol played an important role in the *Wehrmacht* on the Eastern Front, both in battle and in its genocidal violence in the rear, where the intoxication from alcohol and the intoxication from destruction had a dialectically accelerationist relationship. Indeed, there is a good case to be made that alcohol was a more important psychotropic drug for the Nazis than methamphetamine.[38] In any case, drinking was certainly central in the utterly apocalyptic bloodlands of the east.

Stimulants have largely dominated the postwar psychotropic landscape in military affairs. Such was the case in the twentieth century's colonial wars. For example, the French paratroopers who tenaciously defended Dien Bien Phu consumed Maxiton, a brand name for dextroamphetamine.[39] In his epic novel about the *paras*, *The Centurions* (1960), Jean Larteguy draws a picture of the benefits and drawbacks of doing so. During the battle, the paratrooper

225

Lescure consumes a large dose of Maxiton and then "takes part in every attack and counter-attack, living in a sort of secondary state of consciousness." He then suffers through a kind of psychotic withdrawal while in a Vietnamese re-education camp – as spartan an environment for a detox as imaginable – and repeatedly screams out nonsensically, "Some chickens! Some ducks!"[40]

American pilots from Korea onwards have taken amphetamine "go-pills."[41] This was at least the case until 2002's Tarnak Farm Incident, which involved an American F-16 pilot who had taken dextroamphetamine mistakenly bombing a Canadian base, killing four and injuring eight. Afterwards, the USAF began supplying its pilots with a novel non-amphetamine stimulant, modafinil (trade name Provigil).[42] American soldiers and marines on the ground during the so-called "Global War on Terror" did not receive stimulants from the army or corps and relied instead on super-caffeinated diet pills with the inimitable name "Ripped Fuel."[43] American special operators, however, still receive amphetamines. As do their enemies: ISIS and other jihadist fighters take large doses of Captagon, a crude amphetamine analogue.[44] They also sell the drug in Europe's discotheques to fund their murderous ideology.[45] And this is to speak only of stimulants and to say nothing of the bizarre mid-twentieth-century American military obsession with mind-control drugs.[46]

This short history suggests that the will to psychotropic power has been robust and durable in militaries after the First World War; many have sought to manipulate and direct emotional experiences and behaviours with psychotropic drugs. Again, this is not to say that these militaries explicitly copied the technique of psychotropic power earlier exemplified by the French army's alcohol policies on the Western Front. Rather, it is to say that after the First World War, the exercise of psychotropic power became immanent to the conduct of modern war, which is so taxing and hellish as to call out for, or even necessitate, pharmacological help when possible.

The French experiment with the daily, battle, and prohibition systems – as successful as it was – employed, it must be admitted, a rather crude psychotropic. With advances in the medical and pharmacological sciences, more targeted interventions became possible – and ever more targeted interventions are being researched. Yet, while the pharmacopeia available to modern warfighters and those who seek to augment and control them has become much more bountiful, the inner psychotropic logic of the distribution of drugs remains the same as was the case with French alcohol policy on the Western Front – this psychotropic logic is, I would argue, indigenous to the modern conduct of war, which always seeks to optimize the warfighter through biochemical means. The distribution of drugs thought necessary to adapt soldiers to the high-stress physical and emotional environments that come with modern war represents the exercise of biopower on not a molar or somatic scale, but one even finer: the molecular scale. And because soldiers *can* be chemically augmented and enhanced in ways that increase their morale and fighting power, militaries inevitably have sought and will continue to seek the most efficacious means of doing so.

As we have seen, drinking strategically distributed alcohol was central to the experience of soldiering in the French army in the First World War. Through the workings of the daily, battle, and prohibition systems, the army established a progressively more robust psychotropic regime at the front that employed psychotropic power to generate shared emotional experiences and group behaviours among soldiers. These experiences and behaviours were beneficial to generating and maintaining morale because they mobilized the intoxication concepts regarding wine and *eau-de-vie* that already circulated in French culture. The daily system, through the cult of *pinard*, enlivened men and provided them with the physical sensation of patriotism in their bodies; the battle system, through the extraordinary distributions of *gnôle* before battle, prepared them to kill and be killed; and the prohibition system, initially focused primarily on distilled alcohol but, after the mutinies, extended to wine, assured that men only drank when the army wanted them to drink and could surveille their consumption. Controlled alcoholic intoxication, in short, was widely weaponized by the French army on the Western Front. It is impossible to understand the *poilu*'s experience of the war without taking it into account.

But just as important as the peculiar Frenchness of the case study presented in this book and its temporal and spatial boundedness are its broader implications for modern history more generally. The modality of power exemplified by the French army's psychotropic regime was novel: never had state biopower been deployed in such a way and upon such a basis, or at least, not at such a scale and for such duration. It signified the arrival of a particular kind of power relations in advanced liberal societies, one that revolved around the brain and control of its vital processes. The twentieth and twenty-first centuries have witnessed a blossoming of psychotropic mechanisms – both drugs and behaviours, analog and digital – in civilian life, some controlled by the state, others by powerful institutions, and yet others by giant corporations, that have sought to mold emotional experiences and behaviours for power and profit. This is not, of course, to say that French alcohol policy caused any of this. Rather, it is to say that this policy was the avant-garde of a trend that defined the twentieth century and looks to be even more important in the twenty-first.

Notes

Archives Consulted

Archives Nationales Français (ANF)
Archives du Sénat (AS)
Service Historique de la Défense (SHD)

Introduction

1 Louis Barthas, *Poilu* (New Haven, CT: Yale University Press, 2014), 190.
2 Étienne Tanty, *Les Violettes des tranchées: Lettres d'un poilu qui n'aimait pas la guerre* (Triel-sur-Seine, France: Éditions Italiques, 2002), 440.
3 Ibid., 438.
4 Albert Dauzat, *L'Argot de la guerre* (Paris: Armand Colin, 1918), 60–1.
5 A Google Ngram graph of the frequency of the word *pinard*'s usage in the French corpus shows a clear spike in 1914 and decline in 1919. See https://tinyurl.com/pinard (accessed 10 July 2022).
6 Jules Pech, "Le Pinard," *Le Rigolboche* 16 (10 July 1915).
7 Henri Pouzin, "Ode au pinard," *Le 120 court* 30 (1 December 1916).
8 Soldier from the 86è Régiment d'Infanterie, as quoted in Jean Nicot, *Les Poilus ont la parole* (Paris: Éditions Complexe, 1998), 323.
9 At this time in France, the term *"eau-de-vie"* referred to distilled ethyl alcohol produced on an industrial scale. I will use "distilled alcohol" and *eau-de-vie* interchangeably. When referring to the drink in the context of soldiers' culture, I will use their term for the distilled alcohol they received, which was *"gnôle."*
10 Dauzat, *L'Argot de la guerre*, 101–2. Per Dauzat: "Eau-de-vie could equally, following popular conceptions, chase away the mist or create fog in front of one's eyes: it all depends on the temperament and the dose!" The word's popularity shot up with the beginning of the war and collapsed after it. See https://tinyurl.com/gnole1 (accessed 10 July 2022).
11 See the section of Tanquerel's journal titled "The Martyrs," in *"On prend nos cris de détresse pour des éclats de rire": Lettres d'un poilu, 1914–1916*, edited by Dominique Carrier (Paris: L'Harmattan, 2008), 215. Tanquerel suspected the crazed officer

might have taken ether in addition to alcohol, but this is highly unlikely. On the rumour that the army was distributing ether, see ch. 4 of this book.

12 For instance, in a letter home Tanty tersely mentioned drinking *eau-de-vie* before an attack, during which he was shot in the face and invalided from the war. His letters from 24 September to 2 October 1915 cover his participation in the Third Battle of Artois. See Tanty, *Les Violettes des tranchées*, 548–52.

13 Joseph Joffre, GQG-EM no. 7942, March 23 1915, *Service historique de la défense* (SHD), carton 16 N 1575.

14 Joseph Joffre, GQG-EM no. 21091, 29 August 1915, SHD 16 N 1575.

15 Maurice Pellé, GQG-EM no. 108, 1 December 1915, SHD 16 N 1575; Pellé, GQG-EM no. 8562, April 13 1916, SHD 16 N 1575; GQG-EM no. 3298, 5 September 1916, SHD 16 N 1575.

16 Scattered documents related to this network are found in SHD 18 N 190. See also Stéphane le Bras, "'Tracking the Enemy Within': Alcoholisation of the Troops, Excesses in Military Order and the French Gendarmerie during the First World War," in *European Police Forces and Law Enforcement during the First World War*, edited by Jonas Campion et al. (Cham, Switzerland: Palgrave Macmillan, 2019).

17 Some records are found in SHD 18 N 190.

18 Robert Lefort, "La Ballade de la 'gnole,'" *Le Canard enchaîné* 26 (27 December 1916).

19 See here Richard Holmes, *Acts of War: The Behaviour of Men in Battle* (New York: The Free Press, 1985), 244–54; Lukasz Kamienski, *Shooting Up: A Short History of Drugs and War* (Oxford, UK: Oxford University Press, 2016); Norman Ohler, *Blitzed: Drugs in the Third Reich* (New York: Mariner, 2016); Peter Andreas, *Killer High* (Oxford, UK: Oxford University Press, 2020); Nicolas Rasmussen, "Medical Science and the Military: The Allies' Use of Amphetamine during World War II," *Journal of Interdisciplinary History* 42, no. 2 (Autumn 2011): 205–33; and Nicolas Rasmussen, *On Speed* (New York: New York University Press, 2008), 53–86.

20 On the Incas, see Kamienski, *Shooting Up*, 46–50, and Andreas, *Killer High*, 206–7. On the Wehrmacht, see Ohler, *Blitzed*, 40–102; Andreas, *Killer High*, 180–93; and the epilogue to this book.

21 On the Siberians, see Kamienski, *Shooting Up*, 38–45, and Howard D. Fabing, "On Going Berserk: A Neurochemical Inquiry," *The Scientific Monthly* 83, no. 5 (November 1956): 232–7. On Napoleon's men, see Kamienski, *Shooting Up*, 51–7. I am here following Richard Davenport-Hines in defining cannabis as a hallucinogen. See his *The Pursuit of Oblivion: A Global History of Narcotics* (New York: Norton, 2002), 12.

22 On the Greeks, see Kamienski, *Shooting Up*, 31–4, and Andreas, *Killer High*, 141–2. On the Americans, see Kamienski, *Shooting Up*, 68–82, and Jonathan Lewy, "The Army Disease: Drug Addiction and the Civil War," *War in History* 21, no. 1 (January 2014): 102–19.

23 Kamienski, *Shooting Up*, xvii, 1.

24 Ibid., 5–8.

25 Ibid., 6.

26 Andreas, *Killer High*, 56–64.

27 Ibid., 16.

28 Edward B. Westermann, *Drunk on Genocide: Alcohol and Mass Murder in Nazi Germany* (Ithaca, NY: Cornell University Press, 2021), 3.

29 Kamienski and Andreas both provide sketches of drinking in the First World War, but their synoptic histories provide very few details and only superficially consider the French experience. See Kamienski, *Shooting Up*, 18–21, and Andreas, *Killer High*, 49–51.

30 Ernst Junger, *Storm of Steel* (London: Penguin, 2003), 119, 136.

31 Nicholas K. Johnson, "The Germany Army and Intoxication" (2014), https://pointsadhsblog.wordpress.com/2014/06/19/world-war-i-part-4-the-german-army-and-intoxication (accessed 12 October 2022); Lukasz Kamienski, "Drugs" (2019), in *International Encyclopedia of the First World War*, https://encyclopedia.1914-1918-online.net/article/drugs#cite_note-ftn39-39 (accessed 12 October 2022).

32 Robert Graves, *Good-bye to All That* (London: Cassell & Company, 1966), 153, 144. See also Lord Moran, *The Anatomy of Courage* (New York: Carroll and Graf, 2007), 32.

33 On Navy rum, see James Pack, *Nelson's Blood: The Story of Navy Rum* (Annapolis: Naval Institute Press, 1983).

34 Richard Holmes, *Tommy: The British Soldier on the Western Front 1914–1918* (London: HarperCollins, 2004), 329.

35 Ibid., 329–32.

36 *Report of the War Office Committee into "Shell Shock"* (London: His Majesty's Stationery Office, 1922), 151, 153.

37 Ibid., 67–8.

38 "A Tommy," *If I Goes West!* (London: G.G. Harrap, 1918), 30.

39 F.T. Nettleingham, *Tommy's Tunes* (London: E Macdonald, 1917), 31.

40 John Ellis, *Eye-Deep in Hell* (London: Croom Helm, 1976), 133.

41 Ibid., 134.

42 Tim Cook, "'More a Medicine than a Beverage': 'Demon Rum' and the Canadian Trench Soldier of the First World War," *Canadian Military History* 9, no. 1: 7–22; Ellis, *Eye-Deep in Hell*, 134.

43 Ellis, *Eye-Deep in Hell*, 136.

44 Frederic Manning, *Her Privates We* (London: Serpent's Tail, 2013), 59.

45 Christophe Lucand, *Le Pinard des poilus: Une Histoire du vin durant le Grande Guerre* (Dijon, France: Éditions Universitaires de Dijon, 2015), 18.

46 Ibid., 16–18. It is worth noting that this was the argument I put forward in my doctoral dissertation, which was completed and filed several years before Lucand's work. See Adam Derek Zientek, "Wine and Blood" (PhD diss., Stanford University, 2012), esp. 6–12.

47 Charles Ridel, *L'Ivresse du soldat* (Paris: Vendémiaire, 2016), 16. See also 19.

48 Ibid., 85–144.

49 Ibid., 352.

50 For reviews, see Karina P. Abrahao et al., "Alcohol and the Brain: Neuronal Molecular Targets, Synapses, and Circuits," *Neuron* 96, no. 6 (20 December 2017): 1223–38; Elio Acquas et al., "Editorial: Ethanol, Its Active Metabolites, and Their Mechanisms of Action: Neurophysiological and Behavioural Effects," *Frontiers in Behavioural Neuroscience* 12, no. 95 (May 2018); Changhai Cui and George F. Koob, "Titrating Tipsy Targets: The Neurobiology of Low-Dose Alcohol," *Trends in Pharmacological Sciences* 38, no. 6 (June 2017): 556–68; and Michael J. Eckhart et al., "Effects of Moderate Alcohol Consumption on the Central Nervous System," *Alcoholism: Clinical and Experimental Medicine* 22, no. 5 (August 1998): 998–1040.

51 On the energetic content of alcohol, see R. Mattes, "Fluid Calories and Energy Balance," *Physiology & Behaviour* 89, no. 1 (30 August 2006): 66–70.

52 For a recent metanalysis of ethanol's analgesic properties, see Trevor Thompson et al., "Analgesic Effects of Alcohol: A Systematic Review," *The Journal of Pain* 18, no. 5 (May 2017): 499–510.

53 See Reuben A. Hendler et al., "Stimulant and Sedative Effects of Alcohol," *Current Topics in Behavioural Neuroscience* 13 (2013): 489–509.

54 N.L. Harrison et al., "Effects of Acute Alcohol on Excitability in the CNS," *Neuropharmacology* 122 (August 2017): 36–45; Merideth A. Addicott et al., "The Biphasic Effects of Alcohol: Comparisons of Subjective and Objective Measures of Stimulation, Sedation, and Physical Activity," *Alcoholism: Clinical and Experimental Research* 31, no. 11 (November 2007).

55 See here, among many scientific articles, Barry T. Jones et al., "A Review of Expectancy Theory and Alcohol Consumption," *Addiction* 96 (2001): 57–72.

56 See here Norman Zinberg's seminal *Drug, Set, and Setting* (New Haven, CT: Yale University Press, 1984).

57 For overviews, see Jan Plamper, *The History of Emotions: An Introduction* (Oxford, UK: Oxford University Press, 2012); Barbara H. Rosenwein and Riccardo Cristiani, *What Is the History of Emotions* (Cambridge: Polity, 2008); Susan J. Matt and Peter N. Stearns, eds., *Doing Emotions History* (Urbana: University of Illinois Press, 2014); and especially Boddice, *The History of Emotions* (Manchester, UK: Manchester University Press, 2017).

58 Barbara H. Rosenwein, *Generations of Feeling: A History of Emotions* (Cambridge: Cambridge University Press, 2016), 1.

59 See, most recently: Lisa Feldman Barrett, "The Theory of Constructed Emotion: An Active Inference Account of Interoception and Categorization," *Social Cognitive and Affective Neuroscience* 12, no. 1 (January 2017): 1–23; Lisa Feldman Barrett and Ajay B. Satpute, "Historical Pitfalls and New Directions in the Neuroscience of Emotion," *Neuroscience Letters* 693 (February 2019): 9–18; and most importantly, Lisa Feldman Barrett, *How Emotions Are Made* (Boston, MA: Mariner Books, 2018). Feldman Barrett convincingly argues that the large size of the scientific literature on basic emotions is the result of research and funding path-dependencies more than anything else.

60 Feldman Barrett uses James A. Russell's theory of affect. See James A. Russell, "Core Affect and the Psychological Construction of Emotion," *Psychological Review*

110, no. 1 (2003): 145–72, and more recently, Jonathan Posner, James A. Russell, and Bradley S. Peterson, "The Circumplex Model of Affect: An Integrative Approach to Affective Neuroscience, Cognitive Development, and Psychopathology," *Development and Psychopathology* 17, no. 3 (2005): 715–34. For a partial critique of the constructed emotions model, see Ralph Adolphs and David J. Anderson, *The Neuroscience of Emotion* (Princeton, NJ: Princeton University Press, 2018), 290–4.

61 Feldman Barrett, *How Emotions Are Made*, 29, 86.

62 Ibid., 126. My emphasis.

63 The phrase "intoxication concept" is mine, but the idea is drawn from the work of sociologists Craig MacAndrew and Robert B. Edgerton and psychiatrist Norman E. Zinberg. In their classic *Drunken Comportment*, MacAndrew and Edgerton show how people intoxicated by alcohol are not disinhibited in the folk-psychological sense, but rather act out cultural scripts that define what they ought to do with their intoxication. Similarly, as we have seen, Zinberg famously argued in *Drug, Set, and Setting* that the pharmacological properties of a given psychotropic drug cannot explain intoxicated people's behaviour. An "intoxication concept" corresponds roughly with a historically situated "set." See MacAndrew and Edgerton, *Drunken Comportment: A Social Explanation* (New York: Pecheron Press, 2003), 100–64, and Zinberg, *Drug, Set, and Setting*.

64 My concept of "psychotropic power" is derived from my reading of Daniel Lord Smail's *On Deep History and the Brain* (Berkeley, CA: University of California Press, 2008), 112–89, esp. 161–4. See also Boddice's discussion of Smail's ideas in *The History of Emotions*, 154–64.

Chapter One

1 On the theory of degeneration, see Daniel Pick, *Faces of Degeneration* (Cambridge: Cambridge University Press, 1994); William H. Schneider, *Quality and Quantity* (Cambridge: Cambridge University Press, 1990), 11–54; and Joseph A. Nye, *Crime, Madness, and Politics in Modern France* (Princeton, NJ: Princeton University Press, 1984), 121–31. On Bertillon, see Luc Berlivet, "Les Démographes et l'alcoolisme," *Vingtième Siècle* 3, no. 95 (2007): 93–113, and Nye, *Crime, Madness and Politics*, 167.

2 Their respective populations in 1789: France, 26 million; Russia, 25 million; Austria, 18 million; Britain, 12 million; and Prussia, 5 million. In 1914: France, 39 million; Russia, 130 million; Austria, 50 million; Britain, 45 million; and Germany, 63 million. On France's population growth, see Nye, *Crime, Madness and Politics*, 134, and Jack D. Ellis, *The Physician-Legislators of France: Medicine and Politics in the Early Third Republic, 1870–1914* (Cambridge: Cambridge University Press, 1990), 176–8.

3 Jacques Bertillon, *La Dépopulation de la France* (Paris: Félix Alcan, 1911), 22.

4 See here Anne Carol, *Histoire de l'eugénisme en France: Les Médecins et la procréation XIXe–XXe siècle* (Paris: Éditions du Seuil, 1995), 87–114.

5 Jacques Bertillon, *Le Problème de la dépopulation* (Paris: Armand Colin, 1897), 16.

6 Nye, *Crime, Madness and Politics*, 154–8 discusses alcoholism in this context.

7 Ibid., 135. See also Bertrand Dargelos, "Une spécialisation impossible: L'Émergence et les limites de la médicalisation de la lutte antialcoolique en France (1850–1940)," *Actes de la recherche en sciences sociales* 1–2, no. 156–7 (2005): 52–71, and Dargelos, *La Lutte antialcoolique en France depuis le XIXe siècle* (Paris: Dalloz, 2008), 66–73.

8 Pick, *Faces of Degeneration*, 51. On Morel, see Pick, 44–59, and Dargelos, *La Lutte*, 69–71.

9 B.A. Morel, *Traité de dégénérescences physiques, intellectuelles et morales de l'espèce humaine* (Paris: Chez J.B. Baillière, 1857), 80.

10 For instance, Magnan's massive *Recherches sur les centres nerveux* (Paris: G. Masson, 1876) declared one of its primary purposes to be describe the degenerative effects of alcohol on the body. On Magnan, see Pick, *Faces of Degeneration*, 99; Nye, *Crime, Madness and Politics*, 123–4; and Dargelos, *La Lutte*, 76–7.

11 Alfred Fouillée, *La France au point de vue morale* (Paris: Felix Alcan, 1911), 135.

12 L. Viaud and H.A. Vasnier, *La Lutte contre l'alcoolisme* (Paris: Asselin et Houzeau, 1907), vii.

13 Clemenceau's "Préface" to Louis Jacquet, *L'Alcool* (Paris: Masson et Cie, Éditeurs, 1912), i.

14 Joseph Reinach, *Les Lois anti-alcoolique et la guerre* (Paris: Ligue Nationale Contre l'Alcoolisme, 1915), 7. My emphasis.

15 Desiré Deschamps, *L'Alcoolisme et la question sociale* (Lille, France: Descamps & Cie, Libraires-Editeurs, ca. 1900), 7.

16 Paul Griveau, *L'Alcoolisme, fléau sociale* (Paris: Marchal et Billard, 1906), 2.

17 On Huss, see Henri Bernard, "Alcoolisme et antialcoolisme et France au XIXe siècle," *Histoire, économie et société* 3, no. 4 (1984): 609–28; Dargelos, "L'Émergence"; and Dargelos, *La Lutte*, 64–6.

18 Michael Marrus, "Social Drinking in the Belle Epoque," *Journal of Social History* 7, no. 2 (Winter 1974): 117.

19 On the process, see Dubrunfaut, *La Vigne remplacée par la betterave, la pomme de terre, etc…* (Paris: Guiraudet et Jouaust, 1854).

20 Jacquet, *L'Alcool*, 695.

21 On drinking in the north, see Raoul Brunon, *L'Alcoolisme ouvrier en Normandie* (Paris: Masson et Cie, 1899).

22 Charles K. Warner, *The Winegrowers of France and the Government since 1875* (New York: Columbia University Press, 1960), 1–3; Rod Phillips, *French Wine* (Berkeley, CA: University of California Press, 2016), 149–54.

23 On the *phylloxera*, see Warner, *The Winegrowers*, 1–16, and Phillips, *French Wine*, 155–69.

24 Jacquet, *L'Alcool*, 695; Joseph Reinach, *Contre l'alcoolisme* (Paris: Charpentier, 1910), 19–22.

25 Phillips, *French Wine*, 167.

26 Warner, *The Winegrowers*, 11–12; Phillips, *French Wine*, 172–5.

27 "La France est-elle le pays le plus alcoolique de l'Europe?" *Le Matin*, 31 May 1914.

28 James Kneale, "Consumption," in *Alcohol in the Age of Industry, Empire, and War*, edited by Deborah Toner (London: Bloomsbury Academic, 2021), 46.

29 This is the argument of Thomas Brennan, "Towards the Cultural History of Alcohol in France," *Journal of Social History* 23, no. 1 (Fall 1989): 71–92, which is the essential essay on the subject. See also Susanna Barrows, *Distorting Mirrors* (New Haven, CT: Yale University Press, 1981).

30 On the origins of anti-alcoholism in France, see Didier Nourisson, "Aux Origines de l'antialcoolisme," *Histoire, économie et société* 7, no. 4 (1988): 491–506. Nourisson notes that, before the increase in consumption of distilled alcohol, anti-alcohol reformers focused on reducing drunkenness resulting from wine-drinking, but after around 1870, they focused on distilled alcohol. See also Patricia Prestwich, "Temperance in France: The Curious Case of Absinth," *Historical Reflections* 6, no. 2 (Winter 1979): 301–19, and Prestwich, *Drink and the Politics of Social Reform: Antialcoholism in France since 1870* (Palo Alto, CA: SPSS, 1988), 69–74.

31 *Le Vin du midi de la France (du Languedoc) comme aliment parfait* (Montpellier, France: Roumegous et Déhan, 1910), 10–12.

32 Marrus, "Social Drinking," 120.

33 A. Lafont, *Les Dangeurs de l'alcoolisme* (Lyon, France: Bureau de la Société de Tempérance, ca. 1900), 6.

34 Reinach, *Contre l'alcoolisme*, 86.

35 Not all anti-alcohol reformers thought this. Some held (correctly) that wine too could cause alcoholism. See, for instance, Maurice Legrain, *Le Dégénérescence alcoolique*, and Émile Pierret, *Le Péril de la race* (Paris: Perrin et Cie, 1907), both of which held that excessive wine consumption would lead to alcoholism.

36 Émile Mauriac, *Les Vins de Bordeaux* (Bordeaux, France: Peret et Fils, 1907), 17.

37 Gustave Fabre, *La Vigne et la vin* (Paris: Ernest Flammarion, 1898), unnumbered page in "Avant-propos," 10.

38 Dr Ladreit de Lacharrière and A. Joltrain, *Que doit-on boire?* (Paris: Au Siège Sociale de la Sociétés Savantes, 1902), 12.

39 Fabre, *La Vigne et le vin*, 278.

40 Charles Mayet, *Le Vin de France* (Paris: Jouvet & Cie, ca. 1895), vi, 6.

41 Dr Peton, as quoted in Raymond Brunet, *La Valeur alimentaire et hygiènique du vin* (Paris: Librairie Agricole de la Maison Rustique, 1914), 76.

42 Brennan, "Towards the Cultural History of Alcohol in France," 79.

43 Griveau, *L'Alcoolisme*, 40.

44 Hamond, *Le Roi du jour* (Paris: Ancienne Maison Charles Douniol, 1903), 74, 76.

45 Serieux, *L'Alcool* (Paris: Félix Alcan, 1901), 26.

46 Hamond, *Le Roi du jour*, 60.

47 Ibid., 64.

48 Bergeret, *De l'Abus des boissons alcooliques* (Paris: J.B. Baillière et Fils, 1870), 67.

49 Pierret, *Le Péril de la race*, 86.

50 Galtier-Boissière's anti-alcohol handbook, *L'Antialcoolisme en histoires vraies* (Paris: Larousse, 1901), was the standard pedagogical text on the subject at the fin-de-siècle.

51 On that character, see Dargelos, *La Lutte*; Didier Nourisson, *La Buveur du XIXe siècle* (Paris: Michel, 1990); and Prestwich, *Drink and the Politics of Social Reform*, 108–42, esp. 140–2.

52 See Lunier quote in M.J. Gaufrès, "Les Origines de l'antialcoolisme en France," *L'Alcool* (February 1902).

53 Prestwich, *Drink and the Politics of Social Reform*, 108–28.

54 For the official report behind the program, see *Bulletin administratif du ministère de l'instruction publique*, Tome LXI (Paris: Imprimerie Nationale, 1897), 397–414. On the program, see Thierry Lefebvre, "La Propagande antialcoolique en milieu scolaire au début du XXe siècle," *Revue d'histoire de la pharmacie* 309 (1996): 143–50.

55 L. Angot, *Le Livre d'antialcoolisme des écoles primaires* (Paris: Librairie Classique Internationale, 1897), 33–4. See also 78–9.

56 For the first lesson, see ibid., 7–16; for the second, see 17–28. See also A. Lemoine and Villette, *Contre l'alcoolisme* (Paris: Librairie Classique Fernand Nathan, 1902); V.S. Lucienne, *Leçons d'anti-alcoolisme* (Lille, France: Imprimerie-Librairie Camille Robbe, 1899); Jules Steeg, *Les Dangers de l'alcoolisme* (Paris: Librairie Classique Fernand Nathan, 1898); and Galtier-Boissière, *L'Antialcoolisme en histoires vrais*.

57 Angot, *Le Livre*, 78.

58 Lucienne, *Leçons*, 96.

59 Steeg, *Les Dangers*, 22, 72.

60 Galtier-Boissière, *L'Antialcoolisme*, 82.

61 Lucienne, *Leçons*, 95; Lemoine and Villette, *Contre l'alcoolisme*, 50.

62 Galtier-Boissière, *L'Antialcoolisme*, 53–60.

63 Douglas Porch, *The March to the Marne* (Cambridge: Cambridge University Press, 1981), 37. See also Eugen Weber, *Peasants into Frenchmen: The Modernization of Rural France 1870–1914* (Stanford, CA: Stanford University Press, 1976), 292–302.

64 Porch, *The March to the Marne*, 37.

65 Tallon, *La Campagne antialcoolique dans l'armée* (Paris: Berger-Levrault, 1903), 52.

66 Dujardin-Beaumetz to the Minister of War, "M. Viry Médecin Principal 1ère Class," no. 175/98, 24 May 1899, SHD GR 9 NN 7 1031.

67 Dieu to the Minister of War, "Au sujet de l'alcoolisme dans l'armée," April 1899, SHD GR 9 NN 7 1031. Jean de Lanessan, as Minister of the Marine, issued his own circular stating that the sale of distilled alcohol to sailors would be highly regulated, but not banned entirely. See Lanessan, "Circulaire de 1er Juin 1900," SHD GR 9 NN 7 1031.

68 Gallifet, "Circulaire de 3 Mai 1900," SHD GR 9 NN 7 1031.

69 See, for instance, Mme Legrain's letter to Gallifet, no. 6682, 18 May 1900, SHD GR 9 NN 7 1031, which is just one of many pieces of fan mail in the *carton* (her husband, Dr Legrain, was one of France's most prominent anti-alcohol reformers).

70 "L'Alcoolisme," *La France militaire*, 30 June 1900.

71 "L'Alcoolisme et l'armée," *Le Temps*, 5 May 1900.

72 André, "Circulaire de 21 Mars 1901," SHD GR 9 NN 7 1031.

73 On female *cantinières*, Gil Milhaley, "L'Effacement de la cantinière ou la virilisa-tion de l'armée française au XIXe siècle," *Revue d'histoire du XIXe siècle* 30 (2005): 1–19.

74 On this general trend, see Nye, *Crime, Madness and Politics*, 319–21.

75 These measures are all reviewed in the lengthy report "Note sur la lutte contre l'alcoolisme dans l'armée," undated [ca. 1910], SHD GR 9 NN 7 1031.

76 André, "Circulaire de 15 janvier 1901," SHD GR 9 NN 7 1031.

77 M.J. Simonin, "La Prophylaxie de l'alcoolisme dans l'armée. Sa réglementation officielle," in *Le Caducée* 10, no. 2 (22 January 1910); Dujardin-Beaumetz, "Au Sujet de l'alcoolisme dans l'armée," no. 293/00, 26 April 1900, SHD GR 9 NN 7 1031.

78 Gunnebaud, *La Vie à la caserne au point de vue social* (Saint-Brieuc, France: Imprimerie René Prud'homme, 1906), 33–4.

79 Tallon, *La Campagne antialcoolique*, 63.

80 Ibid., 63.

81 Ibid., 6.

82 Simonin, "Prophylaxie."

83 Indeed, Jean de Lanessan, in *La Lutte pour l'existence* (Paris: Félix Alcan, 1903), identified the ration schedule of 1890 as his standard by which to evaluate the nu-tritional deficiencies of the working class. For a discussion of the rations and their caloric content, see Perrier and Guilhaumon, "De l'alimentation dans l'armée," *Bulletin de la Société scientifique d'hygiène alimentaire* 4 (1914): 332–59.

84 The rations schedule is provided in Peyrolle's textbook for use at the École Supérieure de Guerre, *Alimentation et ravitaillement des armées en campagne* (Paris: Imprimerie Librairie Militaire, 1897), 283.

85 E. Lux, *De l'Alimentation rationnelle et pratique des armées en campagne et à l'inte-rieur* (Paris: Librairie pour L'Art Militaire et les Sciences, 1881), 11.

Chapter Two

1 Charles Delvert, *From the Marne to Verdun* (Barnsley, UK: Pen & Sword, 2016), 8.

2 Henri Désagneaux, *A French Soldier's War Diary* (Barnsley, UK: Pen & Sword, 2014), 7.

3 Holger H. Herwig, *The Marne, 1914* (New York: Random House, 2011), 248–9.

4 Herwig argues, for example, that the Germans had effectively lost the war in the West by the end of September 1914. See ibid., 305–19.

5 On the "Race to the Sea," see François Cochet, *La Grande guerre* (Paris: Perrin, 2018), 82–5, and Robert A. Doughty, *Pyrrhic Victory* (Cambridge: Belknap, 2005), 97–100.

6 Herwig, *The Marne*, 319.

7 On the impact of firepower on the battlefield, see Cochet, *La Grande guerre*, 95–103; Eric Leed, *No Man's Land* (Cambridge: Cambridge University Press, 1979), esp. 96–105; Michael Howard, "Men against Fire: Expectations of War in 1914," *International Security* 9, no. 1 (Summer 1984): 41–57; and Jean Norton Cru, *Du Temoignage* (Paris: Allia, 2008), 26–32.

8 Cru, *Du Temoignage*, 50–1.

9 Paul Lintier, *My '75* (London: William Heineman, 1917), 79.

10 Leed, *No Man's Land*, 104.

11 Ibid., 101–2.

12 The gruesome nature of these exit wounds led the belligerents to accuse one another of using "dum-dums" or "expanding bullets," which had been outlawed by the 1907 Hague Conventions. The Germans, in particular, were appalled, and assuming the Belgians were using these illegal munitions, enacted reprisals upon the civilian population.

13 Delvert, *From the Marne to Verdun*, 27.

14 Stéphane Audoin-Rouzeau and Annette Becker argue that avoiding discussion of the obscenity of the violence brought by modern firepower is "tantamount to consenting to a historiographical denial." See their *14–18* (New York: Hill and Wang, 2014), 20–31, esp. 23.

15 Cazin, *L'Humaniste à la guerre* (Paris: Librairie Plon, 1915), 189.

16 All the belligerents faced the same problem. On morale in the British army, see John Baynes, *Morale* (Garden City Park, NY: Avery, 1967); J.G. Fuller, *Troop Morale and Popular Culture* (Oxford, UK: Clarendon Press, 1991); and Alex Watson, *Enduring the Great War* (Cambridge: Cambridge University Press, 2009), which also considers the German armies. No comparable study exists for the French army.

17 See, for example, Christian Mallet, *Impressions and Experiences of a French Trooper 1914–1915* (London: Constable & Co., 1916), 25.

18 Joseph de Fontenioux, *Mon Carnet rouge, vol. 1* (St. Julien, France: Texto, 1997), 78.

19 Maurice Genevoix, *Neath Verdun, August–October 1914* (London: Hutchinson, 1916), 42–3.

20 Christophe Lucand, *Le Pinard des poilus* (Dijon, France: Presses Universitaires de Dijon, 2015), 44–6.

21 "Le 'Vin au soldat'," *Le Temps* (15 November 1914).

22 Andre Lebert, "Rapport sur le ravitaillement en vin des armées" (November 1916), Archives du Sénat 69S 119.

23 Marcel Lachiver, *Vins, vignes, et vignerons: Histoire du vignoble français* (Paris: Fayard, 1997), 485.

24 Louis Martin, "Le vin aux soldats," *Le Radical* (19 October 1914). My emphasis on "right."

25 H. Gomot, "Nos Soldats auront du vin," *Le Petit Journal* (13 November 1914).

26 J. Garat, *La Gazette de Biarritz* (24 November 1914).

27 "Du vin pour nos soldats sur le front," *La Petite Gironde* (6 November 1914).

28 "Le Vin aux soldats," *L'Écho d'Alger* (28 October 1914).

29 "Le Vin aux soldats," *L'Écho d'Alger* (8 November 1914).

30 "Dons de vin d'Algérie aux soldats combattants," *L'Écho d'Alger* (6 December 1914). The newspaper frequently ran lists of hundreds of donations of all sizes.

31 F.V., "Le 'Vin aux soldats,'" *Revue de viticulture* (August–December 1914).

32 de Fontenioux, *Mon carnet rouge, vol. 1*, 20.

33 Pellé, "Note pour la direction de l'arrière," no. 1119, 4 November 1914, SHD 16 N 2644.

34 GQG to Fourth Army in response to letter no. 2208, 4 November 1914, SHD 16 N 2644.

35 Lebert Report (1916).

36 Zacharie Baqué, *Journal d'un poilu* (Paris: Imago, 2003), 84.

37 G. Nony, *L'Intendance en campagne: Cours professé au stage de l'intendance militaire* (Paris: Henri Charles-Lavauzelle, 1914), 91.

38 Ibid., 91–2.

39 In January 1915, there were *stations-magasins* in St. Cyr, Dunkerque, Sotteville les Rouen, Vernon, Le Mans, Orléans les Moulins, Les Aubrais, Auxerre, Nuits sur Ravières, Montereaux, Sens, Besançon, Dôle, Dijon, Chalones sur Saône, Nantes, Moulins, and Lyon. Their number changed over the war, as new *stations-magasins* were built and older ones closed, but always remained around 20.

40 On the *stations-magasins*, see Louis Le Fur, *Pour le ravitaillement des armées: Les Stations-magasins* (Paris: Phillipe Renouard, 1916), 5–8; Franc-Nohain and Paul Delay, *Histoire anecdotique de la guerre: Les Services de l'arrière* (Paris: P Lethielleux, 1915), 9–17; and "How France Subsists Her Armies at the Front," *Professional Memoirs, Corps of Engineers, US Army* 9, no. 48 (November–December 1917): 692–706.

41 See, for instance, the statistical annex to Piston, "Lettre à Monsieur le Général Directeur de l'Arrière, Vitry-le-François," no. 7966, 29 August 1914, in SHD 16 N 2636.

42 Minister of War to the Directeur de l'Arrière, "Fours de construction," no. 1221.4/11, 28 September 1914, SHD 16 N 2635; Minister of War, "Au sujet du ravitaillement en viande congelée de l'armée desservie par la gare régulatrice de Gray," ca. early November 1914, SHD 16 N 2635.

43 Linder, "Note au sujet de la consommation de denrées dont les approvisionnements ne sont pas constitués normalement dans les Stations-Magasins," no. 156, 26 October 1914, SHD 16 N 2635.

44 Laffon de Labdebat, "Note au sujet des commandes aux Stations-Magasins," no. 6182, 1 October 1914, SHD 16 N 2635.

45 Anselin, Letter to the Général Commandant en Chef, no. 7805 2/2, 16 December 1914, SHD 16 N 2635.

46 Le Hénaff and Bornecque, *Les Chemins de fer français et la guerre* (Paris: Librairie Chapelot, 1922), 83; De LaCroix, "Les Chemins de fer pendant la guerre II: L'Effort économique et industriel," *Revue des deux mondes* 50, no. 3 (April 1919): 587, 594.

47 Lebert Report (1916).

48 Cavaillon, Note to the Directeur de l'Arrière, no. 03842-7/5, 4 November 1914, SHD 16 N 2635; Lebert Report (1916).

49 The records of some of these requisitions can be found in ANF F.23.99. In 1916–17, the Third Republic requisitioned 8,099 *wagons-citernes*, more than half of all in France.

50 All statistics below are derived from the monthly logistical reports of the *stations-magasins* in SHD 16 N 2641.

51 These calculations were made with the following assumptions: 1.35 million men received both wine and *eau-de-vie*; wine was 10 per cent ABV and *eau-de-vie* 50 per cent ABV; and a European standard drink contains 10mL of alcohol. An "American" standard drink, not surprisingly, contains more at 14mL of alcohol; I will use the European standard throughout this book.

52 See Charles Ridel, *L'Ivresse du soldat* (Paris: Vendémiaire, 2017), 104–20. Ridel's analysis mentions some of the same men featured in the narrative above.

53 At this time, the ration consisted of 750 g of bread, 500 g of fresh meat (or 280 g of canned meat), 50 g of porridge, 100 g of dried vegetables, 31 g of sugar, 30 g of fat, 24 g of coffee, and 250 mL of wine at 10 per cent ABV or 62.5 mL of *eau-de-vie*.

54 Armand Gautier, "Sur la ration de soldat en temps de guerre," *Comptes rendus hebdomadaires des séances de l'Académie des sciences*, Tome 160 (Paris: Gauthier-Villars, 1915), 159–67.

55 Ibid., 166.

56 *Journal officiel de la Republique française* 47, no. 39 (9 February 1915): 688.

57 M.L., "Le Vin sur le front," *Revue de viticulture* 22, no. 1085 (25 March–1 April 1915): 315–17. My emphasis.

58 Émile-Léon Vidal, "La Ration du vin pour le soldat français," *Le Progrès agricole et viticole* 32, no. 11 (14 March 1915): 251–3.

59 Émile-Léon Vidal, "La Ration de vin du soldat français dans ses rapports avec l'alcoolisme," in *Bulletin de l'Académie de médecine*, Tome 73 (Paris: Masson et Cie, Éditeurs, 1915), 784–91.

60 Armand Gautier, "Dans la ration actuelle du soldat en campagne il faut diminuer la viande et augmenter les légumes et le vin," in *Bulletin de l'Académie de médecine*, Tome 74 (Paris: Masson et Cie, Éditeurs, 1915), 5–13.

61 L. Landouzy, "Le Vin, dans la ration du soldat, moyen de lutte contre l'alcoolisme," in ibid., 53–8.

62 See, for instance, his article "La Guerre et la santé de la race," in *Revue d'hygiène et de police sanitaire* (Paris: Masson et Cie, 1915), 1–17.

63 See the transcript of the debate in *Bulletin de l'Académie de médecine*, Tome 74, 207–13.

64 *Revue de viticulture* 22, no. 1107 (16 September 1915): 216–23.

65 Pierre Viala, "L'Avenir viticole de la France après la guerre," *Association française pour l'avancement des sciences* (Paris: Masson et Cie., 1916), reprinted as *L'Avenir viticole de la France après la guerre* (Paris: Bureaux de la Revue de Viticulture, 1916). I will cite from the latter version. The text was brought to my attention by Rod Phillips, *French Wine* (Berkeley, CA: University of California Press, 2016), 199.

66 Viala, "L'Avenir viticole," 52.

67 Ibid., 47, 51.

68 Ibid., 49.

69 Ibid., 52.

70 Ibid., 57.

71 Duhamel, "Qualité du vin reçu de l'arrière," no. 8068, 12 April 1915, SHD 16 N 2644.

72　The internal review was made in response to a request from the Ministry of War. See Laurent, Ministry of War to GQG, no. 9878/5, 19 August 1915, SHD 16 N 2644, and the responses in the same *carton*.

73　Phillips, *French Wine*, 196.

74　Charles K. Warner, *The Winegrowers of France and the Government since 1875* (New York: Columbia University Press, 1961), 60.

75　Laurent, Ministry of War to GQG, no. 010382-7/5, 20 July 1915, SHD 16 N 2644.

76　Deliveries fell from 824,869,96 hL to 279,551.82 hL; receipts fell from 327,805.85 hL to 63,426.81 hL. See statistics in SHD 16 N 2641.

77　The figure was 345,736.58 hL, from SHD 16 N 2641.

78　On the purchasing and logistics of requisitions, see Lebert's 1916 and 1919 reports.

79　Stéphane Le Bras, "Nous reviendrons pour les vendages: les Aquitains, le vin, et la Grande Guerre," in *La Guerre en Aquitaine*, edited by B. Lachaise and C. Piot (Nérac, France: Éditions D'Albret, 2017), 287–308.

80　Pellé, "Production du vin en France," GQG EM TOE 1er Bureau, 1 January 1916, SHD 16 N 2644.

81　Savoye, no. 12924, 14 December 1915, SHD 16 N 2644.

82　Ministry of War, "Consommation de mélange de cidre et de vin," no. 3655/DA, 31 December 1915, SHD 16 N 2644.

83　Dubois, "Compte-rendu," no. 2076/DA, 19 February 1916, SHD 16 N 2644.

84　André Laurent, Untitled, no. 4766 2/5, 16 March 1916, SHD 10 N 169.

85　Ordre De Mission [Sic], unnumbered, no date, SHD 10 N 169.

86　Wagner, unnumbered, 14 May 1916, SHD 10 N 169.

87　Some of the reports are found in SHD 16 N 2644.

88　Statistics are from SHD 10 N 169.

89　Statistics are from SHD 10 N 169 and Lebert Report (1916).

90　F. Mathieu, "Vins de l'Argentine," 26 Februrary 1916, SHD 10 N 169.

91　Baraton, no. 362, 10 May 1916, SHD 10 N 169.

92　On buying wine from California, see Maurice Meusnier, Letter to the Minister of Commerce, 14 January 1916, Archives Nationales de France (ANF), F.23.99, and the Minister's unenthusiastic response (transport fees were too high) in Minister of War to Minster of Commerce, no. 2450 2/5, 8 February 1916, ANF F.23.99.

93　Warner gives the following figures: in 1914, the French army requisitioned 3 per cent of the harvest; in 1915, 14 per cent; in 1916, 11 per cent; in 1917, 20 per cent, and in 1918, 10 per cent.

94　Statistics are derived from reports in SHD 16 N 2640.

Chapter Three

1　"Wine and Milk," in Roland Barthes, *Mythologies* (New York: Noonday Press, 1972), 58.

2　Chaf, "Le Pinard," *Le Poilu du 37* 2, no. 16 (15 June 1917).

3　Mary Douglas, *Natural Symbols* (New York: Routledge, 1996), 11.

4　Stéphane Audoin-Rouzeau, *Men at War* (London: Berg, 1988), 188.

5 Ibid., 33.

6 Le Hénaff and Henri Bornecque, *Les Chemins de fer français et la guerre* (Paris: Librarie Chapelot, 1922), 58–63.

7 On the spatial organization of the trenches and their social effects, see Leonard Smith, *Between Mutiny and Obedience* (Princeton, NJ: Princeton University Press, 1994), 80–5. For a layer-by-layer tour, see François Cochet, *Survivre au front* (Paris: Soteca 14-18 Éditions, 2005), 95–106.

8 Jean du Nord, "Le Cuistot," *Boum! Voilà!* 10 (June 1915); G.L., "Le Cuistot," *Le 120 court* 19 (June 1916).

9 "Ballade pour le cuistot," *La Première ligne* 16 (March 1916); Lamisol, "Mon cuistot," *Le Camouflet* 6 (September 1916); Henri Pouzin, "La Ballade du cuistot," *Grenadia* 18 (August 1917).

10 Soldiers typically carried a *bidon* with a volume of a litre on their persons. Men on the *corvées* often used larger two-litre *bidons* designed for the task.

11 V. Dufour, "Le Pinard," *Le Diable au cor* 2, no. 26 (14 May 1916).

12 A. Rubben, "Le Bidon," *Le Poilu de 37* 23 (15 April 1918).

13 Jean Mady, "Mon quart," *Le Rigolboche* 35 (20 January 1916).

14 See, for example, Bistouri, "À mon bidon perdu," *Le Rire aux éclats* 5 (1 November 1918); Félix Champion, "Mon bidon," *On les aura* 6 (31 July 1917); G. Cuvier, "Trois amis (mon quart, mon bidon, et moi)," *Bleutinet* 20 (1 August 1916); Robert Desailly, "Compagnon: le quart," *Le Rire aux éclats* 15 (1 October 1917); and Henri Pouzin, "À mon quart," *Le 120 court* 44 (March 1918).

15 R. Dubar, "Corvée de soupe," *Le Bochofage* 5 (25 December 1916).

16 "Corvée de soupe," *Bulletin des Armées de la République* 276 (12 December 1917).

17 Joseph Raymond, *Froc et epée* (Paris: Société d'Éditions Artistiques, 1919), 185. On the *corvée*, see Rémy Cazals and André Loez, *Dans les tranchées de 1914–18* (Paris: Éditions Cairn, 2008), 44–6, 115–20, and Cochet, *Survivre au front*, 115–17.

18 "Corvée de soupe," *Le Crapouillot* 1, no. 1 (1 January 1915).

19 S.A.M., "Le bon 'filon,'" *Echo du camp de Rennbahn* 33 (20 January 1917).

20 Eugène Pic, *Figures et choses du front* (Paris: Recueil Sirey, 1918), 122.

21 Roland Dorgelès, *Les Croix de bois* (Paris: Albin Michel, 1919), 27.

22 For humorous instructions, see Charles Chassé, "Kerbiquette, professeur de dilation," *L'Horizon* 2, no. 8 (2 January 1918).

23 Cam. Dubois, "Corvée de pinard," *Le Poilu* 4, no. 27 (1 November 1916). See also Farigoulet, "La Corvée de pinard," *Le Feuille de Jau-Dignac-Loriac* 2 (June 1917).

24 On the descent, see Cochet, *Survivre au front*, 118–20.

25 René Nicolas, *Carnet de campagne d'un officier français* (Chicago, IL: Benj. H. Sanborn & Co., 1919), 58–9.

26 Cazals and Loez, *Dans les tranchées*, 47–50.

27 Paul Fussell, *The Great War and Modern Memory* (Oxford, UK: Oxford University Press, 2009), 50.

28 Alexandre Arnoux, *Le Cabaret* (Paris: Fayard, 1922), 225.

29 Jean Giono, *Le Grand troupeau* (Paris: Éditions Gallimard, 1937), 116.

30 A. Rubben, "Le Bidon," *Le Poilu de 37* 23 (15 April 1918).

31 See Anthony Clayton, *Paths of Glory* (Croydon, UK: Orion Books, 2003), 83–92; Cochet, *Survivre au front*, 142–6; Cazals and Loez, *Dans les tranchées*, 105–15; and Jacques Meyer, *La Vie quotidienne des soldats pendant la grande guerre* (Paris: Hachette, 1967).

32 J. Belot, "Carnet d'un poilu," *Le Flambeau* 6 (28 May 1916).

33 Jean-Pierre Bernard et al., eds., *Je suis mouton comme les autres* (Valence, France: Édition Peuple Libre & Notre Temps, 2002), 76.

34 Alfred-Marie Job, *Notes d'un chasseur à pied* (Toulouse, France: E Privat, 1922), 51.

35 Raymond, *Froc et epée*, 186.

36 Albert Jamet, *La Guerre vue par un paysan* (Paris: Albin Michel, 1931), 71.

37 Andre Tanquerel, as quoted in *"On prend nos cris de détresse pour des éclats de rire":* *Lettres d'un poilu*, edited by Dominique Carrier (Paris: L'Harmattan, 2008), 206.

38 L.V., "Au pinard! Au pinard!" *Le Diable au cor* 36 (1 May 1917).

39 René Benjamin, *La Guerre sous le ciel de France* (Paris: Fayard, 1916), 219.

40 Snop, "Un Elément de la victoire: le pinard," *La Ligature* 3 (10 September 1916).

41 Francisque Vial, *Territoriaux de France* (Paris: Berger-Levrault, 1918), 45.

42 Émile Durkheim, *The Elementary Forms of Religious Life* (Oxford, UK: Oxford University Press, 2001), 140–7.

43 Ibid., 162–4.

44 Ibid., 154.

45 Randall Collins, *Interaction Ritual Chains* (Princeton, NJ: Princeton University Press, 2005), 32–46.

46 See Goffman's *Interaction Ritual: Essays in Face-to-Face Behavior* (New York: Routledge, 2017), and Collins, *Interaction*, 16–25.

47 Collins, *Interaction*, 65–78.

48 Ibid., 35.

49 Ibid., 39, 102–40.

50 Ibid., xiii.

51 Ibid., 38.

52 J. Dardier, "Le Pinard," *La Première ligne* 18 (February 1916).

53 Gype, "Ballade en l'honneur du pinard," *Le Ver luisant* 2, no. 12 (1 October 1916).

54 "Quand les poilus ont du pinard," *La Première ligne* 33 (15 June 1916).

55 Benjamin, *La Guerre*, 216.

56 Jean Galtier-Boissière, *En Rase campagne* (Paris: Berger-Levrault, 1917), 253. Galtier-Boissière was also the editor of the trench journal *Le Crapouillot* and the son of the anti-alcohol figure Émile Galtier-Boissière from ch. 1. He later became a major French literary figure who, like René Benjamin, was attracted to the far right after the war.

57 H. Pouzin, "Ode au pinard," *Le 120 court* 30 (1 December 1916).

58 Jean de Granvilliers, *Le Prix d'un homme* (Paris: Calman-Lévy, 1919), 54.

59 "Le Pinard," *L'Écho des tranchées* 3, no. 51 (20 July 1916).

60 P. Poitevin, "Le Pinard," *Le Rigolboche* 89 (30 August 1917); Abric, "Au Pinard," *Brise d'entonnoirs* 18 (January 1918); Trissotin, "Le Pinard," *L'Écho des marmites* 12 (20 August 1916).

61 In 1916 there was, for instance, an army public relations campaign with fliers that read "If you want wine, wash the barrels!!!" and contained instructions for how to do so. See example in SHD 16 N 2644. Trench journals too got in on the act. See the inspiring song "Soyez bon pour les tonneaux," in *Gardons la sourire* (December 1916).

62 "Au caveau du 'Bon Pinard,'" *L'Oeil* 2, no. 2 (1 January 1917).

63 Jean-Louis Beaufils, *Journal d'un fantassin* (Paris: L'Harmattan, 2007), 26; Émile Morin, *Lieutenant Morin: Combattant de la guerre, 1914–1918* (Besançon, France: Éditions Cêtre, 2002), 78.

64 Jules Mazé, *Le Carnet de campagne du Sergent Lefèvre* (Tours, France: Maison Alfred Mame et Fils, 1917), 150.

65 Th. G., "Le Pinard," *Le Périscope* 10 (1 July 1916); Princet, "Le Bidon," *La Première ligne* 45 (1 February 1917); A. Lauris, "Invocation," *Le Poilu* 4, no. 28 (1 December 1916); L.V., "Au Pinard! Au Pinard!"

66 Jules Princet, "Le Bidon," *La Première ligne*, no. 45 (1917).

67 Eric Leed, *No Man's Land* (Cambridge: Cambridge University Press, 1979), 110.

68 Étienne Tanty, *Les Violettes des tranchées* (Triel-sur-Seine, France: Éditions Italiques, 2002), 428.

69 Pierre Causse, "Le Pinard," *La Vie poilusienne* 1, no. 2 (1 January 1916). My emphasis.

70 Lucien Boyer, *La Chanson des poilus* (Paris: F. Salabert, 1918).

71 Natal, Untitled poem, *Le Poilu du 37* 30 (30 October 1918).

72 Émile Roudié, *La Légende des poilus* (Paris: Berger, 1916), 76.

73 L.V., "Au Pinard! Au Pinard!"

74 Th. G., "Le Pinard."

75 Louis Hourticq, *Récits et réflexions d'un combattant* (Paris: Hacette et Cie., 1918), 55.

76 "Gloire au Pinard!" *Le Plus-Que-Torial* 8 (15 July 1916).

77 Cochet, *Survivre au front*, 146–59; Cazals and Loez, *Dans les tranchées*, 105–15.

78 Pont, Circular no. 3891, 7 April 1917, SHD 16 N 1575; Debeney, Circular no. 21.317, ca. April 1917, SHD 16 N 1575; Minister of War, no. 8297 4/8B, June 1917, SHD 16 N 2644.

79 Guillaume Apollinaire, "À Italie," in *Caligrammes* (Paris: Mercure de France, 1918), 152.

80 Stello, "Eloge du pinard," *La Première ligne* 46 (March–April 1917).

81 Teulade, "Le 'Pinard.'"

82 Duby, "Ballade du pinard," *Bulletin des Armées de la République* 222 (29 November 1916).

83 Mazé, *Le Carnet de campagne*, 150. See also Jean-Louis Beaufils, *Journal d'un fantassin* (Paris: L'Hartmann, 2007), 72.

84 Rigal, "La Valse du pinard"; Abeille, "Rondel du pinard."

85 J. Chatelain, "En honneur du 'pinard,'" *Le Poilu* 5, no. 49 (1 December 1918).

86 H. Pouzin, "Au Pinard."

87 A. Michoud, "Le Bidon," *Le Diable au cor* 49 (30 August 1918).

88 Natal, Untitled poem; L.V., "Au Pinard! Au Pinard!"

89 Gabriel Chevallier, *Fear* (New York: New York Review of Books, 2011), 61.

90 "Le Pinard," *Le Filon* 3.

91 L.V., "Au Pinard! Au Pinard!"

92 The *cafard* was a cross-cultural syndrome. Charles Carrington, a British officer, describes something similar: he claims that he became "the zombie" during a period of particular stress. See Carrington's *Soldier from Wars Returning* (London: Hutchinson & Co, 1965), 194–7.

93 See here Dominique Kalifa, *Biribi: Les Bagnes coloniaux de l'armée française* (Paris: Perrin, 2009), 75–9, and Michael Vann, "Of *Le Cafard* and Other Tropical Threats," in *France and Indochina: Cultural Representations*, edited by Kathryn Robson and Jennifer Yee (Lanham, MD: Lexington Books, 2005), 95–106.

94 H. Chanot, "Le Cafard," *Le Flambeau* 18 (12 November 1916).

95 Marc Boasson, *Au soir d'un monde* (Paris: Plon, 1926), 119, 127.

96 Joseph Bousquet, *Journal de route 1914–1917* (Bordeaux, France: Éditions des Saints Calus, 2000), 277.

97 Louis Huot and Paul Voivenel, *Le Cafard* (Paris: Bernard Grasset, 1918), 4.

98 Huot and Voivenel, *Le Cafard*, 186.

99 Charles Delvert, *From the Marne to Verdun* (Barnsley, UK: Pen & Sword, 2016), 90.

100 Louis Huot and Paul Voivenel, *Psychologie du soldat* (Paris: La Renaissance du Livre, 1918), 66.

101 Pierre Le Houx, "Salut, pinard!" *L'Écho des gourbis* 28 (1 August 1917); Gaston Lacroix, "Le Pinard!!" *Le Klaxon* 8 (August 1916); A. Lauris, "Invocation"; Abric, "Au Pinard"; Théodore Botrel, "Encore un p'tit coup d'pinard," *Le Clos bleu* 2, no. 15 (1 April 1918); J. Dardier, "Le Pinard."

102 Stello, "À la façon de pinard ou pineau," *La Première ligne* 4 (1 September 1917).

103 Félix Champion, "Mon bidon," *On les aura* 6 (31 July 1917).

104 Stello, "Eloge du pinard"; Teulade, "Le 'Pinard'"; Pech, "Le Pinard."

105 Dufour, "Le Pinard."

106 Natal, Untitled poem.

107 Thaumiaux, "Ballade du pinard."

108 Th. G., "Le Pinard"; "Le Pinard," *Le Petit écho du 21è Régiment d'Infanterie* (1 September 1917); R. Régis-Lamotte, "Le Pinard," *Le Petit journal* (10 September 1916); H. Pouzin, "Ode au pinard."

109 Barbara Rosenwein, *Emotional Communities in the Early Middle Ages* (Ithaca, NY: Cornell University Press, 2007), 2.

110 William Reddy, *The Navigation of Feeling* (Cambridge: Cambridge University Press, 2001), 129.

111 On Rosenwein and Reddy, see Rob Boddice, *The History of Emotions* (Manchester, UK: Manchester University Press, 2018), 62–77.

112 For a summary of the debate, see Pierre Purseigle, "A Very French Debate," *Journal of War and Culture Studies* 1, no. 1 (2007).

113 This school traces itself from Pierre Renouvin, to Jean Jacques-Becker, to Annette Becker, Stéphane Audoin-Rouzeau, and other historians now associated with the *Historial*, an international research centre and museum located in Péronne. See, for instance, Audoin-Rouzeau and Annette Becker, *14–18* (New York: Hill

and Wang, 2014); Jay Winter, *Sites of Memory, Sites of Mourning* (Cambridge: Cambridge University Press, 2014 ed.); and Leonard V. Smith, Stéphane Audoin-Rouzeau, and Annette Becker, *France and the Great War 1914–1918* (Cambridge: Cambridge University Press, 2003).

114 This school is primarily associated with the *Collective de recherche international et de débat sur la guerre de 1914–1918* (CRID). See, for instance, Frédéric Rousseau, *La Guerre censurée* (Paris: Éditions du Seuil, 1999), esp. 64–125; André Loez, *14–18 Les Refus de la guerre* (Paris: Gallimard, 2010); Nicolas Mariot, *Tous unis dans la tranchée?* (Paris: Seuil, 2013); and, most recently, Rousseau, *14–18: Penser le patriotisme* (Paris: Gallimard, 2018).

115 See Cochet, *Survivre au front*, 154–9.

116 For the classic work on the role of political ideology in maintaining morale and combat effectiveness, see Omer Bartov, *Hitler's Army* (Oxford, UK: Oxford University Press, 1992). On primary groups, see S.L.A. Marshall, *Men under Fire* (Norman, OK: University of Oklahoma Press, 2000). On morale more generally, see Gary Sheffield, *Command and Morale* (Barnsley, UK: Pen & Sword, 2014).

117 In the British army, there was a popular song called "We're Here Because We're Here," whose lyrics consisted of that phrase sung over and over to the tune of Auld Lang Syne.

118 See here Giorgio Agamben, *Homo Sacer: Sovereign Power and Bare Life* (Stanford, CA: Stanford University Press, 1998), esp. 119–25.

119 Tanty, *Les Violettes des tranchées*, 462.

120 Le Barrillet, "Chantepinard," *L'Écho de tranchéesville* 35 (22 June 1916).

Chapter Four

1 Recall that *débits de boissons* were officially licensed retail alcohol-sellers such as cafés, bistros, and bars.

2 *Journal officiel de la République française: Débats parlementaires, chambre des députés* (1 February 1916), 179. Per the practice established earlier in this book, I will translate the word *alcool* as "distilled alcohol," which reflects the contemporary French sense of the word.

3 Georges Lecomte, "Respect à nos héros et à nos morts," *Excelsior* (4 February 1916).

4 "Les Soldats insultés par un député," *La Croix* (11 February 1916).

5 "Les Salisseurs," *L'Express du midi* (11 February 1916).

6 Maurice Barrès, "Les Salisseurs" (9 February 1916), in *L'Âme française et la guerre* 8 (Paris: Émile-Paul Frères, 1919), 239.

7 Georges Lecomte, "Que le réparation soit égale à l'offense!" *Excelsior* (21 February 1916).

8 The author took exception to the requisitions program put into place in the early fall of 1915. Pierre Mille, "Il y a pinard et pinot," *Excelsior* (29 December 1915).

9 "Un Banquet de promotion à la popote: le café au salon," *Excelsior* (7 February 1916).

10 Michel Sorbier, "L'Étonnement du père Bicoque," *Excelsior* (8 February 1916).

11 Pierre Mille, "Ce que l'on dit en attendant…" *Excelsior* (2 June 1916).

12 Stephane Lauzanne, *Fighting France* (New York: D. Appelton and Company, 1918), 30.

13 Joseph de Fontenioux, *Mon Carnet rouge Vol I* (St. Julien, France: Texto, 1997), 95.

14 "Le Chemin de la gloire," *Le Rire rouge* 9 (16 January 1915).

15 See, for instance, Jules Mazé, *Le Carnet de campagne du Sergent Lefèvre* (Tours, France: Maison Alfred Mame et Fils, 1916), 89; Alfred F, "La Haine féconde," in Charles Clément, *Au Bruit du canon* (Paris: A. Lemerre, 1916), 102; Léon C., "Le Choc en retour," in *Sous les obus* (Paris: A Lemerre, 1916), 205; Anatole Castex, *Verdun* (Paris: Imago, 1996), 105; and François Blayac, *Carnets de guerre 1914–1916* (Carcassonne, France: Ecomarine, 2006), 181.

16 When drunk, diethyl ether has similar effects to alcohol, although with a much more profound degradation of motor and cognitive skills and a shorter duration. It was, in fact, a favourite among some British temperance reformers, as it could serve as a substitute drink.

17 Marcel Marie, *Sac au dos* (St Croix, France: Presse du Belvédère, 2006), 89.

18 Entry from 29 January 1915 in Raymond Recouly, *La Bataille dans la fôret* (Paris: Hachette et Cie, 1916), 32.

19 Entry from 10 September 1914 in Maurice Genevoix, *'Neath Verdun* (London: Hutchenson, 1916), 98.

20 X, "Réception de fleurs," *Le Poilu* 2, vol. 10 (26 May 1915).

21 Lebret's diary is available at http://www.chtimiste.com/carnets/Lebret/Lebret.htm (accessed 18 August 2022).

22 Belloc's diary is available at http://www.chtimiste.com/carnets/Belloc%20Gilbert/BELLOC%20Gilbert.htm (accessed 18 August 2022).

23 Lucien Barou, *Mémoires de la grande guerre Tome III* (2014), interview with Roger Roche, 258 in pdf.

24 I here mean the term "extraordinary" in two senses: first, that the distributions were large, and second, that they were out of the ordinary, coming only during days of attacks.

25 Barou, interview with François Potin, in *Mémoires Tome III*, 253–4 in pdf.

26 Ibid., 330–1 in pdf.

27 AC, "Pour soutenir le moral," *Le Bochofage* 11 (1917).

28 See, for instance, Frédéric Rousseau, *La Guerre censurée* (Paris: Éditions du Seuil, 1999), 192–200; François Cochet, "1914–1918: L'Alcool aux armées. Représentations et essai de typologie," *Guerres mondiales et conflits contemporains* 2, no. 222 (2006), 19–32; Stéphane Le Bras, "L'Ivresse dans l'armée française pendant la grande guerre. Un mal pour un bien?" in *L'Ivresse entre le bien et le mal, de l'antiquité à nos jours* (Brussels: Peter Lang, 2018), 167–86; and Charles Ridel, *L'Ivresse du soldat* (Paris: Vendémiaire, 2016), 255–7.

29 Rene Arcos, *Caserne* (Paris: F. Rieder et Cie., 1921), 50.

30 Henri Barbusse, *Under Fire* (London: Penguin, 2004), 223. Barbusse, describing the scene before an attack, claims that men were drunk neither "physically nor spiritually," but the attack he describes is set in early 1915, possibly before extraordinary rations became regular.

31 The logistical records in the military archives begin in December 1914. See statistics in SHD 16 N 2641.

32 Louis Barthas, *Poilu* (New Haven, CT: Yale University Press, 2014), 47.

33 Ibid., 79; Victor Chantenay's war diary is hosted at http://www.chtimiste.com/carnets/Chatenay%20Victor/Chatenay%20Victor.htm (accessed 17 August 2022).

34 Antoine Négroni's war diary is hosted at http://www.chtimiste.com/carnets/Negroni/Negroni.htm (accessed 18 August 2022).

35 Étienne Tanty, *Les Violettes des tranchées* (Triel-sur-Seine, France: Éditions Italiques, 2002), 551–2.

36 The term "hyper-battle" is historian François Cochet's. See Cochet, *La Grande guerre* (Paris: Éditions Perrin, 2018), 261–376. For personal narratives, see, in addition to Belloc's diary about Verdun, Marceau Nédoncelle's war diary, hosted at http://www.chtimiste.com/carnets/Nedoncelle/Nedoncelle.htm (accessed 18 August 2022); Paul Frot, *Mon Journal de guerre 1914/1918* (Paris: Connaissances et Savoirs, 2005), 150; and the letter from Louis Corti dated 29 August 1916 in Jean-Pierre Guéno, *Paroles de Verdun: Lettres de poilus* (Paris: Éditions Perrin, 2006).

37 Louis Hobey, *La Guerre? C'est ca!* (Paris: Éditions Librairie du Travail, 1937), 120. On the Chemin-des-Dames, see ch. 5 of this book.

38 Joseph Delteil, *Les Poilus* (Paris: P. Grasset, 1926), 85.

39 Gabriel Chevallier, *Fear* (New York: NYRB, 2011), 217–18. My emphasis.

40 The five volumes can be downloaded from https://www.loire.fr/jcms/lw_1056847/lucien-barou-fait-revivre-la-memoire-des-poilus (accessed 18 August 2022).

41 Barou, *Mémoires Tome III*, 251 in pdf.

42 See Pellé, "Réponse à la télégramme chiffré 19/546 du 28 Juin, no. 77/CDA, 28 June 1916, and the response, Telegram 3517/M (SM Boves à EM Chantilly), 28 June 1916, both in SHD 16 N 2644; Pellé to the Commandant la 6ème Armée, "Allocation de suppléments à la ration forte," 29 June 1916, SHD 16 N 2644.

43 Maistre, "Order Général," no. 961 PC/4, 2 May 1917, SHD 16 N 2644. There are three more such requests from early May in SHD 16 N 2644.

44 Barou, interview with Alphonse Solnon in *Mémoires Tome III*, 255–6 in pdf.

45 The *Syndicat central des distillateurs de France* argued that *alcool* was "indispensable" as a "cordial and cure" that was profitably "used" by the army. See M. Grasset, letter to the Directeurs du Service de Ravitaillement, 30 September 1914, in *Archives Nationales* (AN) F.23.66.

46 Zacharie Baqué had to do it in a letter home on 14 November 1914; Jean Louis-Beaufils did the same ten days later, on 26 November 1914; and Vigne Aimé on 1 May 1915. See Zacharie Baqué, *Journal d'un poilu* (Paris: Éditions Imago, 2006), 74; Jean-Louis Beaufils, *Journal d'un fantassin* (Paris: L'Hartmattan, 2007), 26; and Jean-Pierre Bernard, *Je suis mouton comme les autres: Lettres, carnets, et mémoires de poilus drômois et de leur familles* (Valence, France: Éditions Peuple Libre & Notre Temps), 230.

47 Natal, untitled poem, *Le Poilu du 37* 30 (30 October 1918).

48 W. Tip, Untitled Postcard (ca. 1917).

49 Robert Lefort, "La Ballade de la 'gnole,'" *La Canard enchâiné* 26 (27 December 1916).

50 Edmond Vivier, "La 'Gniole' des armées," *La Mitraille* 5 (June 1916).

51 H. Boyer, "La Gnôle," *Le Rigolboche* 72 (20 February 1917); Robert Raymond, "Odelette à la Gnole," *La Lacrymogène* 15 (December 1917).

52 F.D., "L'Argot de tranchées," *Journal de Roanne* (14 March 1915).

53 Lefort, "La Ballade."

54 Letter from 27 December 1914 in Ernest Benoist's collected letters, hosted at http://www.chtimiste.com/carnets/benoist/benoist.htm (accessed 18 August 2022).

55 Entry for 4 September 1916 in "Carnet de guerre de Louis Élie Decamps," http://www.chtimiste.com/carnets/Decamps%20Louis/Decamps%20Louis%202.htm (accessed 18 August 2022).

56 On the etymology of *gnôle* and a list of its synonyms, see François Déchelette, *L'Argot des poilus* (Paris: Jouve et Cie, 1918), 112–13; Albert Dauzat, *L'Argot de la guerre* (Paris: A Colin, 1919), 79–83; *Dictionnaires des terms militaires et de l'argot poilu* (Paris: Larousse, 1916), 104, 147; and Gaston Ensault, *Le Poilu tel qu'il se parle* (Paris: Éditions Bossard, 1919), 270–1.

57 Beaufils, *Journal*, 26.

58 Eric Leed, *No Man's Land* (Cambridge: Cambridge University Press, 1979), 12–33. See also Victor Turner, *The Ritual Process* (New York: Routledge, 2017), 95, 138. In Leed's thinking, training and mobilization functioned as preliminal rites while life in the trenches provided the liminal, but the nature of the war – impersonal, relentless, inescapable – meant that there could be no resolution or reintegration. The Western Front provided no postliminal resolution; its only exit was injury, insanity, or death.

59 John Keegan, *The Face of Battle* (New York: Penguin, 1976), 229–74.

60 Henri Barbusse, *Under Fire*, 222; Georges Gaudy, *Verdun et le Chemin des Dames* (Paris: Nouvelle Éditions Latines, 1966), 126.

61 Maurice Laurentin, *Le Sang de France* (Paris: Bloud & Gay, 1919), 192-3.

62 "Sous la mitraille," *L'Ouest-Éclair* (6 June 1915).

63 Paul Tuffrau, *Carnet d'un combattant* (Paris: Payot, 1917), 2, 9.

64 Joanna Bourke, *Fear: A Cultural History* (London: Shoemaker Hoard, 2006), 203.

65 Gabriel Chevallier, *Fear* (New York: NYRB Press, 2011), 219.

66 This sense of "tunnel vision" during attacks is well-known and not unique to the experience of the First World War. The French military theorist Ardent du Picq called this rush to the enemy positions the "forward flight." See Richard Holmes, *Acts of War: The Behaviour of Men in Battle* (New York: The Free Press, 1989), 152, 157, and Randall Collins, *Violence: A Micro-sociological Theory* (Princeton, NJ: Princeton University Press, 2008), 85, 121.

67 Chevallier, *Fear*, 220.

68 Paul Dubrulle, *Mon Régiment dans la fournaise de Verdun et dans la Bataille de la Somme* (Paris: Plon, 1917), 233.

69 Barbusse, *Under Fire*, 226–7; see also Gaudy, *Verdun*, 136 for an additional description of this motive force.

70 Barou, interviews with François Potin, Guillaume, Montagne, Roger Roche, and Mathieu Grand, *Mémoires Tome III*.

71 Barou, interview with Marc Délime, *Mémoires Tome III*, 257 in pdf.
72 Barou, interview with Dubuis, *Mémoires Tome III*, 254 in pdf.
73 Barou, interview with Roche, *Mémoires Tome III*, 258 in pdf.
74 Collins, *Violence*, 40–57, 82.
75 David Grossman, *On Killing* (New York: Back Bay Books, 1995), 30–41; Grossman, "Combat: The Universal Human Phobia," in *On Combat* (Millstadt, IL: Warrior Science Publications, 2008), 2–7. The specifics of Grossman's conclusions about violence have not gone uncritiqued. For a blistering critique, see Robert Engen, "Killing for Their Country: A New Look at 'Killology,'" *Canadian Military Journal* 9, no. 2: 120–8. Nevertheless, Grossman's basic point – that killing is hard to do – stands.
76 See Collins, *Violence*, 43–54; S.L.A. Marshall, *Men under Fire* (Norman, OK: University of Oklahoma Press, 2000), 55–73.
77 Ernst Junger, *Storm of Steel* (New York: Penguin, 2003), 241.
78 Barou, interview with Francisque Ferret, *Mémoires Tome III*, 331 in pdf. Many of Barou's interview subjects express similar sentiments.
79 On the subject of distance and killing, see Grossman, *On Killing*, 99–140.
80 Barou, interview with Jean-Marie Quet, *Mémoires Tome III*, 333 in pdf. See also Barou, *Mémoires III*, 326–42, for interviews that describe the act of killing.
81 See also Rousseau, *La Guerre censurée*, 198, and Ridel, *L'Ivresse*, 256.
82 Barou, interview with Marius Dubuis in *Mémoires Tome III*, 254 in pdf.
83 Barou, interview with Georges Montaigne in *Mémoires Tome III*, 256–7 in pdf.
84 Barou, interview with Délime in *Mémoires Tome III*, 257 in pdf.
85 Barou, interview with Guillaume in *Mémories Tome III*, 254 in pdf.
86 On the mechanics of the attack, see Leonard V. Smith, *Between Mutiny and Obedience* (Princeton, NJ: Princeton University Press, 1994), 100–24.
87 Collins, *Violence*, 81–2.
88 Ibid., 85, 87. This is very similar to what Jonathan Shay famously called the "berserk" physiological and psychological state in his groundbreaking *Achilles in Vietnam* (New York: Simon and Schuster, 1995).
89 Ibid., 102–12.
90 Chevallier, *Fear*, 220–1.
91 Letter from 30 May 1915 in "Les Memoires de Pierre Menetrier," http://guerre14menetrier.free.fr/18-lettre/18-30Mai.html (accessed 4 August 2022).
92 Collins reviews some of this evidence from other wars in *Violence*, 94–9.
93 Barou, interview with Potin, *Mémoires Tome III*, 330–1 in pdf.
94 Barou, interview with Antoine Fanget, *Mémoires Tome III*, 257–8 in pdf.
95 See the "Carnet de Victor Chantenay," entry for May 9.
96 See the "Carnet de guerre de Claude Parron," hosted at http://www.chtimiste.com/carnets/Parron%20Claude/Parron%20Claude.htm (accessed 18 August 2022).
97 Barthas, *Poilu*, 79.
98 Barou, interview with Francis Ferret, *Mémoires Tome III*, 253 in pdf.
99 Barou, interview with Charles Fraty, *Mémoires Tome III*, 273 in pdf.
100 Barou, interview with Léon Guichard, *Mémoires Tome III*, 255 in pdf.

101 Barou, interview with Ernest Pigeron, *Mémoires Tome III*, 255 in pdf.

102 Barou, interview with Solnon in *Mémoires Tome III*, 256–7 in pdf.

103 See Grossman, *On Killing*, 70–1, and *On Combat*, 16–27.

104 Barbusse, *Under Fire*, 235. See also Gaudy, *Verdun*, 155–9.

105 Chevallier, *Fear*, 222.

106 Louis Maufrais, *J'étais médecin dans les tranchées* (Paris: Robert Laffont, 2010), 95.

107 Barou, interview with Dubuis in *Mémoires Tome III*, 254 in pdf.

108 Ibid., 254 in pdf.

109 See Mitchell Dean, *Governmentality: Power and Rule in Modern Society* (Los Angeles, CA: Sage, 2010), 118; Catherine Mills, *Biopolitics* (London: Routledge, 2018), 14–15.

110 Michel Foucault, *The Birth of Biopolitics* (London: Picador, 2008), 317, as cited in Dean, *Governmentality*, 119.

111 Mills, *Biopolitics*, 15.

Chapter Five

1 On temperance during the war, see Dan Malleck, "Regulation and Prohibition," in *Alcohol in the Age of Empire, Industry, and War*, edited by Deborah Toner (London: Bloomsbury Academic, 2021), 74–81.

2 Ibid., 67–8; Patricia Prestwich, *Drink and the Politics of Social Reform* (Palo Alto, CA: The Society for the Promotion of Science and Scholarship, 1988), 74.

3 Prestwich, *Drink and the Politics of Social Reform*, 108–42.

4 Ibid., 144; Patricia Prestwich, "Temperance in France: The Curious Case of Absinth," *Historical Reflections* 6, no. 2 (Winter 1979): 301–19.

5 Prestwich, *Drink and the Politics of Social Reform*, 147–8.

6 Ibid., 155–63.

7 Ibid., 163–7.

8 Ibid., 174–8.

9 Jean Finot, "À tous nos lecteurs," *Le Bulletin de l'Alarme* 1, no. 1 (April 1916). See also Finot's *L'Union sacrée contre l'alcoolisme* (Paris: Flammarion, ca. 1916), 55–72.

10 *Le Bulletin de l'Alarme* 1, no. 2 (July 1916).

11 "Plus de liqueurs entre les Repas," *Le Rire aux éclats* 17 (1 March 1918). Yet this, as we have seen, was not strictly true: soldiers did not always get their *gnôle* while in the trenches.

12 "La Gniole," *On les aura* 3 (1 November 1916).

13 Vivier, "La 'Gniole' des armées," *La Mitraille* 5 (June 1916).

14 Robert Lefort, "La Ballade de la 'gnole,'" *Le Canard enchâiné* 26 (1916).

15 Louis Barthas, *Poilu* (New Haven, CT: Yale University Press, 2014), 52.

16 Ibid.

17 Letter from 8 January 1915 in "Correspondances d'Ernest Benoist," http://www.chtimiste.com/carnets/benoist/benoist.htm (accessed 18 August 2022).

18 Letter 45 in Marie-Joëlle Ghouati-Vandrand, *Il fait trop beau pour faire la guerre: Correspondence de guerre d'Elie Vandrand, paysan auvergnat* (Vertaizon, France: Édition "La Galipote, 2000).

19 See the consumption statistics in Louis Jacquet, *L'Alcool* (Paris: Masson et Cie, 1912), 704–5.

20 Joffre, GQG EM no. 7942, 23 March 1915, SHD 16 N 1575.

21 See the "Arrêté concernant la vente et la circulation de l'alcool dans la zone des armées" attached to the letter above, SHD 16 N 1575. Several examples of these large printed *arrêtés* can be found in SHD 18 N 190.

22 Barthas, *Poilu*, 61.

23 Entry for 22 March 1915 in "Les Carnets de guerre de Lucienne Courouble," http://www.chtimiste.com/carnets/Courouble/Lucienne%20Courouble%201914%20 1916.htm (accessed 18 August 2022).

24 Entry from 27 August 1915 in "Carnets de guerre du sergent-fourrier Alexandre Robert," http://www.chtimiste.com/carnets/Robert/Robert%201915.htm (accessed 18 August 2022).

25 Joffre, GQG EM no. 21090, 29 August 1915, SHD 16 N 1575.

26 See the *arrêté* attached to ibid.

27 Pellé, GQG EM no. 1376, 3 September 1915, SHD 16 N 1575.

28 Pellé, GQG EM no. 108, 1 December 1915, SHD 16 N 1575.

29 Pellé, GQG EM no. 1160, 3 December 1915, SHD 16 N 1575.

30 *Débitants* sometimes complained that the closure of their shops was unjust. See SHD 19 N 37 for a few examples.

31 See the *arrêté* that follows Joffre, GQG EM no. 1161, 3 December 1915, SHD 16 N 1575.

32 Pellé, GQG EM no. 8562, ca. May 1916, SHD 16 N 1575; Pont, GQG EM no. 20230, 24 December 1916, SHD 16 N 1575.

33 Stéphane Le Bras, "Tracking the 'Enemy Within': Alcoholization of the Troops, Excesses in Military Order and the French Gendarmerie during the First World War," in *European Police Forces and Law Enforcement in the First World War*, edited by Jonas Campion et al. (Cham, Switzerland: Palgrave Macmillan, 2019), 50.

34 Ruffie to Dubois, 30 December 1915, SHD 18 N 190. For an overview, see "Instruction pour les CA et DI et DES," no. 1/203, 3 October 1916, SHD 18 N 190.

35 "Service des repressions de fraudes sur l'alcool," 22 November 1916, SHD 18 N 190.

36 "Service des repressions de fraudes sur l'alcool," 5 December 1916, SHD 18 N 190.

37 "État nominatif des débitants de boissons situés dans la zône des operations," SHD 18 N 190.

38 Humbert, "Instruction pour les CA et DI et la DMS," no. 1/203, 3 October 1916, SHD 18 N 190; Ruffie, "Rapport au sujet de l'organisation du service special de repression des fraudes sur l'alcool," 16 December 1916, SHD 18 N 190. Le Bras also mentions Royer's activities in a different case in 1918 in "Tracking the 'Enemy Within,'" which suggests Royer was quite busy over the course of several years.

39 Ruffie, "Rapport."

40 Joseph Bousquet, *Journal de route 1914–1917* (Bordeaux, France: Éditions des Saints Calus, 2000), 56.

41 Trissotin, "Le Pinard," *L'Écho des marmites* 12 (20 August 1916).

42 Le Bras, "Tracking the 'Enemy Within.'"

43 François Barge, *Avoir vingt ans dans les tranchées* (Clermont-Ferrand, France: CRDP, 1984), 10.

44 Charles Delvert, *From the Marne to Verdun* (Barnsley, UK: Pen & Sword, 2016), 55–6.

45 Georges Lafond, *Ma Mitrailleuse* (Paris: Arthème Fayard & Cie, 1918), 133.

46 Barthas, *Poilu*, 183–4.

47 Maurice Genevoix, *Ceux de 14* (Paris: Flammarion, 1950), 140.

48 Barge, *Avoir vingt ans*, 10.

49 Letter dated 15 September 1915 in Jules Isaac, *Jules Issac, un historien dans la grande guerre: Lettres et carnets, 1914–1917* (Paris: Armand Colin, 2004). The letter is mentioned in Le Bras, "Tracking the 'Enemy Within,'" and Dominque Fouchard, *Le Poid de guerre: Les Poilus et leur familles après 1918* (Rennes, France: Presse Universities de Rennes, 2013), 119.

50 P. Courel, "Filochard: II—Déplacement," *Marmita: Revue littéraire, anecdotique, humoristique, fantaisiste du 267e* 22 (15 March 1916).

51 On rates of pay, see Elizabeth Greenhalgh, *The French Army and the First World War* (Cambridge: Cambridge University Press, 2014), 29–30, and Ian Sumner, *They Shall Not Pass* (Barnsley, UK: Pen and Sword, 2017), v.

52 The survey of wine prices is found in SHD 19 N 653.

53 Camille Lian, "L'Alcoolisme, cause d'hypertension artérielle," *Bulletin de l'Académie de médecine* 3, no. 74 (1915): 525–8.

54 "L'Estaminet," *Le Filon* 21 (21 April 1918).

55 Émile Morin, *Lieutenant Morin* (Besançon, France: Éditions Cêtre, 2002), 78.

56 Robinson, "Le Café," *Le Pépère: Journal gai du 359e Régiment d'Infanterie* 47 (1 June 1916).

57 Zizi, "Notre repos," *Le Filon* 24 (1918).

58 Charles Ridel, *L'Ivresse du soldat* (Paris: Vendémiaire, 2016), 221.

59 Delvert, *From the Marne to Verdun*, 64.

60 Barbusse, *Under Fire*, 63–71.

61 Trissotin, "Le Pinard."

62 "La Chasse au pinard," from the *Poilu du 37*, reprinted in *Bulletin des armées de la Republique* 13 (17 May 1916).

63 Jean Ménti, "En repos," *Le Klaxon* 5 (15 June 1916). See also Lamisol, "Au Repos," *Le Camouflet* 7 (October 1916).

64 Auguste Allemane, *Journal d'un mobilisé* (Bordeaux, France: Éditions Sud Ouest, 2014).

65 J. Dardier, "Le Mercanti," *La Première ligne* 29 (May 1916).

66 C. Gorce, "Le Mercanti," *La Suippes à demain* 24 (September 1918).

67 See here R.W. Connell, *Masculinities* (Berkeley, CA: University of California Press, 2005), esp. 67–86.

68 On this subject in the British context, see Nicoletta F. Gullace, *"The Blood of Our Sons": Men, Women, and the Renegotiation of British Citizenship during the Great*

War (New York: Palgrave Macmillan, 2002), 73–98, which is concerned with the "White Feather" campaign.

69 Joshua S. Goldstein, *War and Gender: How Gender Shapes the War System and Vice Versa* (Cambridge: Cambridge University Press, 2003), esp. 251–3, 264–72.

70 Per Nye: "[I]n the context of military crisis and national decline that reigned in France in the period 1890–1914, courage was a universally prized quality ... [B]ecause the French lagged behind Germany in both material resources and population, they were obliged to compensate for this deficit by developing superior 'spiritual' qualities, of which courage was perhaps the most important." See Robert A. Nye, *Masculinity and Male Codes of Honor in Modern France* (Oxford, UK: Oxford University Press, 1993), 218–19. See also Frédéric Rousseau, *14–18: Penser le patriotisme* (Paris: Gallimard, 2018), 68–78.

71 Jessica Meyer, *Men of War: Masculinity and the First World War in Britain* (London: Palgrave Macmillan, 2009), 61.

72 Jean G-B, "Le Poilu," *Le Crapouillot* 1, no. 5 (5 January 1915). Jean G-B is presumably Jean Galtier-Boissière, the journal's editor. See also Léon Hudelle, "Le Poilu," *L'Écho côtier* 1, no. 5 (1 May 1917).

73 On Winckelmann and the masculine ideal, see George Mosse, *The Image of Man: The Creation of Modern Masculinity* (Oxford, UK: Oxford University Press, 1996), 29–39. Mosse also discusses *fin-de-siècle* and First World War notions of martial masculinity, 107–19.

74 Delvert, *From the Marne to Verdun*, 68.

75 Joan W. Scott, "Rewriting History," in Margaret Randolph Higonnet et al., *Behind the Lines: Gender and the Two World Wars* (New Haven, CT: Yale University Press, 1989), as quoted in Meyer, *Men of War*, 3.

76 J.T., "Tenir," *Le Poilu marmité* 3, no. 40 (30 April 1917).

77 Max Buteau, *Tenir* (Paris: Plon, 1918), viii.

78 H. Pouzin, "Ode au pinard," *Le 120 court* 30 (1 December 1916).

79 Frédéric Rousseau, *La Guerre censurée* (Paris: Éditions du Seuil, 1999), 266.

80 On masculinity and alcohol-drinking in France, see Anne-Marie Sohn, *"Sois un homme!": La Construction de la masculinité au XIXe siècle* (Paris: Seuil, 2009), 42–50.

81 On singing in the army, see Rémy Cazals et al., *Années cruelles, 1914–1918* (Paris: Atelier du Gué, 1998), 60, and Pascal Cordereix, "Quand Madelon vient nous servir à boire," *Revue de la BNF* 2, no. 53 (2016): 80–1.

82 See the collection of Botrel's songs, along with sheet music, in Theodor Botrel, *Chants de bataille et de victoire* (Paris: Payot, 1920). "Encore un p'tit coup d'pinard" is on p. 47–9. On "Rosalie," see Charles Rearick, "Madelon and the Men – in War and Memory," *French Historical Studies* 17, no. 4 (Fall 1992): 1006.

83 Rearick, "Madelon and the Men." Emphasis in original.

84 Lucien Laby, *Les Carnets de guerre de l'aspirant Laby, médecin dans les tranchées* (Paris: Bayard, 2001), 315; M. Gagneur, *Avec les chars d'assaut* (Paris: Hachette, 1919), 26.

85 "Quand Madelon," *Le Périscope* 2, no. 2 (2 September 1916); there are many such transcriptions of the lyrics in personal narratives and trench journals.

86 Pierre Causse, "Le Moral est bon," *La Vie poilusienne* 9.

87 François Vatès, "Histoire d'un quart de vin," *Le Col bleu* 3, no. 33 (1 January 1919).

88 Christian Benoît, "Le Soldat et l'amour," *Inflexions* 2, no. 38 (2018), 113. See also Mary Louis Roberts, *What Soldiers Do: Sex and the American GI in World War II France* (Chicago, IL: University of Chicago Press, 2013), 59–67.

89 Letter from Henri Aimé Gauthé to Marie-Alice Jeannot in *Paroles de poilus* (Paris: Soleil, 2006), 60.

90 Joseph Delteil, *Les Poilus* (Paris: Bernard Grasset, 1926), 105–13.

91 Jean-Yves Le Naour, "L'Éducation sexuelle du soldat en 14–18," *Bulletin du centre d'étude d'histoire de la médecine de Toulouse* 32 (2000): 1–7; Michelle Rhoades, "Renegotiating French Masculinity: Medicine and Venereal Disease during the Great War," *French Historical Studies* 29, no. 2 (2006): 293–327.

92 Rousseau, *La Guerre censurée*, 307.

93 GQG DA, "Note relative à la prophylaxie des maladies veneriennes," no. 1061/s, 15 January 1916, SHD 16 N 2685.

94 For example, see Lyautey to his commanders, no. 1008-C, 14 March 1917, SHD GR 9 NN 7 1031, along with the attached and detailed note.

Chapter Six

1 EM IV Armée, "Rapport" from the Commissaire spécial adjoint [signature unreadable], no. 14/52, 3 June 1917, SHD 16 N 1521.

2 EM IV Armée, "Compte-rendu a sujet des évènements qui se sont passés dans la soirée du 2 Juin au 221è Régiment d'Infanterie à Mourmelon-le-Petit," no. 6233, 3 June 1917, SHD 16 N 1521.

3 EM IV Armée, "Rapport" from the Commissaire spécial adjoint [signature unreadable], no. 13/52, 3 June 1917, SHD 16 N 1521. See also Denis Rolland, *La Grève des tranchées: Les Mutineries de 1917* (Paris: Imago, 2005), 287.

4 Ritleng to Féraud, no. 232g, 3 June 1917, SHD 16 N 1521. See also the two reports from Saphores and Casamajor, 3 and 4 June 1917 (these reports erroneously date the demonstration to 2 May). Saphores and Casamajor, commanders of the unit, were both punished with sixty days' arrest for a lack of energy in their response. There are numerous reports on the incident in SHD 16 N 1520, many of which mention alcohol consumption among the demonstrators from the regiment. See also Rolland, *La Grève des tranchées*, 245.

5 "Resumé des compte-rendus et rapports parvenus dans la journée du 7 Juin 1917," no. 5/56, SHD 16 N 1521.

6 On Chacrise, see Rébais to the Commander of 6è Corps, no. 109/58, 3 June 1917, SHD 16 N 1521; on Coeuvres and Leury, see VI Armée EM, "Evenements de la nuit du 2 au 3 Juin," no. 2665/3, 3 June 1917, SHD 16 N 1521; on Beuvardes, see Zopff, "Resumé des rapports et compte-rendus parvenus dans la journée du 9 Juin," 9 June 1917, SHD 16 N 1521; on Blérancourt, see IIIè Armée EM, "Rapport," no.

385/A, 9 June 1917, SHD 16 N 1521. See also the invaluable statistics from André Loez, "Annexe à télécharger," to *14–18. Les Refus de la guerre: Une Histoire des mutins* (Paris: Gallimard, 2010), at http://www.crid1418.org/espace_scientifique/ouvrages/Loez_mutins_anx.pdf (accessed 22 August 2022).

7 On the problems that come with quantifying these events, see Nicolas Mariot, "Pour compter des mutins faut-il soustraire des moutons?" in *Obéir / désobeir*, edited by André Loez and Nicolas Mariot (Paris: La Découverte, 2008), 345–72.

8 On the debate as to what to call these acts of collective indiscipline, see Loez, "Annexe," 22. I will use the term "demonstration" to refer to those acts of collective indiscipline that were on the non-violent end of the spectrum, and "mutiny" to refer to those on the violent end.

9 On Beuvardes, see GAN EM, "Rapport," no. 497, 4 June 1917, SHD 16 N 1521. For the others, see Loez, "Annexe." Poincaré was the prime minister.

10 Guy Pedroncini, *Les Mutineries de 1917* (Paris: Presses Universitaires de France, 1967). Two English-language works discussing the mutinies were published before Pedroncini's, but (as Pedroncini showed) they are riddled with errors and practically useless as histories. See Richard M. Watt, *Dare Call It Treason* (New York: Simon and Schuster, 1963), 146–76, and John Williams, *Mutiny 1917* (London: Heinemann, 1962). Moreover, two narratives on the mutinies that sought to rehabilitate Pétain's reputation were also published in the 1950s and 60s: Henri Carré, *Les Grandes heures du Général Pétain 1917* (Paris: Éditions du Conquistador, 1952), and Pétain's own *Une Crise morale de la nation française en guerre, 16 avril–23 octobre 1917* (Paris: Nouvelles Éditions Latines, 1966). Both essentially mirror Pedroncini's thesis, although Pedroncini himself seemed to be unaware of them.

11 Pedroncini, *Les Mutineries de 1917*, 309–13.

12 Leonard V. Smith, *Between Mutiny and Obedience: The Case of the French Fifth Infantry Division during World War I* (Princeton, NJ: Princeton University Press, 1994), 175–214 (quote from 176). See also Leonard V. Smith, Stéphane Audoin-Rouzeau, and Annette Becker, *France and the Great War 1914–1918* (Cambridge: Cambridge University Press, 2003), 117–38, esp. 124.

13 Rolland, *La Grève des tranchées*, 404.

14 Loez, "Annexe," 546, 550.

15 Ministre de la Guerre, ed., *Les Armées françaises dans la grande guerre, Tome V 2è Volume* (Paris: Imprimerie Nationale, 1936), 194.

16 Reports are held in SHD 1519–26, esp. 19–21.

17 Loez, "Annexe," 204–6.

18 David Murphy, *The Breaking Point of the French Army: The Nivelle Offensive of 1917* (Barnsley, UK: Pen & Sword, 2015), 51–2.

19 Ibid., 48–9.

20 Ibid., 44.

21 As quoted in ibid., 67.

22 Ibid., 91.

23 Georges Cuvier, *La Guerre sans galon* (Paris: Éditions du Combattant, 1920), 12. Emphasis mine.

24 Extract 7 in IV Armée Commission de Contrôle Postale de Troyes, "Rapport du 16 Avril 1917, mitrailleuses de position," 16 April 1917, SHD 16 N 1406.
25 Extract 10 in ibid.
26 Murphy, *The Breaking Point*, 94.
27 Richard Doughty, *Pyrrhic Victory: French Strategy and Operations in the Great War* (Cambridge, MA: Harvard University Press, 2008), 354.
28 Ibid., 317. See also Jean-Jacques Becker, *The French People and the First World War* (New York: Berg, 1990), 195–216.
29 Jonathan Shaw, *Achilles in Vietnam: Combat Trauma and the Undoing of Character* (New York: Scribner, 2003), esp. 6. On the subject of moral injury, see also James M. Dubik, "Foreword," in Nancy Sherman, *Afterwar: Healing the Moral Wounds of Our Soldiers* (Oxford, UK: Oxford University Press, 2015), xiv–xvi; Sherman, *Afterwar*, 8; and David Wood, *What Have We Done: The Moral Injury of Our Longest Wars* (New York: Little, Brown and Company, 2016), esp. 7–34.
30 Shaw, *Achilles*, 6.
31 Rolland, *La Grève des tranchées*, 37–9.
32 Ibid., 45.
33 See Loez, "Annexe."
34 As quoted in Rolland, *La Grève des tranchées*, 62.
35 Ibid., 63.
36 As quoted in ibid., 62.
37 Pedroncini, *Les Mutineries de 1917*, 102.
38 Loez, "Annexe," 30.
39 Extract 13 in IV Armée Commission de Contrôle Postal Bureau Frontière, "Unité Contrôlée: 20è Régiment d'Infanterie," 4 May 1917, SHD 16 N 1406.
40 Extract 24 in ibid.
41 Extract 25 in ibid.
42 "Un Vieux poilu paysan," in IV Armée Commission de Contrôle Postal Bureau Frontière, SHD 16 N 1406.
43 Charles Tilly and Sidney Tarrow, *Contentious Politics* (Boulder, CO: Paradigm, 2007), 11–17.
44 Cuvier, *La Guerre sans galon*, 55.
45 Ibid., 56.
46 As quoted in Rolland, *La Grève des tranchées*, 76.
47 Monroe, "Compte-rendu du Général Monroe Cdt. la 69è DI su sujet de la participation de militaires du 267è RI aux événements qui se sont déroulés à Villers-sur-Fère dans la soirée du 27 Mai 1917," no. 569/P, SHD 16 N 1521.
48 Cheneble, "Confidentiel rapport," 23 May 1917, SHD 16 N 1520.
49 Ibid.
50 Passaga, "Au 162è RI," no. 444 S/3, 28 May 1917, SHD 16 N 1521.
51 Cheneble, "Confidentiel rapport," SHD 16 N 1520.
52 Cuvier, *La Guerre sans galon*, 56–7.
53 Rolland, *La Grève des tranchées*, 74.
54 Bertrand, "AS de la situation morale du régiment," 25 May 1917, SHD 16 N 1520.

55 Bertrand, "Le Colonel Bertraud, commandant le 162è Régiment d'Infanterie au Colonel, commandant l'Infanterie divisionnaire de la 69è DI," 27 May 1917, SHD 16 N 1520.

56 "Journal des marches et opérations de 162è régiment d'infanterie," SHD 26 N 702/8.

57 Murphy, *The Breaking Point*, 103.

58 Mareschal, "Au sujet de troubles à Villers," no. 3/1, 28 May 1917, SHD 16 N 1521.

59 Rolland considers the heat to be a proximal cause of the mutinies. See Rolland, *La Grève des tranchées*, 319–20.

60 Ibid.

61 Descoings, "Incidents militaires," no. 282/2.5, 1 June 1917, SHD 16 N 1521.

62 A witness later claimed Mme Assailly's goal was to "excite to the highest degree the men's spirits to prevent them from marching," although it is not clear how trustworthy this witness was. In any case, commanders considered the Assailly family "veritable agents provocateurs" and banished them from the front for the duration of the war. See Rolland, *La Grève des tranchées*, 83, and Mareschal, "Au sujet de troubles à Villers," no. 3/1, SHD 16 N 1521.

63 Mareschal, "Au sujet de troubles à Villers," no. 3/1, SHD 16 N 1521.

64 Ibid.

65 Ibid.

66 Ibid. Two differing accounts are given. One holds that the men attacked Decherf. The other holds that the men attacked one another and the officers got caught in the scrum. Compare the citation above with Hirschauer, "Le Général Hirschauer Commandant le 18è CA à Monsieur le Général Cdt. la Xè Armée," no. 500P, 29 May 1917, SHD 16 N 1521.

67 "Déclarations d'un soldat du 18è Régiment d'Infanterie, condamné à mort," no. 5784D, 15 June 1917, SHD 16 N 1521.

68 The letter is found in État-Major 2è Bureau III Armée, "Contrôle de la correspondance totalite du courrier postal d'arrivée du 36è Régiment d'Infanterie le 6 Juin 1917," no. 363/4, 6 June 1917, SHD 16 N 1521. Like the 18è RI, the 413è RI had fought on the Chemin-des-Dames. It manned the trenches for sixteen straight days between 9 May and 24 May with 118 killed, 472 injured, and 141 missing. See 413è Régiment d'Infanterie, "Journal des marches et opérations," 1 January–8 July 1917, SHD 26 N 770/3.

69 État-Major 2è Bureau III Armée, no. 363/4, SHD 16 N 1521.

70 Smith argues that the fact that soldiers used the language of revolutionary socialism to make their claims does not necessarily mean they were calling for socialist revolution. Rather, this language provided a ready and familiar framework of protest that men found useful in the context of their demonstrations. See Smith, *Between Mutiny and Obedience*, 193–4.

71 "Compte-rendu d'un service de police executé dans les environs de Fère-en-Tardenois," no. 159, 29 May 1917, SHD 16 N 1521.

72 See Loez, "Annexe," 259–69 for a discussion of the "march on Paris" as a motivating idea in the mutinies.

73 Mareschal, "Au sujet de troubles à Villers," no. 3/1, SHD 16 N 1521.

74 "Compte-rendu d'un service de police executé dans les environs de Fère-en-Tardenois," no. 159, SHD 16 N 1521.

75 On this subject, see Loez, "Annexe," 495–503.

76 "Journal des marches et opérations de 133è Régiment d'Infanterie," SHD 26 N 688/12.

77 "Journal des marches et opérations de 41è Division d'Infanterie," SHD 26 N 340/3.

78 See "Rapport sur la prise de Loivre et la voie ferrée entre le boyau de Blanc de Craie et l'Ecluse de Noue Gouzaine," in ibid.

79 On the experience, see Combes, "Impressions du Chef de Batallion Combes au sujet de la dernière offensive," 28 May 1917, SHD 16 N 1521, and Roux, "Réflexions sur les dernières opérations les 16 et 18 Avril 1817," 23 May 1917, SHD 16 N 1521.

80 Mignot, "Rapport du General Mignot," 21 April 1917, SHD 16 N 1521.

81 "Journal des marches et opérations de 41è Division d'Infanterie," SHD 26 N 340/3.

82 Brindel, "Rapport du Lieutenant-Colonel Brindel," 3 June 1917, SHD 16 N 1521.

83 Mignot, "Rapport sommaire du Général Mignot, Commandant la 41è DI," 2 June 1917, SHD 19 N 840.

84 Ibid.

85 Ibid.

86 Mignot, "Rapport Secret du Général Mignot," 11 June 1917, 16 N 1521. An "apache" was an ostensibly degenerate Parisian street hoodlum and criminal.

87 Bulot, "Rapport du Général Bulot Commandant la 82è Brigade d'Infanterie," 4 June 1917, SHD 16 N 1521.

88 "Rapport: Mutiniere des 23è et 133è Régiments d'Infanterie," 4 June 1917, SHD 16 N 1521; Mignot, "Rapport Secret du Général Mignot," SHD 16 N 1521.

89 Piebourg was the commander of the first batallion of the 133è RI. See Piebourg, "Rapport du Chef de Bataillon Piebourg Commandant le 1è Bataillon du 133è RI au sujet des évènements des 1 et 2 Juin 1917," 6 June 1917, SHD 16 N 1521.

90 Mignot, "Rapport Sommaire du Général Mignot, Commandant la 41è DI," SHD 19 N 840.

91 "Rapport: Mutiniere des 23è et 133è Régiments d'infanterie," SHD 16 N 1521.

92 Mignot, "Rapport Sommaire du Général Mignot, Commandant la 41è DI," SHD 19 N 840.

93 Libaud, "Rapport du Capitaine Libaud," 4 June 1917, SHD 16 N 1521.

94 Mignot, "Rapport du Général Mignot Commandant la 41è Division d'Infanterie sur les incidents de la 82è Brigade, pendant les journées des 2,3,4,5 Juin 1917," 6 June 1917, SHD 16 N 1521.

95 Le Verger, "Rapport du Chef de Bataillon Le Verger, Cdt. le DD/41 sur les évène-ments survenus à Bassu dans la soirée du 4 Juin 1917," 6 June 1917, SHD 16 N 1521.

96 Merdriel, "Rapport," 6 June 1917, SHD 16 N 1521.

97 Loez, "Annexe."

98 Ibid. On the one hand, all these reports, of course, must be read with caution. The size estimates were given by men under significant duress and amid an adrenaline high, and they may have exaggerated the figures to excuse their inaction. But on the other hand, these were the estimates of men who were trained and used to ascertaining the number of men at a glance.

99 For the unit's movements, see "Journal des marches et opérations de 5è Division d'Infanterie," SHD 26 N 268/10; "Journal des marches et opérations de 36è Régiment d'Infanterie," 26 N 612/6; "Journal des marches et opérations de 129è Régiment d'Infanterie," SHD 26 N 686.

100 Boucher, "4è Rapport du Colonel Boucher," 3 June 1917, SHD 19 N 305.

101 Boucher, "Rapport," 9 June 1917, SHD 19 N 305.

102 Boucher, "3è Rapport du Colonel Boucher," 3 June 1917, SHD 19 N 305. They were not alone in this. The rumour that Indochinese labourers were machine-gunning women in Paris played a role in the mutinies in fifteen different regiments that mutinied. See Jean-François Jagielski, "Entre fiction et réalité, la rumeur des Annamites massacrant les Parisiennes," in *Obéir / Desobéir*, 141.

103 Captain Mondages, for instance, traced this first night's events to a *"coup de pinard"* taken at the wine-shop in Léchelle. See Boucher, "3è Rapport du Colonel Boucher," 3 June 1917, SHD 19 N 305.

104 Genet, "Rapport du Lt-Colonel Genet, Commandant le 129è Régiment d'Infanterie sur les incidents des 28 et 29 Mai, 1917," 29 May 1917, SHD 19 N 305. Aubergé is also referred to as "Auberger" and "Auberge" in the reports.

105 De Roig, no. 363/P, 29 May 1917, SHD 16 N 1521; Mondages in Boucher, "3è Rapport du Colonel Boucher," SHD 19 N 305.

106 Boucher, "3è Rapport du Colonel Boucher," SHD 19 N 305.

107 Lefrançois's testimony in Boucher, "2è Rapport du Colonel Boucher," 2 June 1917, SHD 19 N 305.

108 Boucher, "3è Rapport du Colonel Boucher," SHD 19 N 305.

109 Mondages's testimony in ibid.

110 Boucher, "Rapport d'ensemble sur les événements qui se sont déroulés et 28 et 29 mai au 129è RI," 9 June 1917, SHD 19 N 305.

111 Ibid.

112 Ibid.

113 Boucher, "3è Rapport du Colonel Boucher," SHD 19 N 305.

114 Extract 21, Alfred Combray, in État-Major 2è Bureau III Armée, "Contrôle des courriers de depart du 3 Juin militaire compromis au 36è Régiment d'Infanterie," no. 334/A, 3 June 1917, SHD 16 N 1521; Menager, "Rapport du Chef de Batallion Menager," 29 May 1917, SHD 19 N 305.

115 Extract 59 in Boeringer, "Rapport," no. 592, 6 June 1917, SHD 19 N 305.

116 Boucher, "4è Rapport du Colonel Boucher," SHD 19 N 305.

117 "Inconnu à Antonia Golliat," in Etat-Major 2è Bureau, "Contrôle de la correspondance de la totalité du courrier postal de depart du 36è Régiment d'Infanterie, mis à la poste le 29 Mai," no. 312/A, 31 May 1917, SHD 16 N 1521.

118 Extract 28, Provoste, in État-Major 2è Bureau III Armée, "Contrôle des courriers de depart du 3 Juin militaire compromis au 36è Régiment d'Infanterie," no. 334/A, SHD 16 N 1521. My emphasis.

119 Rolland, *La Grève des tranchées*, 164.

120 Boucher, "Rapport d'ensemble sur les évenements qui se sont déroulés et 28 et 29 Mai au 129è RI," 9 June 1917, SHD 19 N 305.

121   Smith, *Between Mutiny and Obedience*, 201.

122   Boucher, "Rapport d'ensemble sur les évenements qui se sont déroulés et 28 et 29 Mai au 129è RI," 9 June 1917, SHD 19 N 305.

123   Ibid.

124   Smith, *Between Mutiny and Obedience*, 208.

125   This is André Loez's criticism of Leonard Smith's work, which he accuses is "argument by reduction." See Loez, "Annexe," 363. See also Smith's hostile review of Loez's work in *The Journal of Military History* 74, no. 4 (October 2010): 1301–3, and Loez's equally hostile response in *The Journal of Military History* 75, no. 1 (January 2011): 350–1.

126   For instance, about nine per cent of the mutinies involved such exaggerated signs of respect. Twenty-five per cent showed outright violence, and the rest generic threats and calls for revolution but no actual violence. See Loez, "Annexe," 332.

127   Martenet, "Rapport complémentaire sur les incidents que se sont déroulés les 28 et 29 Mai au 129è Regt. D'Inft," 3 June 1917, SHD 19 N 305. My emphasis.

128   Zopff, "Résumé des rapports et compte-rendus parvenus dans la journée du 9 Juin," no. 16/58, 9 June 1917, SHD 16 N 1521.

129   "Contrôle de la correspondance de la totalité du courrier postal de depart du 36è Régiment d'Infanterie, mis à la poste le 29 Mai," no. 312/A, 31 May 1917, SHD 16 N 1521.

130   As quoted in Rolland, *La Grève des tranchées*, 148.

131   On the influence of the 10è BI's mutiny in the Soissons region, see ibid., 176–82.

132   Ibid., 262.

133   See David I. Kertzer, *Ritual, Politics, and Power* (New Haven, CT: Yale University Press, 1988,) 144–50; Edward Muir, *Ritual in Early Modern Europe* (Cambridge: Cambridge University Press, 2005), 93–124; and Natalie Zemon-Davis, "The Reasons of Misrule: Charivaris in Sixteenth-Century France," *Past & Present* 50 (February 1971): 41–75.

134   "Compte-rendu au sujet de troubles à Villers," no. 3/1, 28 May 1917, SHD 16 N 1521; Bulot, "Rapport," 4 June 1917, SHD 16 N 1521.

Chapter Seven

1   Schniegans, "Rapport: Le Commissaire de guerre de Château-Thierry à Monsieur le Général D.E. du G.A.N à La-Ferté-Milon," no. 12l/86, 5 July 1917, SHD 16 N 1522.

2   George, "Rapport du Lieutenant George … Au sujet des incidents survenus à la gare de Château-Thierry le 3 Juillet à 19 heures," no. 12a/86, 5 July 1917, SHD 16 N 1522. By this point in July, every *train de permissionnaires* was supposed to have a police contingent aboard.

3   Schniegans, "Rapport."

4   George, "Rapport."

5   Ibid.

6   Schniegans, "Rapport."

7   Ibid.

8 Ibid.

9 Ibid.

10 For reasons of clarity, I will refer to the events of the type considered in ch. 5 as the "mutinies at the front." I will refer to those in train stations as *"permissionaires'* revolts" or "rebellions."

11 For instance, Pedroncini nearly ignored events in train stations, which garnered only two pages in his book and which he argued held "only passing interest." See Guy Pedroncini, *Les Mutineries de 1917* (Paris: Presses Universitaires de France, 1967), 175. Similarly, Denis Rolland dismisses the events as largely senseless discharges of emotional energy. See Rolland, *La Grève des tranchées* (Paris: Imago, 2005), 314. Andre Loez characteristically treats the events more seriously in his in *14–18: Les Refus de la guerre* (Paris: Gallimard, 2010), but he too holds that the events in train stations were a mere "halo" of the mutinies at the front, which were the "kernel." "The military situation in the front lines," he argues, "was evidently not threatened" by what happened in train stations. See 246.

12 For instance, Pétain himself explicitly linked the mutinies in the 18è RI on 27 May, in the 10è BI on 28 May, in the 82è BI on 1 June, and the events in train stations into the same mass movement. See Pétain, *Une Crise morale en la nation française en guerre* (Paris: Nouvelles Éditions Latines, 1966).

13 Pedroncini puts the number at 130 unique events, and Rolland at 118. See Pedroncini, *Les Mutineries de 1917*, 175, and Rolland, *La Grève des tranchées*, 312. Both numbers come from official reports, but the reports themselves underestimate the events, which were much more widespread that commanders realized at the time. My own quantitative research found about twice as many events as Pedroncini or Rolland.

14 Rolland, *La Grève des tranchées*, 314. Cf. Nicolas Mariot, "Pour compter des mutins faut-il soustraire des moutons?" in *Obéir / désobéir*, edited by André Loez and Nicolas Mariot (Paris: La Découverte, 2008), 345–72.

15 See Pétain's "Directive Numero 1," AFGG Tome V, Volume 2 Annex 1, 391–2. See also Richard Doughty, *Pyrrhic Victory: French Strategy and Operations during the Great War* (Cambridge: Belknap, 2008), 366–7.

16 Leonard V. Smith, Stéphane Audoin-Rouzeau, and Annette Becker, *France and the Great War 1914–1918* (Cambridge: Cambridge University Press, 2003), 131.

17 Henri-Phillippe Pétain, GQG no. 212, 1 June 1917, SHD 16 N 2644.

18 Pétain, no. 28346, 30 May 1917, SHD 16 N 2644.

19 Pétain, "Le Général en chef à M. le général commandant l' …," AFGG, Tome 5 Volume 2 Annex 1, 647–8.

20 Pétain, no. 16662, AFGG Tome V Volume 2 Annex 1, 870–1.

21 Extract 3 EM IV Armée commission de contrôle postal bureau frontière, "Unité contrôlée: 108è Régiment d'Infanterie," 13 June 1917, SHD 16 N 1406.

22 Micheler, no. 4534/1-4, 2 June 1917, SHD 19 N 840.

23 Fayolle, "Note pour les armées," no. 9387, 8 June 1917, SHD 19 N 840; Fayolle, "Conseils données au rapport du GQG au sujet des incidents recents," 19 N 840.

24 See, for instance, "État nominatif des hommes indésirables proposés pour leur envoi aux colonies par application des prescriptions de la note du GQG no. 11974 du 13 Juin 1917," SHD 16 N 1519. This carton contains many disciplinary records of individual soldiers who were deemed alcoholics and sent to the colonies.

25 See Fayolle, "Note pour les Armées et la DE," no. 126/S, 4 July 1917, SHD 16 N 1519, which lists about 500 men to be sent to the colonies. Rolland provides statistics that list about 2,000 men in total sent. See Rolland, *La Grève des tranchées*, 388–91.

26 Pétain, "Distribution d'alcool aux troupes," Minister of War, no. 5864, 25 May 1917, SHD 16 N 2644.

27 EMA, "Reduction des arrivages de vin aux armées," no. 476 4/11, 13 July 1917, SHD 16 N 2644.

28 Ministre de la Guerre, "Rations gratuits de vin," no. 7985 2/5, 29 October 1917, SHD 16 N 2644.

29 Pétain, "Une Crise morale."

30 Emmanuelle Cronier, *Permissionnaires dans la grande guerre* (Paris: Belin, 2013), 19–20.

31 Ibid., 38.

32 Ibid., 42.

33 Ibid., 48.

34 Ibid., 49. See also Cronier, "Le Rôle des permissionaires parisiens dans la révolte de 1917: Un Front contaminé par Paris?" in *Obéir / désobéir*, edited by André Loez and Nicolas Mariot (Paris: La Découverte, 2008), 125–38.

35 Pétain, "Instruction concernant les permissions, les repos à assurer aux troupes et l'alimentation," no. I/.080, 2 June 1917, SHD 19 N 840.

36 Jean-Louis Robert, *Les Ouvriers, la patrie, et la révolution: Paris 1914–1919* (Besançon, France: Annales Littéraires de l'Université de Besançon, 1995), 124–36.

37 "Peur [?] SD à Loire et Cher," in "Untitled CP report, unité contrôlée: 335è RI," 31 May 1917, SHD 16 N 1393.

38 "Untitled CP report, unité contrôlée: 20è Régiment d'Infanterie," 22 June 1917, SHD 16 N 1393.

39 Commission de Contrôle Postal de GR de Troyes, "Rapport du 5 Juin, 73è RG, 51è DI," 5 June 1917, SHD 16 N 1406.

40 Lallement, "Untitled Report," 27 May 1917, SHD 16 N 1521.

41 Rougier, "Manifestations antimilitaristes, cris seditieux proférés par des militare de passage à la gare de Dormans et aux environs," no. 3/55, 6 June 1917, SHD 16 N 1521.

42 Indeed, this was typically the case: it was the later and last trains to leave Paris that most often revolted, usually around the same time in the evening.

43 "Untitled Report," GAN no. 13/6 9449, 8 June 1917, 16 N 1521.

44 Ibid.

45 Commission Regulatrice Annexe de Noisy-le-Sec, "Incidents concernant la discipline, pendant le journée du 7 Juin 1917," no. 459, 7 June 1917, SHD 16 N 1521.

46 "Untitled Report," GAN no. 13/6 9449; Wenzinger, "Rapport du commissaire militaire sur les événements qui se sont passés pendant le séjour en gare du train Rs Ter le 7 Juin de 18h45–20h05," no. 39a/58, 7 June 1917, SHD 16 N 1521.

47 "Untitled Report," GAN no. 13/6 9449.

48 Ibid.

49 Cassel, "Rapport du commissaire militaire sur les évènements qui se sont passés pendant le séjour en gare du train Rs Ter le 7 Juin de 18h45–20h45," 7 June 1917, SHD 18 N 197; "Untitled Report," GAN no. 13/6 9449.

50 Ibid.

51 Payot, "Compte-rendu d'incidents dans un train de permissionnaires," DCF, 7 June 1917, SHD 16 N 1521; "Le Commissaire spécial, chef du service de sûreté le DE du GAC à monsieur le chef de batallion chargé du SR," no. 5820, 8 June 1917, 16 N 1521; Signature unreadable, "Untitled Report," no. 12/57, 8 June 1917, SHD 16 N 1521.

52 Henri Désagneaux, A French Soldier's War Diary, 1914–1918, trans. Godfrey J. Adams (Morley, UK: The Elmsfield Press, 1975), 39.

53 Ibid., 39.

54 Ibid., 40.

55 Ibid.

56 Bureau frontière 1 Armée commission de contrôle postal, "Rapport du 13 Juin, unité contrôlée: 120è BCP," no. 282/12, 13 June 1917, SHD 16 N 1388.

57 Ibid.

58 Ibid.

59 Ibid.

60 Ibid.

61 Ibid.

62 See, for instance, the records in SHD 16 N 1388, SHD 16 N 1393, and SHD 16 N 1406.

63 Extract 12 in Commission de contrôle postal de GR de Troyes, "Rapport du 5 Juin, 73è RG, 51è DI," 5 June 1917, SHD 16 N 1406.

64 Ibid.

65 Commission de Contrôle Postal de GR de Troyes, "Rapport du 31 Mai, 168è RI, 128è DI," 31 May 1917, SHD 16 N 1406.

66 B-(5)- in Bureau Frontière 1 Armée Commission de Contrôle Postal, "Rapport du 3 Juin, unité contrôlée: 70è Bat Chass Alpins," no. 265/6, 3 June 1917, SHD 16 N 1388.

67 "Soldat- 3è CM, à Serigny Indre et Loire," in "Untitled CP Report, unité contrôlée: 335è RI," 31 May 1917, SHD 16 N 1393.

68 Nadaud, "Au sujet de scènes scandaleuses au passage des trains de permission-naires les 3 et 4 Juin 1917," no. 17/54, 5 June 1917, SHD 16 N 1521.

69 Beausoleil, "Compte-rendu d'incidents en gare d'Angoulême," no. 13/64, 15 June 1917, SHD 16 N 1521.

70 Yves Jaouën, La Crise de Juin 1917: Les Trains de permissionnaires dans les gares de Nantes et de la Loire inférieure (Le Poire-sur-Vie, France: Éditions Opéra, 2017).

71 GQG Section du Chiffre, "Traduction d'un télégramme chiffré," no. 2613/M, 11 June 1917, SHD 16 N 1521.

72 Descoings, "Incidents militaires," no. 282/2.5, 1 June 1917, SHD 18 N 197.

73 Debeney, "Note de service," no. 5395/2, 1 June 1917, SHD 18 N 197.

74 Olivier, "Extrait du rapport journalier du commissare militaire de la gare de Meaux," no. 39a/58, 7 June 1917, 16 N 1521.

75 "Télégramme chiffré: Etat-Major Jonchery à Etat-Major Villers-Allerand," no. V.29083/1-4, 14 June 1917, SHD 19 N 840.

76 "Note de service," no. c18017, 16 June 1917, SHD 19 N 840.

77 Deschamps, "La Capitaine Deschamps, commissaire de gare à Esternay, à Monsieur le commissaire régulateur de Connantre," no. 191/76, 19 June 1917, SHD 19 N 840.

78 "Elements (cavalrie et gendarmerie) disponibles en cas de besoin d'ordre," 26 June 1917, SHD 19 N 840.

79 Debeney, "Note de service," no. 25935, 28 June 1917, SHD 19 N 840.

80 Hourbette, "Surveillence dans les trains de permissionnaires," no. 3250 S.G., 29 June 1917, SHD 16 N 1522.

81 Fayolle, "Note pour les armées et les commissaires régulateurs," no. 556/1, 5 June 1917, SHD 19 N 840.

82 Pétain, "Telegramme chiffre," no. V.28669/1-4, 8 June 1917, SHD 19 N 840.

83 Pétain, "Note aux groupes d'armées et armées," no. 10221, 11 June 1917, SHD 19 N 840.

84 GQG Section du Chiffre, "Traduction d'un télégramme chiffré," no. 2894/M, SHD 16 N 1522.

85 Domercq, "L'Inspecteur Domercq à monsieur le commissaire spécial, chef de la sûreté – DEO du GAN," 19 June 1917, SHD 16 N 1522; Foulon, "Le Lieutenant Colonel Foulon Prévôt de la DE du GAN à monsieur le général DE ouest," no. 7722, 17 June 1917, SHD 16 N 1522; Petit, "Trains de permissionnaires," no. 16f/68, 16 June 1917, SHD 16 N 1522.

86 GQG Section du Chiffre, "Traduction d'un Télégramme Chiffré," no. 3116/M, SHD 16 N 1522.

87 "Note," no. P/182, 11 June 1917, SHD 19 N 528.

88 Georges Humbert, "Note pour MM les généraux commandant les CA, le 1er CC, la 70è DI, et les Brigades Territoriales," 17 June 1917, SHD 19 N 528.

89 Ibid.

90 Georges Humbert, no. PS/197, 19 June 1917, SHD 19 N 528.

91 "Télégramme chiffré, intérieur sûreté à préfects France en communication guerre cabinet," no. 30/65, 17 June 1917, SHD 16 N 1522.

92 Ibid.

93 "Rapport de l'officier de surveillance du train des permissionnaires de Chauny à Surveilliers à monsieur le général Cdt la 53è DI," 18 June 1917, SHD 16 N 1522.

94 Grand Quartier Général des Armées du Nord et du Nord-est, *Instruction sur les dispositions à adopter pour l'installation des gares où sont à séjourner des permissionnaires dans la zone des armées* (Paris: Imprimerie Nationale, 1917), 5.

95 Ibid., 14.

96 Ibid., 11.

97 Ibid., 11.

98   Ibid., 11–12.
99   Ibid., 12.
100 Ibid., 18.
101 Inspecteur de Police Mobile [unreadable], "Rapport," no. 561, 21 June 1917, SHD 16 N 1522.
102 Hourbette, "Surveillance dans les trains de permissionnaires," no. 3301 SG, 10 July 1917, SHD 16 N 1522.
103 Ibid.
104 Signature Unreadable, "Rapport d'ensemble sur les constatations faites par le service de sûreté de l'armée au cours des surveillances exercées dans les cantonnements et les trains de permissionnaires pendant le mois de Juin 1917," no. 3255 SG, 10 July 1917, SHD 16 N 1522.
105 Ibid.
106 Ibid.

Epilogue

1   Christophe Lucand, *Le Pinard des poilus* (Dijon, France: Éditions Universitaires de Dijon, 2014), 111–13; Charles Ridel, *L'Ivresse du soldat* (Paris: Vendémiaire, 2016), 312–14.
2   Stéphane Le Bras identified this highly useful source in "Vin, littérature de guerre et construction identitaire. Le Cas des soldats languedociens pendant la grande guerre," *Siècles* 39–40 (2014).
3   Jules Laurent, ed., *Le Maréchal Pinard: Contes de guerre des écrivans combattants* (Annecy, France: Édition Hérisson Frères, 1938), 3.
4   Ibid., 5.
5   Ibid., 9.
6   Ibid., 36.
7   Rod Phillips, *French Wine: A History* (Berkeley, CA: University of California Press, 2016), 208–12.
8   Ibid., 219.
9   Ibid., 221–8; Charles K. Warner, *The Winegrowers of France and the Government since 1875* (New York: Columbia University Press), 93–122.
10 Phillips, *French Wine*, 231; Sarah Howard, "Selling Wine to the French: Official Attempts to Increase French Wine Consumption, 1931–1936," *Food & Foodways* 12, no. 4 (2004): 197–224.
11 Howard, "Selling Wine to the French," 200.
12 Ridel, *L'Ivresse du soldat*, 321–2.
13 Ibid., 321.
14 See the wartime rations schedule in *Manuel du gradé d'infanterie: Mis à jour à la date du 1er octobre 1939* (Paris: Charles-Lavauzelle & Cie, 1939), 873.
15 Ibid., 978–81.
16 *L'Élève soldat* (Paris: Charles-Lavauzelle & Cie, 1932), 159.

17 Ibid., 159.

18 Émile Condroyer, "Petits restaurants," *Le Journal* (11 September 1939).

19 Barthes is quoted in Louis Dubosc, "Le Ravitaillement général en vins," *Le Midi socialiste* (26 January 1940).

20 Didier Nourisson, *Une Histoire du vin* (Paris: Perrin, 2017), 249.

21 "Fontaines de pinard," *Le Matin* (24 November 1939).

22 "Hymne national," *Je suis partout* (31 May 1940).

23 "Vive le vin chaud," *Le Grand écho de l'Aisne* (9 March 1940).

24 "Le Vin chaud au soldat (1916)," *Revue de viticulture* 2384 (7 March 1940).

25 *Le Progrès de la Côte-d'Or* (27 October 1915); *Le Radical* (26 October 1915); *L'Ouest-Éclair* (31 October 1915); *Le Temps* (26 October 1915).

26 "Le Courage artificiel," *La Petite Gironde* (30 October 1915).

27 Rasmussen, *On Speed* (New York: New York University Press, 2009), 54–5; Lukasz Kamienski, *Shooting Up: A Short History of Drugs and War* (Oxford, UK: Oxford University Press, 2016), 109–16. Quote from Rasmussen, 54.

28 Kamienski, *Shooting Up*, 110. His emphasis.

29 Ibid., 111–13.

30 Dosages were around 3 mg every few hours, which was one-tenth to one-fiftieth of those associated with the Benzedrine-loving Beat poets, who ate the entire contents of inhalers containing 250 mg of amphetamine all at once. See Rasmussen, *On Speed*, 94–9.

31 Kamienski, *Shooting Up*, 114–15.

32 Rasmussen, *On Speed*, 53–85.

33 Ibid., 55–71; Kamienski, *Shooting Up*, 116–20.

34 Kamienski, *Shooting Up*, 121.

35 Ibid., 130–1.

36 Rasmussen, *On Speed*, 82.

37 Kamienski, *Shooting Up*, 22.

38 Edward B. Westermann, *Drunk on Genocide: Alcohol and Mass Murder in Germany* (New York: Cornell University Press, 2021).

39 Richard Holmes, *Acts of War: The Behavior of Men in Battle* (New York: The Free Press, 1985), 247. Dextroamphetamine [D-AMP] (trade name Dexedrine) is the right-hand isomer of amphetamine and produces a less jittery high than levoamphetamine [L-AMP]. Benzedrine is a racemic (i.e. equal parts) mixture of the two; today's popular drug Adderall is a mixture of seventy-five per cent D-AMP and twenty-five per cent L-AMP.

40 Jean Larteguy, *The Centurions* (New York: Penguin Books, 2015), 36–7. Lescure was referring to shells.

41 John A. Caldwell, "Go Pills in Combat Prejudice, Propriety, and Practicality," *Air & Space Power Journal* (Fall 2008): 97–102.

42 J.C. Woodring, "Air Force Scientists Battle Aviator Fatigue," *Air Force Print News* (30 April 2004), https://archive.is/20121212032952/http://www.af.mil/news/story.asp?id=123007615. See also John A. Caldwell et al., "Modafinil's Effects on

Simulator Performance and Mood in Pilots during 37h without Sleep," *Aviation Space and Environmental Medicine* 75, no. 9 (September 2004): 777–84.

43 Christopher Boos et al., "Dietary Supplements and Military Operations: Caution Is Advised," BMJ *Military Health* 156, no. 1 (March 2010): 41–3.

44 Jon Henley, "Captagon: The Amphetamine Fuelling Syria's Civil War," *Guardian* (13 January 2014), https://www.theguardian.com/world/shortcuts/2014/jan/13/captagon-amphetamine-syria-war-middle-east.

45 BBC *News*, "Captagon: Italy Seizes € 1 bn of Amphetamines 'Made to Fund IS'" (1 July 2020), https://www.bbc.com/news/world-europe-53254879.

46 On this subject, see Stephen Kinzer, *Poisoner in Chief: Sidney Gottlieb and the CIA Search for Mind Control* (New York: Henry Holt and Co., 2019).

Index

Académie de médecine, 54–7. *See also* alcoholism

alcohol consumption, 22–4, 26–8; gender and, 149, 152–3; legislation against, 29, 30–1, 127, 136; outside France, 24; physical effects of, 12–14, 43, 54–5, 85, 115–16, 154–5, 233n63; racial degeneration and, 20–1, 26, 30–1, 33–4, 57–8; taxation of, 25, 27, 127–8, 218

alcoholism, 21–2; association with Germans, 96; emergence as a social issue, 24–5; in French army, 132–4, 142–3; French science of, 27–9, 55–6, 142; military discipline and, 31–2, 36, 55, 193–4, 209; national security and, 126–7; public health and, 153, 220

Andreas, Peter, 7–8

anti-war demonstrations, 156–8, 164; in 10è *Brigade d'Infanterie*, 180, 184–5; in 82è *Brigade d'Infanterie*, 160, 174–6, 179–80; causes of, 157–60, 163–4, 182, 201–2; civilians and, 199, 205–6, 207, 211; drunkenness as a cause of, 159–60, 167–8, 173–4, 190–1, 203, 214; effects on overall morale, 201, 204–6, 212, 215; historiography of, 157–9, 213–14; non-violent tactics in, 182–3; official responses to, 192–4, 206–7, 209–10, 213; *permissionnaires* and, 188–91, 197–201; punishments of demonstrators, 168, 171, 174, 179, 184, 189, 192, 199, 208–9; racial anxiety and, 182; rumour and, 170, 180–1, 215; "script" of, 165–6, 176, 186, 200, 214–15; sobriety and break-up of, 176, 178–9; socialism in, 155–7, 167, 171–2, 175, 196, 198, 202–5, 258n70; soldiers' opinions on, 196–7, 201; violence in, 171–2, 177–8, 189, 197–9, 201, 205, 209

Barbusse, Henri, 101, 110, 112, 121, 145, 247n30

Barthas, Louis, 3–4, 101–2, 119, 132–3, 135, 140

Barthes, Roland, 66, 90

Belgium, 38, 39, 42

Bertillon, Jacques, 19–20

billeting of soldiers, 139–40, 144–5, 175. *See also* military logistics

biopower. *See* Foucault, Michel

bourrage de crane [eyewash], 110–11, 150. *See also* war propaganda

British army, 9–11

Canadian army, 11

censorship of letters, 164, 202–3

Chamber of Deputies, 94

Chevallier, Gabriel, 86, 102–3, 112, 117, 121

Clemenceau, Georges, 217

Cochet, François, 91, 101, 248n36

Collins, Randall, 76–7, 113, 116–17, 149

colonial soldiers, 83–4, 188, 260n102

combat: physiological effects of, 40–1; psychotropic characteristics of, 121. *See also* trench warfare